MW01013473

CANADIAN FIREFIGHTER EXAMS

TREVOR EDMONDS

Firefighter
District of North Vancouver Fire
and Rescue Services

BARRON'S

All inquiries should be addressed to:
Barron's Educational Series, Inc.
250 Wireless Boulevard
Hauppauge, NY 11788
www.barronseduc.com

ISBN-13: 978-1-4380-0245-3

Library of Congress Control Number: 2013940524

Printed in the United States of America
9 8 7 6 5 4 3 2

A Note on Pronouns

For purely editorial reasons, the pronoun "he" is used throughout this book when referring to firefighter candidates. No gender bias is intended by this writing style.

10%
POST-CONSUMER
WASTE
Paper contains a minimum
of 10% post-consumer
waste (PCW). Paper used
in this book was derived
from certified, sustainable
forestlands.

ACKNOWLEDGMENTS

Thank you to the following companies for their assistance and cooperation:

Brock University Firefighter Screening Services
Cooperative Personnel Services (CPS)
Fire & Police Selection, Inc. (FPSI)
Stefan, Fraser & Associates, Inc.
York University

The author would also like to thank Jay Chiasson, from CSCS from Innovative Fitness, West Vancouver, for providing the fitness information and training programs in Chapter 4. For more information, visit *www.innovativefitness.com* and *www.jaycfitness.com*.

Additional thanks to:

IAFF 1183
The District of North Vancouver
Vic Penman
Curtis Bremner
Rachel Zuckerman
Corinne Nichols
Haley Oxenham
Keith Edmonds
Ian Bolton
Carla Penman
Keith Sharman
Steve, Janice, and Karly Edmonds
Barbara Van De Water

For any questions or assistance regarding this book, please contact Barron's Educational Series, Inc. at *www.barronseduc.com*.

NOTE:

The intention of this publication is to provide a faithful representation of what potential candidates can expect as they begin testing to become a Canadian firefighter. This publication is not officially endorsed by any of the testing companies discussed in this book. Every effort has been made to contact each of the testing companies mentioned prior to publication in order to ensure the accuracy of these test descriptions and provide as much up to date information as possible. The editor has made every effort to trace the ownership of all copyrighted material and to secure necessary permissions. Should there be any question regarding use of any material, please contact Barron's at *www.barronseduc.com* and proper acknowledgment will be made in future editions.

ACKNOWLEDGEMENTS

CONTENTS

INTRODUCTION: WHAT IT TAKES TO BECOME A FIREFIGHTER

Firefighting is one of the most rewarding occupations in Canada. Firefighters work in a constantly changing, challenging, and very gratifying environment. Every shift, firefighters help people deal with some of the most challenging and difficult days of their lives. Firefighters are the first responders on many types of incidents including fires, motor vehicle accidents, rope rescue, medical aid calls, swiftwater rescue, trench rescue, mountain rescue, electrical, gas, and chemical emergencies, and floods. Firefighting is one of the few jobs available that the right candidate will enjoy for his or her entire career.

There are approximately 180 fire departments across Canada that accept applications for full-time firefighters. These fire departments want to have the best results possible from each intake of applicants. Fire departments can gauge a successful hiring process by the success of the candidates they hire as firefighters. Every municipality has the ability to design their own recruitment process and determine the type of firefighter candidate that would best suit their municipality. Because of this, most municipalities have differences in their recruitment process and qualifications. Fire departments use different minimum qualifications, written tests, physical tests, interviews, ride alongs, and other recruitment tools as a way to narrow candidates down to the ones they see as the best fit for them. Each municipality recognizes the importance of their firefighters in the community and designs its hiring process to hire the best firefighters.

Although the attributes that fire departments across Canada are looking for in firefighter candidates are similar, diversity is also an important part of hiring. Diversity in firefighter candidates can be described as the differences or qualities that make each person unique. Fire departments look at a candidate's diversity as an asset because the municipality can better serve the public if their firefighters have a broader skill set. Diversity comes in many forms, including life experience, education, culture, work experience, age, sex, economic background, ethnicity, geopolitical designation, and geographic background, among others.

All fire departments across Canada strive for fair, equitable, and effective hiring practices. Recruitment and firefighter hiring processes aim for employment equity and are required to follow the provisions of the human rights legislation applicable in their province or territory. In most jurisdictions in Canada, discrimination in employment situations is prohibited on the grounds of race or colour; religion; physical or mental disability; age; sex (including pregnancy and childbirth); marital status; family status; sexual orientation; national or ethnic origin; and ancestry or place of origin. Some jurisdictions prohibit discrimination on the grounds of language; social condition or origin; source of income; political belief or other associations; and criminal or summary convictions and records. Fire departments commonly use written and physical tests that have been validated for diverse groups. Essentially, this means that the tests given have been studied to assure they are job related, fair, and predictive of firefighting performance. When hiring, municipalities have an obligation to accommodate a candidate who falls under any of the prohibited grounds. Disabilities, including those that are hidden such as learning disabilities, are an example that may be relevant to a firefighter candidate.

There are many different ways to become an excellent firefighter candidate. To become a successful candidate will take effort and motivation. It is rare for firefighters to be hired with only the minimum qualifications. Municipalities receive hundreds or thousands of firefighter applications annually and competition for a position is fierce. In some hiring processes, less than 1% of the applicants receive job offers. The purpose of any hiring process is to find the best possible candidates to serve the community. Therefore, the goal of any person trying to become a firefighter should be to do everything possible to become the best and most qualified candidate in the hiring process.

One of the most important parts of becoming a good candidate is to be as successful as possible during the written and physical testing portion of the process. This book is designed to provide you with the tools to do that. Be sure to learn as much as possible about the specific testing done by the department you are applying for. Check the Internet, network with other candidates, talk to local firefighters, recruiters, and human resources. The main purpose of these tests is to narrow down the field of applicants into a more manageable group. If successful, the fire department that is hiring will have what they see as the most mentally and physically capable candidates to move on to the next stage of the process.

When applying, make sure that your resumé clearly shows the best you have to offer. If you have applied in the past, your resumé and application should demonstrate that you are clearly improving and evolving as a candidate. Often, the application form is one of the best places to learn how to improve as a candidate. Most application forms have space to include things like preferred qualifications, work experience, and volunteer experience. Use this along with any other experience you have as a firefighter applicant to identify your strengths and weaknesses. When you know your strengths, you can use them to your advantage. When you know your weaknesses, you can work on improving them.

Correcting your weakness can be either easy or hard, and inexpensive or expensive. It depends on the individual candidate. It can be as simple as using this book to improve your scores on a particular part of a written or physical test. If you have identified your work experience as a weakness, consider changing to a job that is more related to firefighting. If you feel your qualifications are weak, take some fire-related courses. Make sure that when you take a firefighter-related course it is recognised by the fire department you are applying for (usually listed as a preferred qualification). These courses are not only beneficial because of knowledge gained, but they also demonstrate to the hiring fire department your ability to learn fire department related information.

Although almost all hiring processes across Canada are at least slightly different, they all exist to achieve the same goal. That goal is to hire the best firefighters possible. The purpose of long application and screening processes is to increase the chances that the successful applicants will be good firefighters. Each stage of the recruitment process is another chance for the fire chiefs, HR, and other fire department members to learn about your character, attitude, and abilities. Essentially, each candidate who is hired can be viewed as a 20-30 year investment for the hiring fire department. It is important for the future of the fire department that it invests in quality candidates. Your job as a recruit is to become a valuable commodity by proving yourself as an excellent applicant.

Getting a job as a firefighter may be one of the biggest moments of your life. Remember that moment will be the result of many smaller moments before it. Your success will depend on those small moments. This book is designed to help you put the small pieces together.

SECTION ONE
WHAT YOU NEED TO KNOW

Written Tests Commonly Used in Canada

1

GENERAL ADVICE

No two calls a firefighter responds to during his or her career will be exactly the same. Every day, firefighters respond to an assortment of incidents that require a variety of mental skills and abilities. To be successful and competent, a firefighter must have the aptitude and personality to deal with these incidents as effectively as possible. Firefighters use many of the competencies covered on firefighter written tests to deal with various scenarios during the course of their shifts. Fire departments want to be sure when they are hiring that new firefighters have a thorough grasp of these competencies so they can effectively deal with the large variety of incidents they will see over the course of their career. This is the main reason fire departments use written testing. When hiring, many fire departments see new firefighters as an investment—they use written testing to try to lower the risk of making a poor investment. Because of this, today's entry level firefighter tests seek to identify the candidates that have the skills required to be a successful firefighter. All written tests, cognitive or behavioral, are designed to identify the firefighter candidates who will mentally be effective firefighters.

To reach your full potential when writing an entry level firefighter test, it is important to have some general knowledge of how the test you are taking will be scored and a general idea of what the test will cover. This chapter is designed to provide candidates with a basic understanding of some of the written tests used in Canada and how those tests are scored. Just like with every portion of the hiring process, you should learn as much as possible about what is involved in the written testing stage. There is no disadvantage in knowing too much. Having some knowledge and understanding of scoring systems and the actual test content may help you relax and focus on your studying. Keep in mind that test content means types and numbers of questions on the test so you can study effectively, not the actual questions—never, ever cheat or use pirated tests. Usually when a fire department is hiring, they will post this information on their website. If you can't find the information you need online or through networking with other candidates, contact the human resources department of the municipality that is recruiting. If you do decide to contact HR, remember to treat your contact as part of the hiring process. As with any contact you have with people who may be involved in hiring you in the future, act and dress (if in person) appropriately and respectfully. Also, be prepared for your conversation. Make sure you are knowledgeable about the fire department and recruitment process. Try to make sure you don't ask questions that you should know the answer to (for example, a question that could easily be answered by looking at the municipal website).

There are multiple tests commonly used by fire departments throughout Canada. Generally (but not always) fire departments use written tests that are designed by a company that specializes in producing aptitude tests. Surprisingly, most of the tests used in Canada are written, designed, and produced in the United States. One of the main reasons fire departments use outside testing companies is that they will have gone through a process to determine that the test will be effective for identifying quality firefighter candidates. Another reason fire departments use written tests that are designed by testing companies is because they are validated and legally defensible. A validated test means that the company providing the test has gone through a process to make sure their test accurately reflects the key competencies that will be predictive of on-the-job performance. A test is usually validated by showing a connection between on-the-job firefighting skills and the test (content validity) or by showing a statistical correlation between the test results and a known result (criteria-related validity). Usually, part of this process will also involve firefighting experts (subject matter experts—SME's) reviewing the questions on the tests. Along with this, most testing companies will also conduct a thorough firefighter job analysis as part of their design process. Common questions found on firefighting tests could involve reading and oral comprehension, spatial perception, mathematical ability, mechanical aptitude, situational questions, and personality profiling type questions.

BASIC WRITTEN TEST SCORING SYSTEMS (APTITUDE TESTS)

Written tests can be scored based on a number of systems. These systems can be used several different ways. For a test to be valid, its scores have to be interpreted properly. It's a good idea for firefighter candidates to understand the basic systems that will *most likely* be used to score their test. This can help candidates understand how the recruitment process functions. Sometimes, your written test score will be weighted and combined with your scores from other stages of the recruitment process.

Pass/Fail—This means that firefighter candidates pass a test if they are above a certain score and fail if they are below it. For example, if the passing grade is 70% all candidates that answer 70% or more of the test correctly will move to the next stage of the recruitment process. While this is a simple system, the difficulty lays in setting the pass/fail mark. There are many ways to set this threshold. Some examples are:

- The fire department sets their own arbitrary pass/fail. Fire departments will usually not set an arbitrary pass/fail point (usually to avoid lawsuits).
- The fire department relies on written testing companies to provide predetermined pass/fail points. This is often not recommended by testing companies. This is sometimes because of the diversity in the group used by the testing company to determine the pass point (eg. volunteer departments, non-volunteer departments, different requirements, etc.). It could also be because a testing company does not want to be involved in a lawsuit that is based on pass point.
- The fire department that is recruiting sets a pass point based on their needs. This could be a set pass point based on number of positions or duration of their hiring list. The pass point could also be based on the number of candidates that can be handled in the next stage of the recruitment process.
- The fire department sets a pass point based on the scores achieved on the test. For example, some fire departments may wish to only move candidates who score one standard deviation above the median (middle) score further through the process.

Banding—Essentially, banding is separating candidates' scores into different groups (bands) based on standard error of difference. This means that firefighter candidates will be put into groups that are considered equally qualified based on the competencies measured by the test. Fire departments will use this type of scoring when they feel that small differences in scores are not always representative of the best candidate.

Ranking—Generally, this means hiring candidates from top score to bottom score (usually with a cutoff for the bottom score).

THE MOST COMMONLY ADMINISTERED TESTS THROUGHOUT CANADA
Cooperative Personnel Services (CPS Test)

www.cps.ca.gov

Designed by CPS HR Consulting in California, CPS tests are probably the most widely used firefighter tests for Canadian fire departments. They are mostly cognitive tests that are designed to identify candidates who will become good future firefighters. CPS offers nine different tests, and these are widely considered to be the most challenging.

CPS tests are two hours long and are taken with paper and pencil, multiple choice format. No previous firefighter training is required to do well on these tests. All of the questions on the test have been researched and validated and can be answered using common sense and the information in this book. It is very important to have a thorough grasp of all of the math explained in Chapter 2 of this book to do well on this test.

Following is a breakdown of the components of the nine tests offered:

	Understanding Oral Information	Reading/ Understanding Written Information	Mathematical Ability/ Numerical Skills	Mechanical Ability/ Reasoning, Maps, Diagrams	Teamwork/ Public Relations/ Community Living	Total Questions
Test 2102M (Metric)	20	20	20	20	20	100
Test 2105M (Metric, available in French)	20	30	25	25	N/A	100
Test 2112A-M (Metric)	20	20	20	20	20	100
2127M (Metric)	20	20	20	20	20	100
2129M (Metric)	20	20	20	20	20	100
2134	N/A	30	30	25	15	100
2151	20	30	25	25	N/A	100
2177	N/A	30	30	25	15	100
2187	N/A	30	30	25	15	100

CONTENT AREAS

Understanding Oral Information

This section involves the proctor reading a passage to the firefighter candidates writing the test. This will usually consist of one passage that is less than ten minutes long. Some tests may have two shorter passages read back to back. After the passage is read, the test booklet will be distributed and candidates will answer questions based on what has just been read to them by the proctor. All of the answers for the Understanding Oral Information section will be contained in the passage(s) read by the proctor.

Reading/Understanding Written Information

The questions in this section are to gauge a firefighter candidate's ability to read and understand written information. The section contains several paragraphs or passages with one or more questions following the text. The answers for each question are found in the text relating to the question.

Mathematical Ability/Numerical Skills

Many candidates describe this as the most difficult section of the test. It is very important to be well prepared for this portion of the exam. Questions can involve addition, subtraction, percentages, multiplication, division, ratio, proportions, perimeter, algebra, and fractions among others. The Math Questions section of this book covers everything you will need to understand to be successful. Be sure you know and thoroughly understand the entire math section in Chapter 2 of this book (especially the algebra, ratios, and proportions section).

Mechanical Ability/Reasoning, Maps, and Diagrams

This section will have 20–25 questions. It will involve many different questions that are very related to the job of a firefighter. Be sure to study and understand the Mechanical Aptitude and Spatial Perception section of this book. Questions cover gears, pulleys, inclined planes, wheel and axle, direction, torque, levers, measurement, and shapes among others. Some questions in this section could be considered more mathematical than mechanical.

Teamwork, Public Relations, Community Living

This section could contain up to 20 questions. Some CPS tests do not contain any of these questions. Be sure to read the Situational Judgment questions section of this book in Chapter 2 for an understanding of these types of questions. Remember that CPS is an American company. Because of this, the questions were most likely designed and validated based on American firefighter responses, culture, and opinions (for example, most fire departments in the United States do not have a seniority system like most Canadian fire departments).

Answer the questions from your point of view as a firefighter, NOT as a rookie. Remember not to overthink or read into the questions.

The International Public Management Association for Human Resources (IPMA-HR)

www.ipma-hr.org/

The International Public Management Association for Human Resources (IPMA-HR) is an organization based in the state of Virginia. IPMA offers six entry level firefighter tests. They also offer fire departments the choice to use fully or partially customized tests. These tests are mostly cognitive tests that are designed to identify candidates who will become good firefighters in the future.

All IPMA tests are well validated using criteria-related validation studies and job analysis. No previous firefighter training is required to do well on these tests. All of the questions on the tests can be answered using your own common sense and the information in this book. The tests are paper and pencil tests that use a multiple choice format. The tests have varying time limits. Some candidates report difficulty finishing some of the IPMA tests in the allotted time. Good time management is essential for these tests.

Following is a breakdown of the various IPMA tests:

FF EL 100 Series—Two Tests

1. **FF EL 101** (formerly B3R)—90 questions, 2-hour time limit
2. **FF EL 102** (formerly B4R)—90 questions, 2-hour time limit

Both tests assess 10 content areas:

Content Area	# of Questions FF-EL 101	# of Questions FF-EL 102
Reading Comprehension	26	24
Interpreting Tables	9	10
Situational Judgment	10	10
Logical Reasoning	6	6
Reading Gauges	3	2
Applying Basic Math Rules	8	9
Mechanical Aptitude	5	6
Spatial Sense	9	10
Map Reading	7	6
Vocabulary	7	7

Overall, the FF-EL 101 and 102 are the only IPMA tests that assess a firefighter candidate's Mechanical Aptitude, Spatial Sense, and Vocabulary.

CONTENT AREAS

Reading Comprehension

This section is similar to tests from other companies. There will be a section of text followed by questions that are related to that text. The answers to the questions are found in the text for each question. This section uses charts, word recognition, and reading passages to assess a candidate's ability to read and comprehend information.

Interpreting Tables

This assesses a firefighter candidate's ability to read and interpret tables. See the Mechanical Aptitude and Spatial Perception section of this book for all information necessary to do well on this section.

Situational Judgment

This section assesses a candidate's situational judgment in different fire-related situations. To be well prepared, read the Situational Judgment questions section of this book. Remember that IPMA-HR is an American company. Because of this, the questions were most likely designed and validated based on American firefighter responses, culture, and opinions (for example, most fire departments in the United States do not have a seniority system like most Canadian fire departments). Answer the questions from your point of view as a firefighter, NOT as a rookie. Remember not to overthink or read into the questions.

Logical Reasoning

These questions will assess a candidate's ability to use logical reasoning to solve problems. Some questions may require the firefighter candidate to read and understand text similar to fire departments' operational guidelines and then use those guidelines to solve problems logically.

Reading Gauges

This section assesses a candidate's ability to read and interpret gauges. See the Mechanical Aptitude and Spatial Perception section of this book for all information necessary to do well in this section.

Applying Basic Math Rules

This is a very fire department–related math section. The Math Questions section of this book covers all the information required to answer all of the content in this section.

Spatial Sense

This section of the test measures a firefighter candidate's spatial sense. For example, a candidate may be required to read floor plans or decipher shapes. See the Mechanical Aptitude and Spatial Perception section of this book for information that will be required to do well in this section.

Map Reading

This very job-related section requires candidates to read and interpret maps. See the Mechanical Aptitude and Spatial Perception section of this book for all information necessary to score well in this section.

Vocabulary

This content area asks for the definition of 7 different words.

FF EL 200 Series—Two Tests

1. **FF-EL 201-NC (TIP)** (formerly B5)—100 questions, 2-hour time limit (plus 20 minutes for the TIP)
2. **FF-EL 202 (TIP)** (formerly B5A)—80 questions, 1-hour and 45 minute time limit (plus 20 minutes for the TIP)

Content Area	# of Questions: FF-EL 201-NC	# of Questions: FF-EL 202
Ability to learn, remember, and apply information (TIP)	35	35
Reading Comprehension	15	15
Fire Interest Questionnaire	20	N/A
Situational Judgment	13	13
Logical and Mathematical Reasoning Ability	17	17

FF-EL 300 Series—Two Tests

1. **FF-EL 301-NC (TIP)**—100 questions, 2-hour time limit (plus 20 minutes for the TIP)
2. **FF-EL 302 (TIP)**—80 questions, 1-hour and 45 minute time limit (plus 20 minutes for the TIP)

Content Area	# of Questions: FF-EL 301-NC	# of Questions: FF-EL 302
Ability to learn, remember, and apply information (TIP)	35	35
Reading Comprehension	15	15
Fire Interest Questionnaire	20	N/A
Situational Judgment	12	12
Logical and Mathematical Reasoning Ability	18	18

- The FF-EL 201-NC and the FF-EL 202 contain the exact same questions aside from the Fire Interest Questionnaire.
- The FF-EL 301-NC and the FF-EL 302 contain the exact same questions aside from the Fire Interest Questionnaire.
- There are no Mechanical Aptitude questions on these tests.

CONTENT AREAS

Ability to Learn, Remember, and Apply information (TIP)

This section involves firefighter candidates reading a Test Information Packet (TIP) that will be taken away after a period of time. You will not be allowed to take notes. Some of the questions in the test will be based on the information packet. All answers required for these questions will be contained in the information packet. This tests firefighter candidates' ability to absorb and recall information they have read. See the "Learning, Remembering, and Applying Information Questions" section of this book to find ways to improve your score.

Reading Comprehension

In this section of the test, firefighter candidates will read a paragraph and answer a question based on that paragraph. The answers to the question will always be contained in the paragraph.

Fire Interest Questionnaire (FF-EL 201-NC and FF-EL 301-NC only)

This section of the test asks candidates to choose between different activities or interests. It is intended to assess a firefighter candidate's interest in work as a firefighter. It is more common for fire departments that do not require pre-service training to use this. Remember to be very honest and consistent.

Situational Judgment

This section will give firefighter candidates a fire-related scenario and then ask them to choose the appropriate solution from several answers. Be sure to read the Situational Judgment Questions section of this book. Remember that IPMA is a U.S. company. Because of this, the questions were most likely designed and validated based on American firefighter responses, culture, and opinions (for example, most fire departments in the United States do not have a seniority system like most Canadian fire departments). Answer the questions from your point of view as a firefighter, NOT as a rookie. Remember not to read into or overthink the questions in this section.

Logical and Mathematical Reasoning Ability

This section of the test aims to measure firefighter candidates' ability to reason using logic and math. Many candidates describe this as an easier section when compared to other tests that are available to select entry level firefighters (CPS, for example).

Fire and Police Selection, Inc. (FPSI)

FPSI.com
Nationalfireselect.com

Fire and Police Selection, Inc. is a company from Folsom, California that provides testing services for fire and police departments. FPSI offers multiple entry level and promotional firefighter exams to fire departments. The questions included on the written tests provided by FPSI are usually fire related.

Most FPSI tests include the common competencies that are used in other entry level firefighter tests. These competencies include math, human relations (situational judgment), reading comprehension, and mechanical aptitude type questions. Chapter 2 of this book covers the information firefighter candidates need to be successful.

All FPSI tests have been thoroughly validated using experts in the field. It is important when answering situational type questions that firefighter candidates remember that FPSI is a U.S.-based company. Although the questions were thoroughly validated, they were designed using American firefighting experts based on their opinions, culture, and responses (most fire departments in the United States do not have a seniority system like most Canadian fire departments). Answer the questions from your point of view as a firefighter, NOT as a rookie.

In Canada, the most commonly used FPSI tests for entry level firefighters are the National Fire Select Test, CEB, PST, and WSI.

National Fire Select Test

This test provides a blend of aptitudes that includes reading and writing, math, mechanical aptitude, and work styles questions. This test is taken in either paper and pencil format or online at a time that is convenient for the test taker. The score will then be distributed to fire departments that are participating in National Fire Select Testing.

Comprehensive Exam Battery (CEB)

The Comprehensive Exam Battery is a series of tests developed to measure the traits required to be a successful firefighter. FPSI used the assistance of over 200 fire departments across the United States to determine relevant questions that cover firefighter candidates' reading ability, general cognitive ability, and important human relations characteristics. See Chapter 2 for strategies specific to the types of questions found in this test.

Questions involve:
Reading Ability
Writing Ability
Mathematics
Teamwork, Decision Making, Interpersonal Skills
Map Reading
Human Relations Test Questions

Practical Skills Test (PST)

This test is designed to predict a firefighter candidate's mechanical aptitude. The test covers the operation and maintenance of tools. It also has fire-related questions involving decision making and problem solving. The Practical Skills Test may be used on its own or combined with other tests. It is a 90 minute paper and pencil test.

Questions Involve:
Math
Vocabulary
Reading Charts
Mechanical Aptitude
Spatial Perception

Work Styles Inventory (WSI)

The Work Styles Inventory (WSI) is a 30 minute test that is usually combined with other types of written testing. The WSI was designed to identify the traits that are essential for a successful firefighter. This test is intended to measure work style traits in a less obvious way than traditional personality profiling tests. It is important for firefighter candidates to remember not to try to fake their way through this test. As with all tests designed to measure these traits, it is important to be honest and consistent when answering questions.

Questions Involve:
Teamwork
Attention to detail
Commitment
Receiving and responding to orders/instruction
Working with others

Ergometrics & Applied Personnel Research, Inc.

Ergometrics.org

Ergometrics & Applied Personnel Research, Inc. is a human resources firm located in Lynnwood, Washington that provides video and job simulation aptitude and personality profiling testing across the United States and Canada. Ergometrics entry level firefighter tests are mostly video based. The tests are designed to identify candidates with the skills that are critical to becoming a successful firefighter.

Ergometrics offers four tests—the FireTEAM Human Relations Video Test, the FireTEAM Mechanical Reasoning Test, the FireTEAM Math Test, and the FireTEAM Reading Test. When fire departments receive the scoring for ergometrics tests, in addition to receiving numerical scores, they also receive "dimensional" scores based on firefighter candidate response patterns. This type of scoring is done to provide further insight into a candidate's strengths and weaknesses.

Ergometrics tests are paper and pencil tests that use a multiple choice format. The tests have varying time limits that are explained below. Some candidates report difficulty finishing some of the questions on ergometrics tests before the video moves to the next question (particularly during the FireTEAM Mechanical Reasoning test). Good time management and focus during these tests are essential for a high score. Following is a breakdown of the four Ergometrics tests:

FIRETEAM HUMAN RELATIONS VIDEO TEST

- 28 scenarios
- 76 questions
- 56 minutes

As with most of their testing, Ergometrics uses a different way of presenting their questions compared to a traditional test. Questions are presented as a short video that depicts a firefighting-related scenario. Test questions play continuously without stopping. Candidates are given 10 seconds to answer each question. Usually, they are asked to pick the best solution to the questions, then the worst solution. Answers are recorded on a bubble sheet in a multiple choice format.

Any information needed to answer the questions is provided in the video. Make sure you pay attention and focus during the test. It is important not to miss any information. When answering the questions, it is essential that you answer honestly and do not read into the test questions. Make sure you base your responses on common sense and the information provided. Remember, there are no trick questions.

The FireTEAM Human Relations Video Test is given in a video-based format in two parts:

PART 1 involves situational and personality profiling type questions that are designed specifically for firefighter candidates. The test is designed to identify firefighter candidates with the teamwork and interpersonal skills that are considered predictive of successful future firefighters.

PART 2 of the human relations test is immediately after part 1. Firefighter candidates will observe individual firefighters in different situations. The questions in part 2 will be directly related to the actions of these firefighters.

It is important when answering situational judgment questions that firefighter candidates remember that Ergometrics is a U.S.-based company. Although the questions were thoroughly validated, they were designed using American firefighting experts and their opinions based on American firefighter culture (for example, most fire departments in the United States do not have a seniority system like most Canadian fire departments). Answer the questions from your point of view as a firefighter, NOT as a rookie.

FIRETEAM MECHANICAL REASONING TEST

- 36 items
- 43 minutes

This video-based test is sometimes called "the brick factory test." Firefighter candidates will be shown an animated brickmaking factory and how some of the parts of the factory work. Questions are based on this information. Some of the questions are trouble shooting questions where firefighter candidates may be asked to find problems involving things such as valves or water pressure. Test takers should remember that all of the questions can be answered using the information provided in the video. It is essential that firefighter candidates pay attention and focus during this test. Questions will not be replayed and some candidates have difficulty keeping up. The Mechanical Aptitude section of Chapter 2 covers the principles candidates will need to do well on this test.

FIRETEAM MATH TEST

- 31 items
- 25 minutes

This video-based test involves questions intended to identify if test takers can do basic firefighter-related math. This test includes addition, subtraction, multiplication, division, and proportions. Most firefighter candidates find this section easier than the firefighter mathematics testing on other firefighter exams. All of these principals are covered in the Math Questions portion of Chapter 2.

FIRETEAM READING TEST

- 25 items
- 15 minutes

This test is designed to identify candidates that have the reading skills necessary to be successful firefighters. Questions involve activities such as placing the correct word (of four choices) in a paragraph. Most firefighter candidates find this section easier than the reading comprehension testing designed by other companies. The Reading Comprehension section in Chapter 2 of this book covers this type of question thoroughly.

Stefan, Fraser & Associates, Inc.

www.stefanfraser.com

Stefan, Fraser & Associates, Inc. have provided screening assessments for municipal fire services in Canada for over 30 years. The Stefan-Fraser Test consists of approximately four hours of paper and pencil testing and is typically conducted in a group setting. The testing is based on current findings from research literature with respect to the factors that predict success as a firefighter "on-the-job." Three main areas are assessed: general learning ability and specific aptitudes (e.g., mechanical reasoning); personality traits associated with success as a firefighter; and career interest patterns.

It is difficult to "study" for this assessment. Remember that it is important to be honest and use consistent answers for the personality traits section of the test (see the Personality Profiling section of Chapter 2 for more information). Also, make sure you are familiar with the information provided in Chapter 2 to score well on the general learning and specific aptitudes portion of the test (math, mechanical aptitude, and reading comprehension in particular).

The Occupational Specific Assessment for Firefighters (OS Test)

www.gledhill-shaw.ca

The Occupational Specific Assessment for Firefighters Test (OS Test) is considered a "Functional Characteristics Assessment" that municipalities can use as part of their recruitment process to help identify various qualities that are important for a successful firefighter candidate. This is not an aptitude test. The OS test is an objective assessment designed using firefighting experts to identify the essential occupational requirements that are necessary for the maintenance of public safety in firefighting.

The OS test is a 2¼ hour test that contains 250 questions. Firefighter candidates can complete their rough work in the question booklet and then transfer it to a multiple choice style bubble sheet. Questions are usually grouped to reflect the following characteristic areas that the recruiting fire department believes are essential for firefighters.

1. Dealing with Group and Team Issues
2. Decision Making in Stressful Situations
3. Coping with Stressful Situations
4. Professional Responsibility
5. Mechanical and Mathematical Computations and Problem Solving
6. Interpersonal Communication and Style

Some of the questions on the OS test require test takers to choose a correct answer from several choices. Other questions will ask candidates to rate their responses to different situations presented in the questions. Recruiting fire departments are provided with scoring for each candidate that indicates whether or not the candidate scored in the target range for each of the six "Characteristics Areas." Firefighter candidates are rated as successful, borderline, or unsuccessful in each of the "Characteristics Areas." An overall score out of 200 is also provided.

Keep in mind that this is not an aptitude test. Questions on this test relate to emergency situations and other specific work place scenarios. Firefighter candidates are required to solve and respond to these situations. Basic math and logic questions are also included.

It is important to be honest and use consistent answers (sometimes similar questions will be asked several times). To prepare, use real life situations and think about what solutions would be best. For example, use situations from work or emergency incidents you see in the news. The Situational Judgment section of Chapter 2 discusses in greater detail how to score well on this type of test.

CWH Research, Inc.

www.cwhms.com

CWH is a company based in Colorado. They offer different services including various types of testing for firefighters. CWH offers an entry level firefighter test called the Selection Solutions Test. This test is considered a skills test; it is intended to measure a firefighter candidate's ability to solve problems, understand complex situations, interact with people, and deal with other job related abilities. CWH tests are thoroughly validated using standard practices that involve firefighter subject matter experts, job analysis, and extensive research. All answers are based on research.

The CWH fire department entry level test is a 3 hour and 15 minute paper and pencil multiple choice test. Questions can have between two and ten possible answers depending on the question. The test contains 140 test items. The scores in each component are combined into a total score that is used for the final ranking of firefighter candidates.

The entry level test is designed to assess a candidate's overall fit using that person's strengths and weaknesses. The test has questions that attempt to measure a candidate's personal, intellectual, and emotional skills. During the test, firefighter candidates will answer mostly situational questions that attempt to gauge a candidate's ability to deal with problems, interact with people, and handle stress. The CWH test does not attempt to gauge a firefighter candidate's specific personality type.

The test measures:

Basic Educational Skills

This portion of the test measures the knowledge a firefighter candidate has acquired over the course of his or her life that he or she will need to be a competent firefighter. This includes math, reading, writing, and grammar skills. Also measured is the firefighter candidate's ability to comprehend, learn, and retain information.

Practical Skills

This section measures a firefighter candidate's ability to deal with everyday challenges. Questions involve problem solving ability, judgment, and common sense.

Interpersonal Skills

Questions on this section of the test assess a firefighter candidate's ability to relate to and get along with others. This portion of the test involves compassion, diversity, and teamwork.

Emotional Skills

This section gauges a firefighter candidate's emotional response to different situations. Questions involve respect for authority, work ethic, ethics, and handling stress.

Mechanical Aptitude

This portion of the test intends to assess a firefighter candidate's mechanical ability including knowledge of basic principles of physics. Questions cover leverage, reading gauges, gears, and pulleys.

It is important for firefighter candidates to remember not to try to fake their way through the portions of this test that measure character traits. It is important to answer honestly and pick the question that is closest to the way you would respond in real life. Remember to be consistent when answering questions.

Preparing for the Written Tests

2

This chapter is designed to help prepare you for any firefighter written exam that you will take in Canada. In it, you will find plenty of valuable information that could help you achieve your goal and become a firefighter, but it is your responsibility to apply the information. Being hired as a firefighter is very competitive; some fire departments may only hire 1–2% of their applicants or less. At every firefighter written exam you attend there will be many other candidates who have spent countless hours studying and preparing for that exam. Always remember that to be a successful applicant will take effort and motivation. A little extra preparation could be the difference between being hired or not being hired. It's your responsibility to provide the drive to be a successful candidate.

GENERAL ADVICE

When writing any type of aptitude test, it is important to remember some very basic but important things to do before you begin the test. Every step of the process can be considered part of an interview. Have respect for the position you are applying for and do everything you can to show fire department personnel that you are an excellent candidate. If you act like a good firefighter, it will help you be seen as one. Remember: You are being watched during all stages of the recruitment. Even if there are thousands of people taking a test, if you are remembered, it is better to be remembered in a positive light than a negative one.

APPEARANCE AND PERSONAL PRESENTATION

Dress appropriately. Business casual for men and women is a minimum (unless physical testing is on the same day). This means crisp, neat attire including dress pants (no jeans or shorts), a collared shirt, leather belt, and shoes (no athletic shoes). Remember that it is better to be overdressed than underdressed. Many people come to written tests wearing a suit (jacket can be put on the chair while writing). A good rule of thumb is to never be dressed more casually than the firefighters in attendance.

Public image is very important to fire departments. How candidates dress for each stage of the recruitment can be an indicator of how seriously they will take the job and how they will represent the department in the future.

Groom appropriately. Almost all fire departments have a grooming policy. The best plan is to follow traditional firefighter grooming. Basically this means that you are clean shaven (mustache is acceptable); if you have long hair it is worn up. Wearing a hat is not a good idea.

General attitude. It is important to be yourself, but remember: respect the position you are in and the job you are applying for. Be humble and respect everyone.

Learn about the test you are taking. This is a very important part of test preparation. Be sure to study as effectively as possible and bring everything you will need during the test. The more you know about a test, the more effectively you can prepare.

Learn about the fire department you are writing the test for. Learn everything you can as something may come up that could give you an edge. Check the Internet, network with other candidates, talk to firefighters, recruiters, and HR.

Learn what you need for the test. The night before the test prepare the materials you will need during and before the test. This includes photo identification (drivers license), pencils, erasers, etc. Human resources will usually tell firefighter candidates what materials they will be required to bring to the test. If you are unsure, contact human resources in the municipality where you are writing the test. As always, make sure you could not have easily answered your own question before you call (for example, a question that could easily be found by looking at the municipal website).

Show up on time. Be early if possible. Never, ever, be late. Plan your trip to the test location ahead of time. Leave ample time for traffic or other problems.

Advice for people with learning disabilities. If you have a recognized learning disability, notify HR. This will not and cannot (legally) be held against you.

STUDYING AND PREPARING FOR THE TEST

It is important to develop good study habits as you lead up to your firefighter written test. This will help you make good use of your study time and be more prepared and confident when you take the test. Always remember: every extra correct answer on the day of the test could be the one that gets you a job. Even 20 minutes of extra studying or preparation could be what helps you reach your goal of becoming a firefighter.

Study in an environment similar to the test. Study somewhere quiet and try to simulate test conditions to the best of your ability. Just focus on studying. Try not to listen to music or study in front of the TV. When it comes to test time, using similar testing conditions will help you relax and focus on doing well on the test.

Maintain a healthy diet and regular exercise schedule. A healthy body helps create a healthy mind. Eating well and exercising regularly are also well documented ways of lowering stress.

Make a study schedule. Regular, scheduled daily study times will help you make studying a priority.

Study effectively. Stay focused and concentrate on absorbing the information you are covering. The more you practice, the more you will learn; but that practice has to be effective. Just like working out a muscle at the gym, if you don't exercise effectively you will see few gains. The more effectively you work out your brain, the greater the improvements will be.

Be completely confident in your ability to do every type of question covered in this book. Make sure you understand every type of question explained in this chapter and every question and answer in the sample tests.

Focus on your weaknesses. After some study time your strengths and weaknesses should become apparent. Make sure you focus on your weaknesses.

WRITING THE TEST

Get a good night's sleep the night before the test. Sleep in if you need to. The more alert you are for your test the better.

Get to the test early. Not only will this be a good sign for recruiters, it should help you be less stressed and more comfortable during the test. This should help you score better. Make sure you have planned your route to the test and have left ample time to get there.

Understand all of the instructions for the test. If you don't understand some of the instructions given at the start of the test, make sure you ask. Be clear on time limits, how to fill in your answer sheet, and other instructions.

Pay attention to the time while you write the test. Make sure you know how much time you have to write the test so you can use your time efficiently. Wear a watch and keep track of time during the test. Testing companies often use similar methods for determining the time limits for their written tests. Usually, 1 minute is given for each question, in addition to 30 extra minutes.

Make sure your questions and answers line up. Check several times while you are writing the test to make sure your answers line up with the question (for example, If you are answering question number 67, make sure you are filling in question number 67 on the answer sheet).

Completely fill in the bubbles. Fill in the bubbles on the answer sheet completely. Only the answer sheet will be scored, so make sure your answers are clear by fully filling in the corresponding circle on the answer sheet. If you know the answer but do not fill in the correct bubble, it will be marked wrong.

Make sure you erase completely. If you change an answer, erase your old pencil mark as completely as possible.

Don't pay attention to patterns on the answer key. Patterns in the answer key mean nothing. Never answer a question based on a pattern on the bubble sheet.

Your first thought is usually the right answer. If you have an answer to a question before you read the possible answers, pick the answer that is the closest. The wording may not always be exactly as you might expect.

Read every question thoroughly. If you skim a question because you think it is easy or you are rushing, you may mark the wrong answer down. For example, if you mix up the words "does" and "doesn't", you could easily mark down the wrong answer.

Base your answers on the information provided. Take questions at face value and do not read into them. Usually your first answer is correct.

Read all of the options before you select an answer. Remember to select the *best* answer to the question.

Don't waste time on the difficult questions. Pass over difficult questions and come back to them at the end of the test. Easy and difficult questions are worth the same towards your total score. Your goal is to complete 100% of the test; don't run out of time focusing on one difficult question and miss 10 easy ones.

Don't leave any blank answers. Go back when you are finished the test and make sure there are no blank spaces on the answer sheet. If you don't know the answer to the question, refer to the "Guidelines for Guessing on Multiple Choice Questions" section in this chapter.

Answer all of the questions the same if time is running out. If time is running out and you don't have time to read and answer the remaining questions, answer them all the same. For example, fill in all the answers as "C". Chances are you will get at least 25% of them right (if there are 4 possible answers). If you have time remaining and don't know the answer to the question, refer to the "Guidelines for Guessing on Multiple Choice Questions" in this chapter.

Go over your answers. If you finish the test before time expires, review your answers. Remember not to read into questions.

Write down difficult questions after you leave. If you can remember some of the questions you had difficulty with (even just the type of question), write it down. This will help you study for your next test (if you have to take one).

GUIDELINES FOR GUESSING ON MULTIPLE CHOICE QUESTIONS

If you do not know the answer, your best option is to take your best educated guess. Below are some guidelines to follow that should help you narrow down the correct answer.

Eliminate the answers that you know are wrong. Cross these answers out in the test book. Don't go back and re-read the answers you have crossed out.

Think about how the test was written. If you are unsure, look at the words used in the question. Always remember (as explained in Chapter 1) that tests have almost always been validated question by question. The right answer needs to be defendable if challenged. Words that provide little movement for test designers often indicate a wrong answer (e.g., everybody, nobody, never, always, etc.). Often correct answers will use words that are easier to defend because they provide test designers with more flexibility (e.g., sometimes, often, possibly, etc.)

Eliminate similar answers. Similar choices are *usually* a sign of incorrect answers. Similar answers means answers that have the same meaning.

Consider specific answers. Answers that contain very specific details or lots of information are often correct.

Look closely at choices with opposite meanings. Choices with opposite meanings (e.g., Does, does not) may indicate that one of these choices is right. Read them both carefully and then return to the question to try to determine the correct answer.

Look closely at how the answers relate to the question grammatically. Options that grammatically don't fit with the question may indicate a wrong answer.

Consider "All of the above" or "None of the above". If more than one of the answers seems correct then "All of the above" or "None of the above" may be the best option.

Remember that most tests are written in the United States. This is usually only applicable for situational type questions. If you have researched the test you are taking, you will know where the test has been designed. Test questions on American tests were most likely designed and validated based on American firefighter responses, culture, and opinions (e.g., most fire departments in the United States do not have a seniority system like most Canadian fire departments). When considering which answer to choose, look at the answers from your point of view as a firefighter and NOT as a rookie.

ORAL COMPREHENSION QUESTIONS
What Are They and Why Are They Used?

Firefighters have to be able to communicate effectively. If a firefighter can't effectively listen to and understand his or her co-workers, it will be impossible to be a successful firefighter. Oral comprehension testing is used to assess candidates' ability to absorb, understand, remember, and apply information that they receive orally.

Most written tests that contain an Oral Comprehension section will involve the proctor reading a passage out loud to the firefighter candidates. After the proctor is finished reading, the candidates will receive the test and be allowed to answer questions based on what the proctor has read. Usually candidates will not be allowed to take notes while the proctor reads the passage. All the answers required for the oral comprehension portion of the test will be contained in what is read by the proctor. It is essential for firefighter candidates to absorb the information read by the proctor to the best of their ability so they can use it effectively to answer the questions in the test.

How Can I Score Higher?

Before the test:

Practice in a way that works for you. Many people remember oral information differently; practice will help you find out what works best for you. You can think of your brain as a filing cabinet. You need to figure out how to create files that will work most effectively for you. That way when you are listening to the oral comprehension portion of your firefighter written exam you can file the information in your memory in a way that will make it easier for you to retrieve. For example, some people try to relate the information they are hearing during written tests to life experiences they have had that are related in some way. This way they can "file" the information temporarily using certain related memories to make the information easier to remember.

Once you know what works, practice regularly. When you know what works best to help you recall information, use it as much as possible. You can practice your oral comprehension skills during your day-to-day life when you are watching TV, listening to the radio, or talking to people. Ideally, you can have someone read information to you (from this book, short stories, magazine articles, firefighter material, even instruction manuals). If you work with someone, you can simulate the exam (for example, by having someone read a newspaper article to you) and they can ask you practice questions after. It is very important to focus and listen to everything that is said. Try not to daydream or let your mind drift. Make sure you get all of the important details as well as the overall message(s) that is being conveyed.

During the test:

Make sure you can hear. Be sure that you sit in a place where you can hear clearly. If you can't hear the proctor properly, there is nothing wrong with asking politely to move to a place where you can hear better.

Concentrate. Pay attention; all of the information you need to answer the oral comprehension questions will be read by the proctor. If you don't pay attention while the proctor is reading the passage, you won't absorb all of the information being read. If you don't absorb all of the information being read, you will not be able to answer all the questions and you will not score well. Do not let your mind drift from what is being read by the proctor.

Notice details. Pay attention to the specific details mentioned by the proctor. Often, the questions on the test involve specific details that are read by the proctor. For example, these details could be numbers, time, addresses, names, or places.

Focus on remembering the key points and important information. Try to pick out important information or key points while listening. These are most likely to be used as questions.

Take notes if possible. Write down notes of specific details and other key points in short form. Most exams do not allow candidates to write anything down (this defeats the purpose of absorbing, understanding, remembering, and applying information). If you are allowed to take notes during the exam, be as thorough as possible.

Answer the questions as soon as you can. When you get the answer booklet, answer the Oral Comprehension questions as soon as possible. This will help you recall the appropriate information because the information, and hopefully the answers, will be fresh in your mind.

Read and answer the questions carefully. Make sure you understand all of the instructions and exactly what the questions are asking. Draw your answers from what the proctor has read only.

READING COMPREHENSION QUESTIONS
What Are They and Why Are They Used?

It is important for firefighters to read and comprehend many different types of written material. Throughout his or her career, a firefighter will be required to read and interpret a vast amount of information. This includes things like manuals, textbooks, operational guidelines, policies, rules and regulations, safety information, training material, and many other things. A firefighter's ability to comprehend that information will directly affect his or her ability to perform and be successful.

When a person reads something, he or she should come away with a good understanding of the ideas and meanings presented in the text—this is reading comprehension. Firefighter exams almost always have a section containing reading comprehension questions. These questions are designed by test manufacturers to gauge a firefighter candidate's ability to read and understand written information. Reading comprehension tests generally contain several paragraphs or passages with a number of related questions following the text. The answers for each question will always be found in the text relating to the question.

It is also important to remember that aside from the "Reading Comprehension" portion of your firefighter written test, all questions on the test will require some level of reading comprehension. Even math and mechanical aptitude questions require a certain level of reading comprehension to understand what the question is asking. Because reading comprehension is part of every question, it is one of the most important skills for a firefighter candidate to have in order to be successful on a firefighter exam.

COMMON TYPES OF READING COMPREHENSION QUESTIONS FOUND ON WRITTEN TESTS

Questions that ask for a general idea presented in the text. This means that the question will be looking for the overall idea presented in the text related to the question. You may have to rearrange sentences to do this but the information will be found in the text for the question. The answer to the question may not come from one particular sentence but it may come from a combination. Be sure to fully read all of the options before answering this type of question and don't choose an answer that's only half correct.

Questions that ask for a solution to a problem or situation. These questions may not have the exact answer in the text provided; they will usually require the test taker to predict the answer from the information provided. To find the answer, you may have to create an answer or conclusion based on facts gathered from the text. When determining your answer, make sure you always use facts that are found in the text. It will also help to try to think about the question from the author's point of view and use common sense.

Questions that ask what a paragraph or section of text means. This type of question asks a firefighter candidate for the meaning of a section of text. To find the correct answer, you may have to read between the lines and interpret the true meaning of the text.

Questions that ask for specific facts or details contained in the text. These questions will ask the test taker for exact details that will be found in the text for the question. To answer this question correctly, you may need to find a concept or rule in the text that fits the question or find a connection between events related to the question. Answers for these types of questions will always be found in the text related to the question.

Questions that ask for information to be put in the correct order. These questions measure a candidate's ability to place information in the correct order for use in a situation. Usually rules or instructions are given as part of the question. To answer these questions correctly, you will need to find the required information in the text and then use the instructions or rules provided to put the information in the correct order.

Questions that ask for the meaning of a word. These questions will test your vocabulary. Usually even if you don't know the meaning of the word, you can guess fairly accurately by inferring its meaning from the sentence it is in (although sometimes questions will just ask you for the meaning of a word that is not in a sentence). Remember to always look up the meaning of words you don't know in your day-to-day life. This will help you answer these types of questions.

How Can I Score Higher?

Before the test:

You can improve your reading comprehension in your daily life simply by reviewing the things you read in newspapers, books, magazines, and on the Internet. Take a second to pause after you have read each paragraph. Make sure you have completely absorbed all of the information included in the paragraph, especially the main idea presented. Train yourself to take the time to read and comprehend the meaning of a passage by reading the text completely and never skimming.

Make sure you practice frequently. The more time you spend practicing, the more efficient and effective you will become. Practice using the techniques listed below in the "during the test" section. When you practice, you will begin to discover the techniques that work best for you and you can begin to apply them successfully.

If you come across a word you don't know the meaning of, take the time to learn it. Google the word or look it up in the dictionary. A firefighter candidate with a larger vocabulary will be much better at grasping the ideas presented in the text during a test. This will make answering questions easier and more efficient. Aside from helping with your general reading comprehension, this will also help you score higher when vocabulary questions are included on firefighter aptitude tests.

During the test:

This process works best for many people when answering Reading Comprehension questions:

Skim the text that relates to the question(s). This could be one paragraph or more. The purpose is to get a quick general idea of what is contained in the text. This will help make it easier when you need to find the information you require to answer the questions that are related to the text.

Read the question. Do this quickly. This will tell you what information you are looking for in the text. Make sure you understand what the question is asking. If you remember anything related to the question from skimming the text in step 1, go back and underline or highlight it during step 3 (if you bring multiple colors of highlighters to the test then you can highlight using different colors for each question to avoid confusion).

Read the text thoroughly. Focus and concentrate on what you are reading and the answer you are looking for. Don't let your mind drift. Make sure you are absorbing everything and looking out for information that is related to the question(s). When you find information related to the question(s), underline or highlight it and use it to answer the question.

> Note: Because different tests present their reading comprehension questions in different ways, this may have to be adjusted to fit the test you are writing. For example, some tests use very long reading sections that have many questions after the text, while other tests have one question per paragraph. Use your judgment.

Answer the question. Make sure you have a good reason for choosing your answer (the answer will always be in the text—either directly or implied). Be sure to read the question and answer thoroughly and follow the "Writing the Test—General Advice" section from this chapter to be sure you are making the correct selection.

LEARNING, REMEMBERING, AND APPLYING WRITTEN INFORMATION QUESTIONS

What Are They and Why Are They Used?

Learning, Remembering, and Applying Written Information questions test firefighter candidates' ability to absorb and recall information they have read. This is very similar to a firefighter's job in that many times during the course of a shift, firefighters may need to recall information they have read as part of their training and use it during a call. The ability to learn and apply information is crucial for efficient and competent firefighters.

As part of a firefighter written exam, Learning, Remembering, and Applying Written Information sections are essentially a combination of the Oral Comprehension and Reading Comprehension sections discussed earlier in this chapter. Usually at the beginning of the test, candidates will be given an information packet/booklet (commonly several paragraphs long based on something related to firefighting) to read for a set amount of time. The candidates will be asked to read the information provided and remember what they can (usually notes are not allowed to be taken). After a pre-determined amount of time, the information packet will be taken away from candidates and they will receive their test. A section of the test will be based on the information packet they have just read. As with other questions that deal with recalling information, all of the answers to the questions will be contained in the information package that was read by the candidates.

How Can I Score Higher?

Before the test:

Practice in a way that works for you. Just like with remembering oral information, people remember written information in many different ways. You need to figure out what will work most effectively for you. That way when you are reading the related portion of your firefighter written exam you can file the information in your memory in a way that will make it easier for you to retrieve. Sometimes it is useful for people to try to relate what they are reading to their own life experiences. This way you can use those related experiences to form a connection with the information in the text.

When you know what works, practice regularly. When you know what works best to help you recall information, use it as much as possible. You can practice your Learning, Remembering, and Applying Written Information skills during your daily life by reading newspapers, books, magazines, the Internet, and other things (especially the practice tests in this book, any reading comprehension can be used this way). Ideally you can work with someone who can ask you questions based on what you have read.

During the test:

Use your time with the information packet as effectively as possible. Try to stay focused; you will not get another chance with this information. If you finish reading before the time is up, read it again. Be sure you are absorbing as much of the important information contained in the passage as possible.

Think of what the questions might be while you are reading. If you are reading something that might make a good question, remember that information.

Focus on remembering the key points and important information. As mentioned above, questions will most likely be based on details, key points, and critical information.

Stay focused. Concentrate and focus while reading and when the test booklets are being collected. Make sure you don't forget the information you have read while you are waiting for the booklets to be collected and the questions to be handed out.

Answer the questions as soon as possible. Open the test and do the Learning, Remembering, and Applying Written Information as soon as the proctor allows you to open the test and start answering questions. An effective way to reduce the information lost between reading the passage and answering the questions is to write down everything you can remember from the test information packet as soon as you are allowed to start the test and then answer the questions. This works better for some people than others. Use your judgment and experience from your practice.

Read and answer the questions carefully. Make sure you understand all of the instructions and exactly what the questions are asking. Draw your answers from what you have read in the test information packet only.

MATH QUESTIONS
What Are They and Why Are They Used?

Math questions test a firefighter candidate's ability to successfully complete job-related mathematics. Firefighters often use mathematics at work. It could be for something as simple as adding up several lengths of hose or for something more complicated such as determining the friction loss in a hose while relay pumping over a long distance.

The answers to simple math question are either right or wrong. There are no grey areas. This is why it is essential to completely understand the types of math questions you will see on your test. What follows is a review of the types of math that you may see on your test—addition, subtraction, multiplication, and division.

Addition

Addition is combining two or more numbers to make a new total.
An easy example:

2 + 2 = 4

or

two plus two equals four

or

```
 2
+2
 4
```

When adding larger numbers, "column" addition is used.

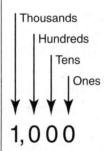

1,000

For example:

```
 24
+24
 48
```

This is done by adding the numbers vertically (4 + 4 = 8 and 2 + 2 = 4).

If the number you are adding vertically becomes a two digit number, you need to split the number and carry it to the next column (called the "tens" column).
For example:

```
  1
 29
+18
 47
```

(9 + 8 = 17, so the 1 is moved to the left and added to 2 and 1)

This works the same with numbers in the 100's and 1,000's, etc. and with decimals:
For example:

```
 4098.17
+3286.26
```

STEP 1 Add up the first column (on the right). 7 + 6 = 13. The 1 is carried to the next column.

$$\begin{array}{r}
{\scriptstyle 1} \\
4098.17 \\
+\ 3286.26 \\
\hline
3
\end{array}$$

STEP 2 Add up the second column. 1 + 1 + 2 = 4

$$\begin{array}{r}
{\scriptstyle 1} \\
4098.17 \\
+\ 3286.26 \\
\hline
.43
\end{array}$$

STEP 3 Add up the third column. 8 + 6 = 14. The one is carried to the next column.

$$\begin{array}{r}
{\scriptstyle 1\ \ 1} \\
4098.17 \\
+\ 3286.26 \\
\hline
4.43
\end{array}$$

STEP 4 Add up the fourth column. 1 + 9 + 8 = 18. The one is carried to the next column.

$$\begin{array}{r}
{\scriptstyle 1\,1\ \ 1} \\
4098.17 \\
+\ 3286.26 \\
\hline
84.43
\end{array}$$

STEP 5 Add up the fifth column. 1 + 0 + 2 = 3.

$$\begin{array}{r}
{\scriptstyle 1\,1\ \ 1} \\
4098.17 \\
+\ 3286.26 \\
\hline
384.43
\end{array}$$

STEP 6 Add up the sixth column. 4 + 3 = 7.

$$\begin{array}{r}
{\scriptstyle 1\,1\ \ 1} \\
4098.17 \\
+\ 3286.26 \\
\hline
7384.43
\end{array}$$

The answer is 7,384.43.

The decimal stays where it was.

This also works for multiple numbers.

Remember: No matter what order you add numbers in or how you write them, the answer will be the same. This is called being associative ((a + b) + c = a + (b + c)) and commutative (a + b = b + c).

For example:

```
 9891
 7995
+5432
```

(STEP 1) Add up the first column (on the right). $1 + 5 + 2 = 8$.

```
   9891
   7995
 + 5432
-------
      8
```

(STEP 2) Add up the second column. $9 + 9 + 3 = 21$. The two is carried to the next column.

```
    2
   9891
   7995
 + 5432
-------
     18
```

(STEP 3) Add up the third column. $2 + 8 + 9 + 4 = 23$. The two is carried to the next column.

```
   22
   9891
   7995
 + 5432
-------
    318
```

(STEP 4) Add up the fourth column. $2 + 9 + 7 + 5 = 23$.

```
   22
   9891
   7995
 + 5432
-------
  23318
```

The answer is 23,318.

Remember: When adding numbers, it may be easier to break the numbers down into more easily manageable groups to make the addition easier. Then you can add them back up at the end. This way the addition can be done in your head and save you time.

An easy example:

$235 + 245 + 110 = ?$

This can be broken down into:

$200 + 200 + 100 = 500$

and

$35 + 45 + 10 = 90$

Then add the numbers back up:

$500 + 90 = 590$

Therefore:

$235 + 245 + 110 = 590$

An example you may see on your written test:

Question: There are 2 lengths of 50 foot hose being used as an exposure line. Your captain asks you to extend the line 50 more feet. After you extend the line, how much hose will you have?

Answer:

Just add up the three lengths of hose:

$50 + 50 + 50 = 150$ feet of hose

Subtraction

Subtraction is taking one number away from another number. It is the opposite operation to addition.

An easy example:

$3 - 2 = 1$

or

three minus two equals 1

or

$$\begin{array}{r} 3 \\ -2 \\ \hline 1 \end{array}$$

When subtracting larger numbers, there are several methods that can be used. Subtraction with regrouping (also called borrowing) is the most common.

Usually you subtract by placing the larger number on top.

For example:

$$\begin{array}{r} 65 \\ -43 \\ \hline 22 \end{array}$$

(STEP 1) Subtract the first column (on the right). $5 - 3 = 2$
(STEP 2) Subtract the second column. $6 - 4 = 2$

The answer is 22.

Sometimes when you put the larger number on top, some of the numbers on the top will be less than the numbers on the bottom. This is when subtraction with regrouping (borrowing) can be used.

For example:

20578
−3699

(STEP 1) Subtract the first column (on the right). 8 is less than 9 so you need to "borrow" from the column to the left. The 7 in the left column becomes 6 and the 8 in the right column becomes 18. The right column is now 18 − 9 = 9.

$$
\begin{array}{r}
6 \\
205\cancel{7}8 \\
-\ 3699 \\
\hline
9
\end{array}
$$

(STEP 2) Subtract the second column. 6 is less than 9 so you need to "borrow" from the column to the left. The 5 in the left column becomes 4 and the 6 in the right column becomes 16. The right column is now 16 − 9 = 7.

$$
\begin{array}{r}
4\,6 \\
20\cancel{5}\cancel{7}8 \\
-\ 3699 \\
\hline
79
\end{array}
$$

(STEP 3) Subtract the third column. 4 is less than 6 so you need to "borrow" from the column to the left. Because you can't borrow from 0 you need to borrow from the next two columns to the left (the "20"). The 20 on the left becomes 19 and the 4 in the right column becomes 14. The right column is now 14 − 6 = 8.

$$
\begin{array}{r}
19\,4\,6 \\
\cancel{2057}8 \\
-\ 3699 \\
\hline
879
\end{array}
$$

(STEP 4) Subtract the fourth column. 9 − 3 = 6.

$$
\begin{array}{r}
19\,4\,6 \\
\cancel{2057}8 \\
-\ 3699 \\
\hline
6879
\end{array}
$$

(STEP 5) Subtract the fifth column. 1 − 0 = 1.

$$
\begin{array}{r}
19\,4\,6 \\
\cancel{2057}8 \\
-\ 3699 \\
\hline
16879
\end{array}
$$

The answer is 16,879.

If you have to subtract more than two numbers, you have to do them two at a time. They cannot be stacked like when adding groups of numbers.

For example:

$53,014 - 16,498 - 8,897 = ?$

Answer $53,014 - 16,498$ first using the method described above. $53,014 - 16,498 = 36,516$.

$$\begin{array}{r} 53,014 \\ -16,498 \\ \hline 36,516 \end{array}$$

Next subtract 8,897 from 36,516 using the method above. $36,516 - 8,897 = 27,619$.

$$\begin{array}{r} 36,516 \\ -8,897 \\ \hline 27,619 \end{array}$$

The answer is 27,619.

Remember: When subtracting numbers, it may be easier to break the numbers down into more easily manageable groups to make the subtraction easier. Then add the numbers back up at the end. This way the subtraction can be done in your head and save you time.
An easy example:

$255 - 120 = ?$

This can be broken down into:

$200 - 100 = 100$

and

$55 - 20 = 35$

Then add the numbers back up:

$100 + 35 = 135$

Therefore:

$255 - 120 = 135$

An example you may see on your written test:
Question: The truck you work on carries 1,000 ft of 2.5 inch hose. At the end of a fire, you have 200 ft of hose left over. How much 2.5 inch hose was used?

   Answer: To find the answer, subtract the 200 ft of remaining hose from the 1,000 ft that was on the truck originally.

   $1000 - 200 = 800$ ft of hose was used at the fire.

Multiplication

Multiplication is essentially a way of adding up or combining groups of numbers.

   For example, 4×5 is easier to write than $5 + 5 + 5 + 5$ but means the same thing (four fives). 4×5 can also mean $4 + 4 + 4 + 4 + 4$ (five fours). Multiplication can be viewed as a more effective way of adding multiples of numbers.

Remember: No matter what order you multiply numbers in or how you write them, the answer will be the same. This is called being associative ((a × b) × c = a × (b × c)) and commutative (a × b = b × a). This is the same as addition.

For example:

$6 \times 5 = 30$
$5 \times 6 = 30$

$$\begin{array}{r} 5 \\ \times 6 \\ \hline 30 \end{array}$$

$$\begin{array}{r} 6 \\ \times 5 \\ \hline 30 \end{array}$$

Multiplication problems can be made a lot easier by memorizing the multiplication tables:

	1	2	3	4	5	6	7	8	9	10	11	12
1	1	2	3	4	5	6	7	8	9	10	11	12
2	2	4	6	8	10	12	14	16	18	20	22	24
3	3	6	9	12	15	18	21	24	27	30	33	36
4	4	8	12	16	20	24	28	32	36	40	44	48
5	5	10	15	20	25	30	35	40	45	50	55	60
6	6	12	18	24	30	36	42	48	54	60	66	72
7	7	14	21	28	35	42	49	56	63	70	77	84
8	8	16	24	32	40	48	56	64	72	80	88	96
9	9	18	27	36	45	54	63	72	81	90	99	108
10	10	20	30	40	50	60	70	80	90	100	110	120
11	11	22	33	44	55	66	77	88	99	110	121	132
12	12	24	36	48	60	72	84	96	108	120	132	144

When multiplying larger numbers, *long multiplication* is used. This involves carrying numbers.

For example:

$$\begin{array}{r} 34 \\ \times 24 \\ \hline \end{array}$$

STEP 1 Multiply the first or "ones" column. $4 \times 4 = 16$. Place the 6 in the "ones" column and "carry" the 1 to the top of the "tens" column.

```
    ₁
   34
 × 24
    6
```

STEP 2 Finish multiplying the first or "ones" column. $4 \times 3 = 12$. Add the 1 from Step 1. $12 + 1 = 13$. Place the 13 in the row next to the 6.

```
    ₁
   34
 × 24
  136
```

STEP 3 Place a zero in the "ones" column as shown. This is important because the next step is to multiply the "tens" column; therefore numbers will not be placed in the "ones" column.

```
    ₁
   34
 × 24
  136
    0
```

STEP 4 Multiply the "tens" column as shown to the first digit in the top row . $2 \times 4 = 8$. Place the 8 in the "tens" column.

```
    ₁
   34
 × 24
  136
   80
```

STEP 5 Finish multiplying the "tens" column. $2 \times 3 = 6$. Place the 6 next to the 8 as shown.

```
    ₁
   34
 × 24
  136
  680
```

STEP 6 Add the numbers that have resulted from the multiplication done in steps 1–5. $136 + 680 = 816$. Make sure you do the addition properly as described in the section above.

```
    ₁
   34
 × 24
  136
  680
  816
```

The answer is 816.

This system works for larger numbers as well. Remember to put the numbers in the correct column as you multiply (ones, tens, hundreds, thousands, etc.).

For example:

4562
× 318

STEP 1 Multiply the first or "ones" column. 8 × 2 = 16. Place the 6 in the "ones" column and "carry" the 1 to the top of the "tens" column.

```
     1
  4562
× 318
     6
```

STEP 2 Multiply the next number in the "ones" column. 8 × 6 = 48. Add the 1 from Step 1. 48 + 1 = 49. Place the 9 in the row next to the 6. Carry the 4 to the top of the "hundreds" column.

```
  41
  4562
× 318
    96
```

STEP 3 Multiply the next number in the "ones" column. 8 × 5 = 40. Add the 4 from Step 2. 40 + 4 = 44. Place the 4 in the row next to the 9. Carry the 4 to the top of the "thousands" column.

```
  441
  4562
× 318
   496
```

STEP 4 Multiply the last number in the "ones" column. 8 × 4 = 32. Add the 4 from Step 2. 32 + 4 = 36. Place the 36 in the correct row next to the 4 as shown.

```
  441
  4562
× 318
 36496
```

STEP 5 Place a zero in the ones column as shown. This is important because the next step is to multiply the "tens" column; therefore numbers will not be placed in the "ones" column.

```
   441
  4562
× 318
 36496
     0
```

STEP 6 Multiply the "tens" column as shown to the first digit in the top row. 1 × 2 = 2. Place the 2 in the "tens" column.

```
   441
  4562
× 318
 36496
    20
```

STEP 7 Multiply the "tens" column as shown to the second digit in the top row. 1 × 6 = 6. Place the 6 in the "hundreds" column.

```
   441
  4562
× 318
 36496
   620
```

STEP 8 Multiply the "tens" column as shown to the third digit in the top row. 1 × 5 = 5. Place the 5 in the "thousands" column.

```
   441
  4562
× 318
 36496
  5620
```

STEP 9 Finish multiplying the "tens" column. 1 × 4 = 4. Place the 4 next to the 5 as shown.

```
   441
  4562
× 318
 36496
 45620
```

STEP 10 Place a zero in the "ones" and the "tens" column as shown. This is important because the next step is to multiply the "hundreds" column; therefore numbers will not be placed in the "ones" or the "tens" column.

```
    4 4 1
   4562
  × 318
  36496
  45620
     00
```

STEP 11 Multiply the "hundreds column." 3 × 2 = 6. Place the 6 in the "hundreds" column.

```
    4 4 1
   4562
  × 318
  36496
  45620
    600
```

STEP 12 Multiply the next number in the "hundreds" column. 3 × 6 = 18. Place the 8 in the row next to the 6. Carry the 1 to the top of the "hundreds" column.

```
      1
    4 4 1
   4562
  × 318
  36496
  45620
   8600
```

STEP 13 Multiply the next number in the "hundreds" column. 3 × 5 = 15. Add the 1 from Step 2. 15 + 1 = 16. Place the 6 in the row next to the 8. Carry the 1 to the top of the "thousands" column.

```
    1 1
    4 4 1
   4562
  × 318
  36496
  45620
  68600
```

STEP 14 Multiply the last number in the "hundreds" column. $3 \times 4 = 12$. Add the 1 from Step 13. $12 + 1 = 13$. Place the 13 in the correct row next to the 6 as shown.

```
    ( (
   4-4-(
   4562
 × 318
  36496
  45620
1368600
```

STEP 15 Add the numbers that have resulted from the multiplication done in steps 1–14. $36496 + 45620 + 1368600 = 1,450,716$. Make sure you do the addition properly as described in the section above.

```
     ( (
    4-4-(
    4562
  × 318
   36496
   45620
 +1368600
 1,450,716
```

The answer is 1,450,716.

Remember: Multiplication is basically adding up multiples of numbers. You can multiply numbers by adding them up based on what the number is being multiplied by.

For example:

```
245
× 4
```

This is the same as 245×4. 245×4 is the same as $245 + 245 + 245 + 245$.

$245 + 245 + 245 + 245 = 980$

Therefore $245 \times 4 = 980$

An example you may see on your written test:
Question: There are 7 fire trucks in your station. Each truck carries 24 lengths of 1.5 inch hose. How much 1.5 inch hose is there on all the trucks in your station?

Answer: To find the answer, multiply the number of fire trucks by the amount of 1.5 inch hose on each truck.

$7 \times 24 = 168$ lengths

There are 168 lengths of 1.5 inch hose loaded on all the trucks in the station.

Division

Division is separating (or dividing) numbers into equal groups. It is the opposite of multiplication.

Remember: Although there are several ways division problems can be written, the order the numbers are written in is very important. Unlike multiplication, if the numbers are reversed the answer will be different.

For example:

$20 \div 2 = 10$ but $2 \div 20 = 0.1$

or

$10 / 5 = 2$ but $5 / 10 = 0.5$

or

$3\overline{)15}^{\,5}$ but $15\overline{)3}^{\,.2}$

or

$\dfrac{100}{50} = 2$ but $\dfrac{50}{100} = .5$

Remember: Knowing your multiplication tables can help you with division. This is because division is the opposite of multiplication.

For example:

$36 \div 6 = ?$

We know from the multiplication tables that $6 \times 6 = 36$.
   Therefore,

$36 \div 6 = 6$.

Sometimes you will need to use *long division* to find the answer to a problem.

For example:

$25\sqrt{625}$

STEP 1 Divide the first number of the dividend by the divisor. $6 \div 25 = 0$ remainder 6. Because 6 can't be divided by 25, there is no whole number result and the remainder is 6.

Divisor | Dividend

$$25\sqrt{625}$$

STEP 2) The whole number is placed at the top (in this case 0) above the first number of the dividend. The remainder (6) is ignored.

$$\begin{array}{r} 0 \\ 25\overline{\smash{)}625} \end{array}$$

STEP 3) The whole number from Step 1 is multiplied by the divisor. $0 \times 25 = 0$. The answer is placed under the first number of the dividend as shown.

$$\begin{array}{r} 0 \\ 25\overline{\smash{)}625} \\ 0 \end{array}$$

STEP 4) The result of step 3 is subtracted from the first number of the dividend as shown. $6 - 0 = 6$.

$$\begin{array}{r} 0 \\ 25\overline{\smash{)}625} \\ \underline{0} \\ 6 \end{array}$$

STEP 5) The second number of the dividend is brought down next to the 6.

$$\begin{array}{r} 0 \\ 25\overline{\smash{)}625} \\ \underline{0} \\ 62 \end{array}$$

STEP 6) Divide 62 by the divisor. $62 \div 25 = 2$ remainder 12. To figure this out in your head, find out how many times 25 will fit in 62 (2) and then multiply that number by 25 ($2 \times 25 = 50$) and subtract it from 62 to find the remainder ($62 - 50 = 12$).

$62 \div 25 = 2$ remainder 12

STEP 7) The whole number is placed at the top (in this case 2) above the second number of the dividend as shown. The remainder (12) is ignored.

$$\begin{array}{r} 02 \\ 25\overline{\smash{)}625} \\ \underline{0} \\ 62 \end{array}$$

STEP 8) The whole number found in Step 6 (2) is multiplied by the divisor. $2 \times 25 = 50$. The answer is placed under the 62 as shown.

$$\begin{array}{r} 02 \\ 25\overline{\smash{)}625} \\ \underline{0} \\ 62 \\ 50 \end{array}$$

STEP 9 The result of step 8 (50) is subtracted from 62. 62 − 50 = 12.

```
        02
   25√625
        0
       62
       50
       12
```

STEP 10 The third number of the dividend is brought down next to the 12 found in Step 9 as shown.

```
        02
   25√625
        0
       62
       50
      125
```

STEP 11 Divide 125 by the divisor. 125 ÷ 25 = 5 remainder 0.

125 ÷ 25 = 5

STEP 12 The whole number is placed at the top (in this case 5) above the third number of the dividend as shown.

```
       025
   25√625
        0
       62
       50
      125
```

STEP 13 The whole number found in Step 11 (5) is multiplied by the divisor. 5 × 25 = 125. The answer is placed under the 125 as shown.

```
       025
   25√625
        0
       62
       50
      125
      125
```

STEP 14 The result of step 13 (125) is subtracted from 125. 125 − 125 = 0.

```
       025
   25√625
        0
       62
       50
      125
      125
        0
```

The answer is 25. There are no more numbers in the dividend to bring down.

Things to remember about long division:

The steps repeat themselves until there are no more numbers from the dividend to bring down:

STEP 1 Divide number in dividend by divisor.

STEP 2 Place whole number on top.

STEP 3 Multiply whole number found by divisor and place below.

STEP 4 Subtract

STEP 5 Bring the next number of the dividend down.

Repeat until no numbers remain in the dividend.

If there are no more dividends to bring down and your last subtraction does not equal zero, you will have a remainder.

For example:

$$20\sqrt{230}$$

The answer is 11 remainder 10.

The above answer can be expressed another way by adding a decimal place (decimals are explained more thoroughly later in this chapter) and a zero to the dividend and then finishing the calculation:

```
        011.5
 20√230.0
     0
    23
    20
     30
     20
     100
     100
       0
```

Note: When the subtraction equals 0, you stop. If the subtraction gives a number more than 0, you can continue to as many decimal places as you want.

For example:

Some problems can be solved fairly easily with simple multiplication, addition, and subtraction. One of the problems above was $25\sqrt{625}$. If you know that there are four 25's for every 100, you can multiply 4 (25's) × 6 (100's) and get 24. Then because you know there are 24 25's in 600, you can just add one more 25 to get to 625. The answer is 25.

An Example You May See on Your Written Test

Question: You are performing a trail rescue. Four firefighters are carrying the victim in the rescue basket which weighs 280 lbs. Approximately how much weight is each firefighter carrying?

Answer: To find the answer, divide the weight by the number of firefighters.

TIP

Sometimes you can use simple multiplication to find the answer to long division problems.

$280 \div 4 = 70$

Each firefighter is carrying approximately 70 lbs.

Positive and Negative Integers

Numbers can be positive or negative. Negative numbers are indicated by the – sign, e.g. (–3). Positive numbers are represented by the + sign or no symbol, e.g. +3 or 3.

Below is the number line. An understanding of the number line will help you understand adding and subtracting positive and negative integers.

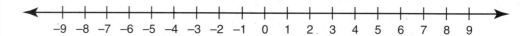

ADDING AND SUBTRACTING POSITIVE AND NEGATIVE INTEGERS

When you are adding or subtracting negative and positive numbers, you can think of the number line.

Always remember

2 positives (+ +) = positive
2 negatives (– –) = positive
2 opposites (+ –) = negative

A good way to remember this is two of the same signs equal a positive, whereas two different signs equal a negative. Remember that subtraction is the opposite of addition—if you do the opposite twice, you get back to the original.

For example: $9 + (-3) = +6$
(the two opposite signs mean that the $9 + (-3)$ becomes $9 - 3$)

Use the number line:

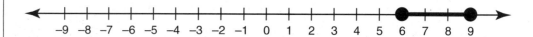

Another example: $5 - (-3) = +8$
(you are "taking away" the minus 3; it becomes addition)

Use the number line:

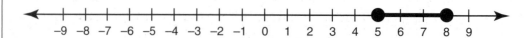

MULTIPLYING AND DIVIDING POSITIVE AND NEGATIVE INTEGERS

Multiplying and dividing positive and negative integers can be done in two easy steps:

(STEP 1) Multiply or divide as usual, ignoring any positive or negative numbers.
(STEP 2) Add the negative or positive symbol to the answer using the rules.

2 positives (+ +) = positive
2 negatives (− −) = positive
2 opposites (+ −) = negative

For example:

$(-2) \times (-2) = 4$
$(-3) \times 2 = -6$
$3 \times 6 = 18$

Fractions

Fractions are used for counting parts of a whole.

For example:
1/3 means one third. An easy way of thinking about this is to imagine a hose cut into three pieces. If you took one of those pieces, you would have one of three pieces or 1/3.

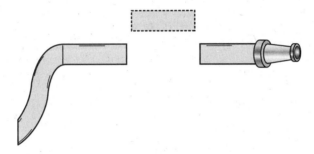

Some fractions have the same value. For example, 1/3 means the same as 2/6 or 3/9.

For example:
If you further cut the hose into six pieces and removed two pieces, you would have the same amount of hose as when the hose was cut into three pieces and you removed one.

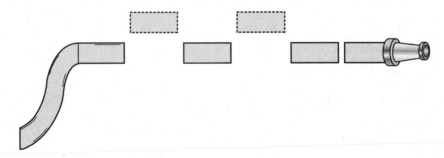

When looking at fractions, the top number is called the numerator and the bottom number is called the denominator.

For example: $\dfrac{2}{3}$ – numerator
– denominator

This number is read as two thirds.
When the numerator is the same as the denominator, this is equal to one.
For example 2/2 is 1, 4/4 is 1, etc. This is called a whole number.

There are three types of fractions:

- In **proper fractions**, the numerator is smaller than the denominator.
  For example: 1/3, 5/8, 2/9, etc.
- In **improper fractions**, the numerator is larger than or equal to the denominator.
  These can be converted to mixed fractions.
  For example: 3/1, 8/5, 9/9, etc.
- In **mixed fractions**, whole number plus proper fractions.
  For example: 1⅔, 3⅘, 1, ¼, etc.
- In **equivalent fractions**, the fractions are different but have the same value. When you multiply both the numerator and denominator by the same number, the fractions keep their value. When an equivalent fraction can't be broken down (into a smaller fraction) any further, this is called a simplified fraction.

For example:

These fractions have the same value:

$$\frac{1}{2} = \frac{2}{4} = \frac{4}{8}$$

ADDING AND SUBTRACTING FRACTIONS

Adding fractions can be done in three steps:

(STEP 1) Make sure the denominator is the same. If it's not the same, make it the same.

(STEP 2) Add or Subtract the numerator.

(STEP 3) Simplify the fraction if you need to.

For example:

4/8 + 2/8

(STEP 1) Not needed because the denominator is the same.

(STEP 2) $\dfrac{4}{8} + \dfrac{2}{8} = \dfrac{6}{8}$

(STEP 3) $\dfrac{6}{8}$ is the same as $\dfrac{3}{4}$

The answer is $\dfrac{3}{4}$

Another example:

2/3 + 3/9

(STEP 1) The number 9 is three times bigger than the number 3. To make the denominator of the 2/3 fraction the same as the 3/9 fraction, multiply both the numerator and denominator by 3. You get 6/9.

(STEP 2) $\dfrac{6}{9} + \dfrac{3}{9} = \dfrac{9}{18}$

(STEP 3) $\dfrac{9}{18}$ is the same as $\dfrac{3}{6}$ (divide the numerator and denominator by 3). This can be further simplified to ½, which is the answer.

MULTIPLYING FRACTIONS

Multiplying fractions can be done in three steps:

(STEP 1) Multiply the numerators.
(STEP 2) Multiply the denominators.
(STEP 3) Simplify the fraction if you need to.

For example:

$6/8 \times 5/6$

(STEP 1) $6 \times 5 = 30$
(STEP 2) $8 \times 6 = 48$

(STEP 3) $\dfrac{30}{48} = \dfrac{5}{8}$

The answer is 5/8.

Another example:

$4/5 \times 8/6$

(STEP 1) $4 \times 8 = 32$
(STEP 2) $5 \times 6 = 30$

(STEP 3) $\dfrac{32}{30} = 1\dfrac{1}{15}$

The answer is $1\dfrac{1}{15}$.

Remember: When the numerator is equal to or greater than the denominator, a mixed fraction can be used. In this case, 30/30 represents a whole number. This leaves 2/30 which can be reduced to 1/15.

DIVIDING FRACTIONS

Dividing fractions can be done in four steps:

(STEP 1) Invert (flip) the fraction you want to divide by. This is called a reciprocal, and is the easiest way to do this operation. (The reason this works is because, as discussed earlier in this chapter, division is the opposite of multiplication. Therefore, if you multiply the inverse number, you are actually dividing.)
(STEP 2) Multiply the top numbers.
(STEP 3) Multiply the bottom numbers.
(STEP 4) Simplify the fraction if you need to.

For example:

$1/3 \div 4/5$

(STEP 1) $\dfrac{4}{5}$ becomes $\dfrac{5}{4}$

(STEP 2) $\dfrac{1}{3} \times \dfrac{5}{4} = 5$

STEP 3 $\frac{1}{3} \times \frac{5}{4} = \frac{5}{12}$

STEP 4 This fraction does not need to be simplified.

The answer is $\frac{5}{12}$.

Remember: If a question asks you to divide mixed fractions, you should convert the mixed fraction to an improper fraction.

For example: 1½ = 3/2.

Place Value

Place value is important to be aware of in order to understand decimals. It is very important to maintain place value when solving math questions. When the decimal is moved, that changes the value of the number. Place value was briefly discussed earlier in this chapter when the ones, tens, hundreds, and thousands columns were introduced. Below is an expanded explanation.

An example of place value names for a whole number:

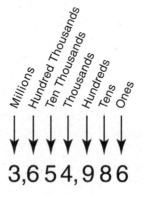

An example of the same number with decimal points added:

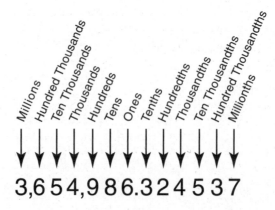

Notice in the above example that as you move to the left the numbers get ten times bigger and as you move to the right the numbers get ten times smaller.

Decimals

Basically, a decimal is another way of writing a fraction. It represents the portion of the number that is not a whole number.

For example:

2 ½ is the same as 2.5

You can turn a fraction into a decimal by dividing the numerator by the denominator. Decimals can make things easier to compare than fractions.

For example:

$$\frac{3}{4} = .75$$

$$1\frac{12}{16} = 1.75$$

With a good understanding of place value, it is easy to turn decimals into fractions.

For example:

$2.1 = 2\frac{1}{10}$ (Notice that the numbers after the decimal go to the tenths place)

$2.11 = 2\frac{11}{100}$ (Notice that the numbers after the decimal go to the hundredths place)

Adding and Subtracting Decimals

Adding or subtracting with decimals can be done in three steps:

(STEP 1) Line up the decimals.
(STEP 2) Fill in the spaces with zeros (this does not change the result of the equation, it just helps keep the numbers lined up properly).
(STEP 3) Add or Subtract.

For example:

25.12 + 2.3 + 1.3333 + 1.24435 = ?

(STEP 1)
```
   25.12
    2.3
    1.3333
+   1.24435
```

(STEP 2)
```
   25.12000
    2.30000
    1.33330
+   1.24435
```

(STEP 3)
```
   25.12000
    2.30000
    1.33330
+   1.24435
   29.99765
```

The answer is 29.99765.

Another example:

14.339 − 3.5 = ?

STEP 1 14.339
        −3.5

STEP 2 14.339
        −3.500

STEP 3

    14.339
    −3.500 (notice that "borrowing" had to be used)
    10.839

The answer is 10.839.

Multiplying Decimals

Multiplying Decimals can be done in three steps.

STEP 1 Remove the decimal points.
STEP 2 Multiply the numbers as you would normally.
STEP 3 Add up the decimal places that were removed and reinsert them.

For example:

$2.023 \times 3.2 = ?$

STEP 1 2023
       ×32

STEP 2   2023
        × 32
      4046
     60690
     64736

STEP 3 64,736 becomes 6.4736 (Because you removed 3 decimal places for 2.023 and 1 decimal place for 3.2, you need to add 4 back).

The answer is 6.4736.

Dividing Decimals

When dividing using decimals, it is important to always divide by a whole number.

For example:

$1.4 \div 7 = ?$

This problem can be solved using normal long division. Ignore the decimal point and put it back in when you are finished. Make sure you put it back directly above the decimal point in the dividend.

$$\begin{array}{r} 0.2 \\ 7\overline{)1.4} \\ \underline{0} \\ 14 \\ \underline{14} \\ 0 \end{array}$$

The answer is 0.2.

Dividing When Both the Numbers Contain Decimals

Sometimes you will have to temporarily move the decimal places on both the dividend and divisor to give yourself a whole number to divide by. This can be done in two steps.

(STEP 1) Move the decimals on both numbers until the divisor is a whole number.
(STEP 2) Divide the dividend by the divisor and find your answer.

For example:

$2.4 \div 0.08 = ?$

(STEP 1) Move the decimals on both numbers until the divisor is a whole number.

$2.4 \div 0.08 = ?$

$240 \div 8 = ?$

(STEP 2) Divide

$240 \div 8 = 30$
$2.4 \div 0.08 = 30$

The answer is 30 (notice that 240/8 is the same as 2.4/0.08).

Remember: Only the divisor needs to be a whole number. If you make the divisor a whole number and the dividend is still a decimal point, remember to place the decimal point in the answer directly above the dividend.

Percentages (%)

Percent essentially means "per 100" or out of 100. All percentages are fractions with a denominator of 100. The % (percent) symbol is a fast way to write "out of 100" or /100.

For example:

50% is the same as 50 parts out of 100 (50/100).

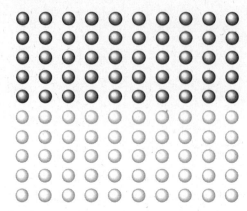

100% is the same as 100 parts out of 100 (100/100). This means that if a firefighter has 100% of his turnout gear on, there is no gear left to put on.

It is important to have a thorough grasp of fractions and decimals to understand percentages.

For example:

Three quarters of something can be as:

As a decimal: .75

As a fraction: 3/4

As a percentage: 75%

Converting a Percentage to a Decimal

Percentages can be converted to decimals by dividing by 100 (same as moving the decimal two spaces to the left) and removing the % symbol.

For example:

Question: Convert 44% to a decimal.

$44 \div 100 = .44$

The answer is .44

Converting a Decimal to a Percentage

Any decimal can be converted to a percentage by multiplying by 100 (same as moving the decimal two spaces to the right) and adding the % symbol.

For example:

Question: Convert .34 to a percentage.

$.34 \times 100 = 34$

The answer is 34%

Converting a Percentage to a Fraction

To convert a percentage to a fraction, remember that all percentages are fractions.

For example:

Question: Convert 20% to a fraction.

$$20\% = \frac{20}{100}$$

Now all you need to do is simplify the fraction.

$$\frac{20}{100} = \frac{1}{5}$$

The answer is 1/5.

Converting a Fraction to a Percentage

(Finding the percentage when you have a given amount and a total amount)

The first step in solving this sort of problem is to realize you have a fraction.

For example:

$$\frac{\text{Given amount}}{\text{Total amount}}$$

The best way to convert a fraction to a percentage is to divide the top number by the bottom number and then multiply by 100.

For example, you may see a question like this on your firefighter written test:
Twenty firefighters are at a house fire. Seven firefighters are busy doing an interior attack. What percentage of the firefighters are doing an interior attack?

To find the answer, you should first realize that 7 (given amount) firefighters out of 20 (total amount) is a fraction: 7/20.

To find the percentage, first divide the top (7) number by the bottom (20).

$7 \div 20 = .35$

Next, multiply .35 by 100.

$.35 \times 100 = 35$

Next add the % sign to 35 and you have the correct answer.

Answer = 35% of the firefighters are doing an interior attack.

Calculating Numbers Based on Percentages

For example, you may see a question like this on your firefighter written test:

Your fire truck has 1,200 ft. of hose on it. How much is 25% of that hose?

To find 25% of 1,200, convert 25% to a decimal and multiply by the total amount (1,200). Note that the "of" in the question indicates that you will need to multiply.

.25 × 1,200 = 300

The answer is 300 ft.

Remember: The reason 25% was converted to .25 is because all percentages are numbers "out of" 100.

Therefore: $25\% = \dfrac{25}{100} = .25$

Exponents

An exponent represents the amount of times that number is multiplied by itself. In other words, it is short-hand notation for several multiplications (just like multiplication is short-hand notation for several additions).

For example:

5^4 means $5 \times 5 \times 5 \times 5$
5^4 equals 625

Exponents can also be called powers.

For example:
2 to the power of 3 is the same as 2^3.
2 to the power of 3 means $2 \times 2 \times 2$.
2 to the power of 3 equals 8.

Exponents make it easier to write multiple numbers.

For example:

8^7 is easier to write than $8 \times 8 \times 8 \times 8 \times 8 \times 8 \times 8$.

Scientific notation: This is a way to write large numbers using exponents.

For example:

$34,000 = 34 \times 10^3$

or

$29,600,000 = 296 \times 10^5$

As you can see the number is written in two parts.

1. the digits
2. ×10 to a power (exponent) that puts the decimal in its correct place

Algebra

Basic algebra and its rules are important to understand for firefighter written tests.

The algebra contained on a firefighter entry tests will be written so that both sides of the equation are in the form of an equality. The questions will involve determining the value of an unknown variable (usually represented by a letter—x in the examples below). The value of the variable can be isolated using addition, subtraction, multiplication, division, or cross-multiplication to simplify parts of the equation. Since both sides of the equation are equal you must do the same things to both sides to preserve the equality. Also, you can do anything to each side.

For example:

Using Addition (Add to Both Sides)

(to solve a subtraction problem because addition is the opposite of subtraction):

For example:

$x - 12 = 4$
$x - 12 + 12 = 4 + 12$
$x = 16$

(adding 12 to the left side of the equation "cancels" out the original 12, giving you the answer of 16 (on the right side = 4 + 12 = 16))

Using Subtraction (Subtract from Both Sides)

(to solve an addition problem because subtraction is the opposite of addition):

For example:

$x + 10 = 24$
$x + 10 - 10 = 24 - 10$
$x = 14$

(Subtracting 10 from the left side of the equation "cancels" out the original 10, giving you the answer of 14 (on the right side = 24 − 10 = 14))

Using Multiplication (Multiply Both Sides)

(to solve a division problem because multiplication is the opposite of division):

For example:

$x \div 3 = 15$
$x \div (3 \times 3) = 15 \times 3$
$x = 45$

(Multiplying the left side of the equation by 3 "cancels" out the original 3, giving you the answer of 45 (on the right side = 15 × 3 = 45))

Using Division (Divide Both Sides)

(to solve a multiplication problem because division is the opposite of multiplication)

For example:

$x \times 4 = 20$
$x \times 4 \div 4 = 20 \div 4$
$x = 5$

(dividing the left side of the equation by 4 "cancels" out the original 4, giving you an answer of 5 (on the right side = 20 ÷ 4 = 5)).

Cross Multiplication

(cross multiplication is used to remove fractions from equations)

For example:

$$\frac{a}{b} \diagdown \frac{c}{d}$$

$ad = bc$

Remember: If there are decimals in the equation, change them to a whole number. This can be done by multiplying by 10, 100, 1,000, etc., depending on how many decimal places are involved.

Remember: Whatever you do to one side of the equation you have to do to the other.

Remember: Always check your answer by putting it in the original equation to see if it works.

BEDMAS

BEDMAS is the order of operations. It stands for:

Brackets
Exponents
Division
Multiplication
Addition
Subtraction

Using this order of operations ensures that problems are solved in the right order. If you do not use the correct order of operations, you will not get the correct answer.
    BEDMAS works like this:

$3^2 + (45 - 3 \times 5) \div 6 = ?$

Brackets

First do the math in the brackets.

$3 \times 5 = 15$ (multiplication is first because it is ahead of subtraction in the order of operations)
$45 - 15 = 30$

Now you have $3^2 + 30 \div 6 = ?$

Exponents

Next do any exponents (this step includes powers and roots).

$3^2 = 9$

Now you have $9 + 30 \div 6 = ?$

Division and Multiplication

Next do any division or multiplication.

$30 \div 6 = 5$

Now you have $9 + 5 = ?$

Addition and Subtraction

Next do any addition or subtraction.

$9 + 5 = 14$

The answer is 14.

BEDMAS Works the Same for Algebra

For example:

$x + (3 \times 3 + 1) = 60 \div 4$

Brackets

$3 \times 3 = 9$
$9 + 1 = 10$

Now you have $x + 10 = 60 \div 4$

Exponents

There are no exponents in this equation.
   You still have $x + 10 = 60 \div 4$

Division and Multiplication

$12 \div 4 = 3$

You now have $x + 10 = 15$

Addition and Subtraction

Now you just have to isolate the value of the variable.

$x + 10 - 10 = 15 - 10$

The answer is $x = 5$.

Ratios

A ratio is basically a way to compare two different things. Ratios can be used to compare many things including gears, people, equipment, etc.

For example:
Let's say there are 3 ladder trucks and 9 engines at an industrial fire.
The ratio is 3 to 9 (3 ladder trucks to 9 engines).
This ratio can also be written like this:

3 : 9

or

3 per 9

or

3/9

or

$\frac{3}{9}$

Notice that the three comes first every time. This is very important. If you put the 9 first, it would mean 9 ladder trucks to 3 engines instead of the correct 3 ladder trucks to 9 engines.

You can simplify a ratio the same way you would with a fraction.

For example:
The fire truck you are working on has pumped 1,200 gallons of water in the past 10 minutes. How many gallons will the truck pump in the next minute assuming the truck has been and will be pumping at a consistent rate?

(STEP 1) Find the ratio: $\frac{1200\,\text{gal}}{10\,\text{min}}$ or 1,200 gallons per 10 minutes.

(STEP 2) Simplify the fraction (ratio) $\frac{120}{10}$ or 120 gallons per 1 minute.

The answer is 120 gallons.

Proportions

Proportions are made from ratios. A proportion is two ratios that are equal to each other.

For example:

1/2 = 10/20 is a proportion because the two ratios are equal to each other.

It can also be written like this:

1/2 : 10/20

Sometimes a proportion will be missing a number. Because we know the two ratios are equal, we can solve the equation. This is a very common type of question used on firefighter exams.

For example:

A fire truck has taken 4 minutes to travel 6 kilometres. How many minutes will it take the fire truck to travel the remaining 9 kilometres back to the firehall (assuming the truck travels at the same speed)?

STEP 1 Recognize this can be solved using the proportion presented.

$$\frac{4 \text{ minutes}}{6 \text{ kilometres}} = \frac{x \text{ minutes}}{9 \text{ kilometres}}$$

STEP 2 Cross multiply. Use the algebra you learned earlier in this chapter.

$$36 = 6x$$

STEP 3 Divide both sides of the equation by 6 (again, use the algebra from this chapter).

$$36 \div 6 = 6 \div 6x$$
$$6 = x$$

Answer: It will take the truck 6 more minutes to travel back to the firehall (check your answer by inserting it into the original equation).

Geometry/Circles

The **diameter** of a circle is the length of a straight line that passes through the center of a circle and ends on each edge.

For example:

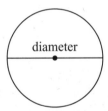

The **radius** of a circle is ½ of its diameter. It is the distance from the center of the circle to the outside edge.

For example:

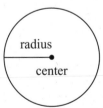

The **circumference** of a circle is the distance around the outside edge of a circle.

For example:

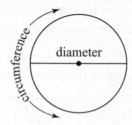

Pi (π) is the ratio of circumference of a circle to its diameter.

This means that if you had a large circle and you completely walked its circumference, you would have walked 3.14 times the distance of the diameter.

Pi (π) = 3.14 (for fire department written exam purposes). π can be used to calculate the circumference of a circle.

For example:

Using Diameter. You can find the circumference by multiplying pi (π) by the diameter of a circle.

$(\pi)d$ = Circumference

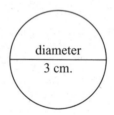

$3 \times 3.14 = 9.42$

The circumference is 9.42 centimetres.

Using Radius. Because the radius of a circle is half its diameter, you can find the circumference of a circle by multiplying pi (π) by the radius of a circle then multiplying by 2.

$(\pi)r \times 2$ = Circumference

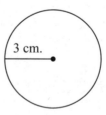

$3 \times 3.14 \times 2 = 18.84$

The circumference is 18.84 centimetres.

Calculating diameter using a circle's circumference. To calculate diameter using circumference, all you need to do is divide the circumference by π.

For example:

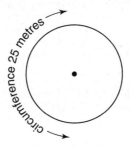

$25 \div 3.14 = 7.96$

The diameter is 7.96 metres.

Calculating radius using a circle's circumference. To calculate radius using circumference, all you need to do is divide the circumference by pi (π) to get the diameter and then divide the answer by 2 (because radius is half of diameter).

Using the example above:

$25 \div 3.14 = 7.96$

The diameter is 7.96 metres.

$7.96 \div 2 = 3.98$

The radius is 3.98 metres.

Perimeter is the border around the outside of a two-dimensional object. You can calculate perimeter by adding the lengths of all of the sides together.

For example:

The perimeter of this triangle is the sum of its sides:

$3 + 3 + 3 = 9$

The perimeter is 9.

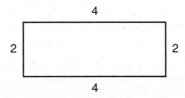

The perimeter of this rectangle is the sum of its sides:

$4 + 4 + 2 + 2 = 12$

The perimeter is 12.

Area is the space inside the perimeter of a two-dimensional shape.

Area of a Square or Rectangle:

Area = Length × Width

For example:

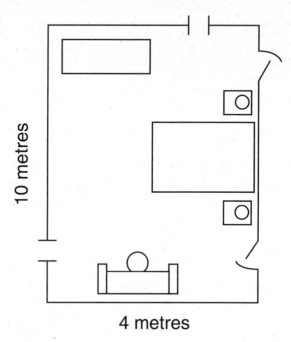

Area of the room = 10 × 4 = 40

The area of the room is 40 m² (square metres)

Area of a Triangle

Area= ½ × base × vertical height

For example:

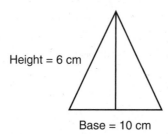

Height = 6 cm

Base = 10 cm

Area of the triangle = ½ × 10 × 6 = 30

The area of the triangle is 30 cm².

Area of a Circle

Area= $\pi(r^2)$

For example:

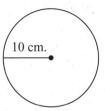

Area of the circle = 3.14×10^2

$3.14 \times 100 = 314$

The area of the circle is 314 cm^2

Area of More Complicated Shapes

To find the area of a more complicated shape, divide the shape into more manageable shapes, find their area, and then add them up.
For example:

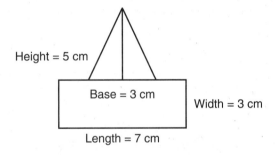

Separate the shapes into a rectangle and a triangle.

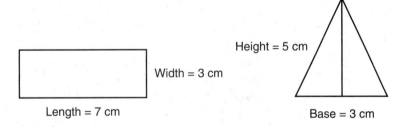

Find the area of the rectangle:

$A = 7 \times 3$
$A = 21$ cm^2

Find the area of the triangle:

$A = ½ \times 3 \times 5 = 7.5$
$A = 7.5$ cm^2

Add the two areas together:

$21 + 7.5 = 28.5$

The area of the shape is 28.5 cm^2.

Volume is the space inside a three-dimensional shape. For firefighter tests, you will need to know how to find the volume of a cube, the volume of a triangular shape, and the volume of a cylinder.

Finding the Volume of a Cube

To find the volume of a cube, multiply the length of the cube by the width of the cube by the height of the cube.

Volume = Length × Width × Height

For example:

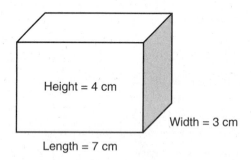

Height = 4 cm
Width = 3 cm
Length = 7 cm

$V = 7 \times 3 \times 4 = 84$

The volume of the cube is 84 cm³.

Finding the Volume of a Triangular Shape

To find the volume of a triangular shape (like the inside of a roof), calculate the area of the two-dimensional triangular portion of the shape and multiply that by the length of the shape.

For example:

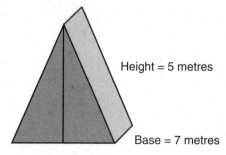

Height = 5 metres
Base = 7 metres
Length = 10 metres

First find the area of the triangular portion:

Area= ½ × base × vertical height
Area = ½ × 7 × 5 = 17.5

Next multiply the area by the length of the shape:

17.5 × 10 = 175

The volume of the shape is 175 metres³.

Finding the Volume of a Cylinder

To find the volume of a cylinder (like a barrel), calculate the area of the two-dimensional circular portion of the cylinder and then multiply that by the length of the cylinder.

For example:

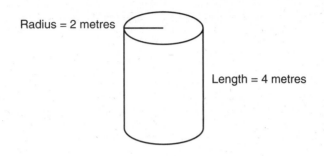

Radius = 2 metres

Length = 4 metres

First find the area of the cylindrical portion:

Area = 3.14×2^2
Area = 12.56

Next multiply the area by the length of the cylinder:

$12.56 \times 4 = 50.24$

The volume of the cylinder is 50.24 m^3.

MECHANICAL APTITUDE AND SPATIAL PERCEPTION QUESTIONS
What Are They and Why Are They Used?

Mechanical Aptitude and Spatial Perception questions are included on almost all firefighter written exams. These questions come in many forms; some expect you to make sense of the use of simple machines or predict an outcome and others may ask you to visualize the movement of objects in an environment. Essentially, all questions aim to evaluate your basic understanding of some of the basic principles of physics, along with your ability to understand the arrangement of your surroundings and how you relate to them.

True Mechanical Aptitude and Spatial Perception questions will focus on basic physics, basic machines, and your ability to orient objects and your environment. Usually, firefighter written tests will provide any formulas that are needed to calculate mechanical aptitude problems. Therefore, it is more important to understand how to solve the problems than to memorize the formulas.

It is very important for firefighters to have a good understanding of mechanical aptitude and spatial perception. A firefighter will use this knowledge constantly during their shift. Good mechanical aptitude and spatial perception skills help firefighters understand how their tools work and how to use them effectively, how to remain safe at work, how to accomplish tasks more efficiently and have many other beneficial effects for successful firefighters. What follows is a review of the types of Mechanical Aptitude and Spatial Perception questions you may see on your firefighter exam.

How Can I Score Higher?

MECHANICAL APTITUDE/GEARS

Gears are basically rotating machines (like a wheel) with teeth. Gears are usually attached to a gear shaft and can be used to increase or decrease speed, increase or decrease torque (force), or to change direction.

There are two basic types of gears that you should understand for your firefighter written test:

1. external gear (teeth on the outside)

2. internal gear (teeth on inside)

When two external gears meet, the second gear will always turn in the opposite direction of the drive gear (no matter what direction it turns). Following this principal, we can see that every odd gear (1, 3, 5, 7, 9, etc.) will turn the same direction as the drive gear, and every even gear (2, 4, 6, 8, etc.) will turn the opposite direction. The exception to this principal is an external gear inside an internal gear. It will turn the same direction as the gear it is inside. The key is to think of the direction the gears teeth are pushing the next gear.

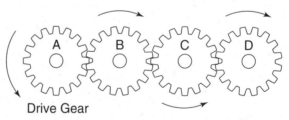

Drive Gear

Larger gears will spin more slowly than if attached to a smaller drive gear but will provide more torque (torque is the force of the twist—think that the larger gear has a longer lever).

Small gears will spin faster when attached to larger gears but will have difficulty transmitting torque.

We can use the teeth on each gear to determine the gear ratio simply by counting their teeth (refer to ratios in the math section of this chapter). For example, if a smaller drive gear has 16 teeth and the larger driven gear has 32 teeth the gear ratio would be 2:1, because the smaller gear will have to turn two times for every one time the larger gear turns. This means that the larger gear has two times the torque but only turns at half the speed.

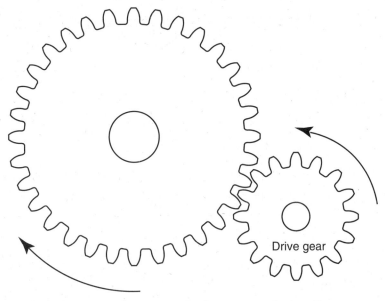

In comparison, if the drive gear above were the larger gear, the smaller gear would have half the torque but go twice the speed.

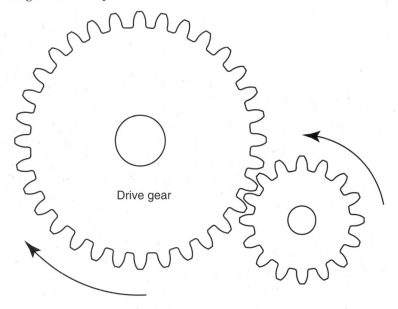

BELT DRIVES

Belt drives are very similar to gears except they use a belt to turn instead of teeth.

A very important thing to remember about belt drives for your firefighter written test is that if the belt is twisted, the wheels will spin in opposite directions. If the belt is not twisted, the wheels will turn the same way. The easiest way to figure this out during your test is to draw arrows on the belt that will show you the direction the wheels are turning.

For example:

Twisted Belt:

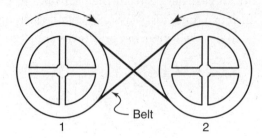

Non-Twisted Belt:

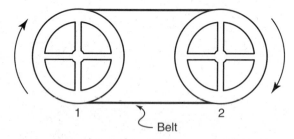

Belt drives are used the same way as gears to increase or decrease speed, increase or decrease torque (force), or to change direction.

For example:

The first wheel in the belt drive below is the drive wheel and is 1/3 the size of the second wheel. Therefore, the second wheel will travel at 1/3 the speed of the first and have 3 times the torque.

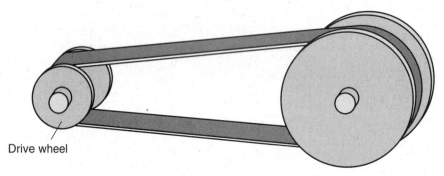

Drive wheel

PULLEYS

It is very important for competent firefighters to understand pulleys. Pulleys are used by firefighters during many different types of calls, particularly during technical rescue calls. Firefighters can use pulleys to change the travel direction of ropes (cable, etc.) or to build mechanical advantage systems.

Mechanical advantage is the factor (amount) that a machine multiplies the force that has been applied to it.

When the rope (or cable, etc.) runs through the pulley, a bend is created (the pulley reduces friction compared to other option—e.g., carabiner). In the picture that follows, the rope runs through a fixed pulley. This is called a 1:1 and offers no mechanical advantage, only a direction change. Fixed pulleys are for changes in travel direction. They do not increase or decrease mechanical advantage.

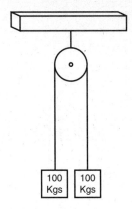

DETERMINING THE MECHANICAL ADVANTAGE OF A SYSTEM

To determine the mechanical advantage that a system of pulleys creates, you can just count the number of ropes that run through moving pulleys (excluding the rope being pulled, unless it comes from a moving pulley—this is just a directional change). Another way to think about this is to count the ropes that are getting shorter.

For example:

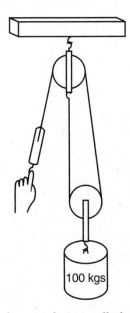

PICTURE A- This is a 2:1 because the rope being pulled comes from a fixed pulley.

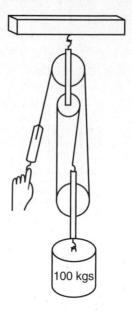

Picture B- This is a 3:1 because the rope being pulled comes from a moving pulley.

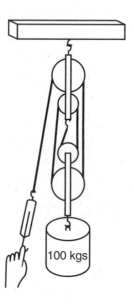

Picture C- This is 4:1. We know this by counting the ropes and subtracting the rope being pulled because it come from a fixed pulley.

An easy way to check that you have calculated the right mechanical advantage is to remember this simple phrase:

ODD LOAD, EVEN ANCHOR

This means that if the start of the rope (cable, etc.) being pulled (the knot) is at the load (whatever is being pulled), the mechanical advantage system will be an odd number (e.g. 3:1, 5:1). If the knot (start of the rope) is at the anchor, the mechanical advantage system will be even (e.g. 2:1, 4:1).

PIGGY BACKING (COMPOUND SYSTEMS)

Sometimes one system of pulleys can be "piggy backed " or added onto another system to increase mechanical advantage. To find the new mechanical advantage, simply multiply the mechanical advantage of the original system by the mechanical advantage of the new "piggy back" system. These can also be called compound systems.

For example:

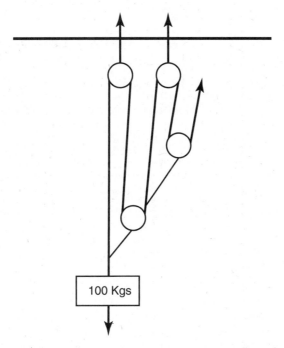

The mechanical advantage is now 9:1. This is because the 3:1 system is being pulled on by a 3:1 system.

CALCULATING EFFORT REQUIRED WHEN USING PULLEYS TO GAIN MECHANICAL ADVANTAGE

Sometimes, as a firefighter—and on firefighter written tests—you will need to calculate the effort required to pull an object when using a system of pulleys for mechanical advantage. Below is the formula used:

Effort = Weight / Mechanical advantage

For example:
If you are lifting 500 kgs using a 2:1 mechanical advantage system, you can just divde 500 by 2. Therefore the effort required to lift the 500 kgs is 250 kgs of force. See math below.

Effort = 500 ÷ 2
Effort = 250 kgs

If you do not know the weight being lifted but you do know the force being used and the mechanical advantage, the same equation can be used.

For example, if the effort being used is 100 kgs and you are using a 4:1 mechanical advantage system, you know that you are lifting 400 kgs. See next page for math:

$100 = x\ /\ 4$

$100 \times 4 = x \times 4$

$400 = x$

The weight being lifted is 400 kgs.

Remember: When you gain mechanical advantage, you gain force but lose distance travelled with each pull. When you lose mechanical advantage, you lose force but gain distance with each pull.

For example:

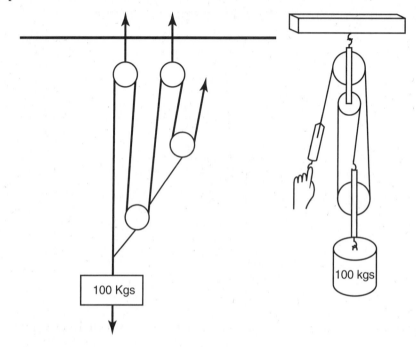

WHEEL AND AXLE

The wheel and axle is basically a larger diameter wheel attached to a smaller diameter axle (a smaller wheel). The larger wheel creates a mechanical advantage that makes it easier to turn the axle. The axle is doing the work.

One of the most commonly seen wheel and axle systems is the one that is positioned over a well to raise a bucket of water.

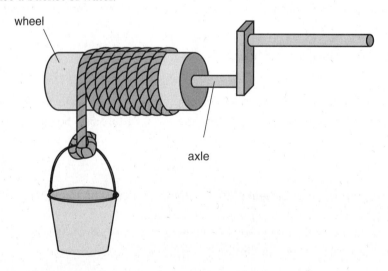

Other common wheel and axles are screwdrivers, door knobs, and hand-operated can openers.

Some questions on firefighter written exams may ask you to determine the effort used to turn the large wheel or the resistance being moved by the large wheel. The equation is the same for both:

(Effort) × (Circumference of drive wheel) = (Resistance) × (Circumference of support wheel)

For example: If we want to find the effort it takes to raise an 80 kg bucket of water out of a well with a wheel and axle, and we know the circumference of the large wheel (drive wheel) is 20 cm and the circumference of the axle (support wheel) is 10 cm, all we need to do is put that information into the equation.

$E \times 20 = 80 \times 10$
$E \times 20 = 800$
$E \times 20 \div 20 = 800 \div 20$
$E = 40$

Effort required is 40 kgs.

Notice that the effort was half of the resistance, just like the circumference of the large wheel was half of the axle (small wheel).

Remember: Always use the same units for effort as resistance when calculating.

Remember: Every time the large wheel turns once the small wheel turns once.

INCLINED PLANES

An inclined plane is essentially a ramp that is used to make it easier to raise objects by connecting a low point to a high point. An inclined plane reduces the force required to move an object up because it provides a path for an object to move on (this reduces the force necessary to overcome gravity).

For example:
If a firefighter had to lift a 400 kg barrel into the back of a tow truck, he could make the job require less effort and force by rolling the barrel up a ramp from the ground to the back of the tow truck. The longer the ramp is, the less force that is needed to push the barrel because the slope would be less (the amount of work would stay the same because of the longer distance the tire would have to be pushed).

To find the amount of effort required to get the barrel on the truck (or for any other problem involving an inclined plane) a formula can be used:

effort × length of inclined plane (effort distance) = resistance × height (resistance distance)

For example:

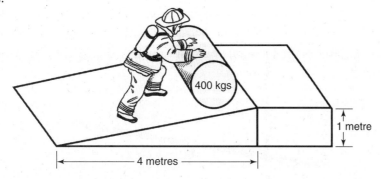

How much effort will it take to move this barrel into the tow truck?

Effort × 4 = 400 × 1

Effort = 400 ÷ 4

Effort = 100 kgs

It will take 100 kgs of effort to move the tire into the tow truck.

WEDGES

Wedges are very similar to inclined planes, but there are two important differences to understand for your firefighter test.

1. A wedge can move while in use (can be forced between or under objects) while an inclined plane stays in one spot.
2. The effort and force is applied to the edge of a wedge while it is applied to the slope of an inclined plane.

The sharper the edge of the wedge, the more force it can produce.

There are many examples of different types of wedges firefighters use at work including: door wedges, axes, knifes, nails, wheel chalks, etc.

LEVERS

A lever is an object used with a fulcrum to multiply mechanical force. Some examples from firefighting are a pry bar, halligan, or a crow bar.

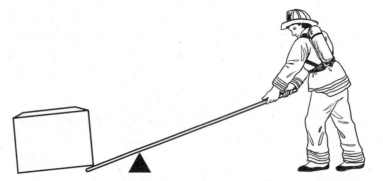

To understand how a lever works, think of a teeter totter. If two equal weights sit at the same spot on each end of the teeter totter, it should balance on the fulcrum.

If one weight was heavier, that side would fall to the ground, but if the heavier weight was moved closer to the fulcrum the teeter totter would once again balance. If the heavier weight was moved even closer to the fulcrum, eventually the lighter side of the teeter totter would fall to the ground.

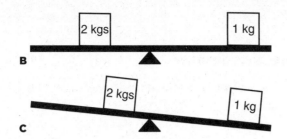

There are three types of levers:

First Class:

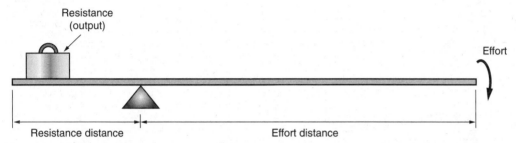

Examples: pry bar, halligan

Second Class:

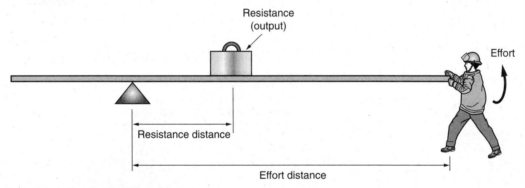

Example: wheelbarrow

Third Class:

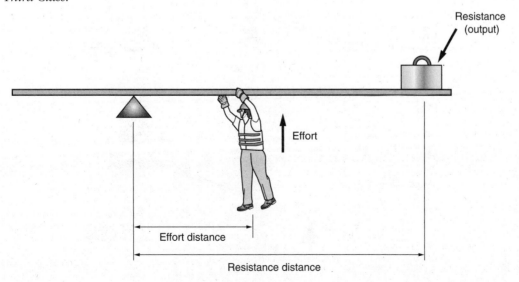

Example: your arm

Two important things to remember:

Remember: The closer the weight being lifted (resistance) is to the fulcrum, the less effort that will be required to lift it.

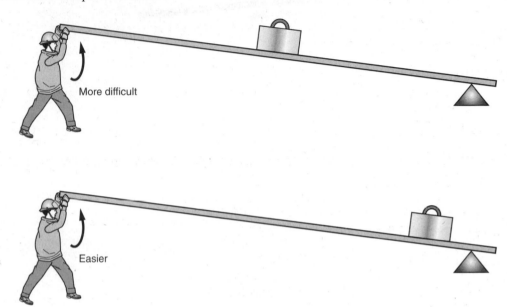

More difficult

Easier

Remember: The longer the lever is (the further the effort is from the fulcrum—called effort distance), the less effort that will be required to lift the resistance.

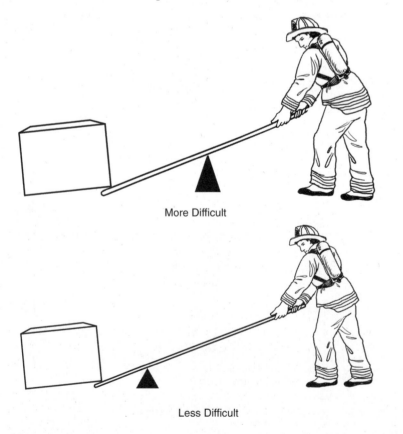

More Difficult

Less Difficult

The equation used with levers to determine their benefits is below (notice this is the same as we used with the inclined plane and other simple machines):

effort × effort distance = resistance × resistance distance

For example:

Question:
How much effort does it take for a firefighter to lift a 300 kg weight with an 8 metre long lever if the fulcrum is 2 metres from the weight?

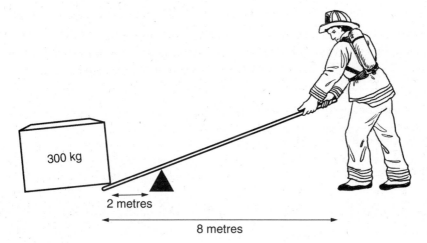

Answer:
This is known from the question:

Effort distance (distance from fulcrum to effort) = 6
Resistance= 300
Resistance distance (distance from fulcrum to resistance) = 2

Now put the numbers in the equation:

Effort × 6 = 300 × 2
Effort = 600 ÷ 6
Effort = 100 kgs

Notice: The lever in the above question was 3:1 and the effort required was 1/3 of the weight.

SCREWS

A screw is basically a rod with an inclined plane wrapped around it. The inclined plane that wraps around the screw is called a thread. The threads will be at a certain pitch that is determined by the distance between the threads. The pitch of a screw is critical for determining the mechanical advantage it can produce. Every time a screw is turned one revolution, it will move a distance that depends on its pitch.

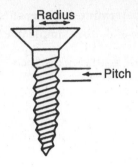

The screw can be used for many things. Screws can be used in construction to screw (actually wedge) materials together. Firefighters use screws for many things, including the water supply valve intake on the fire truck, fire hydrants, and screw jacks (used for lifting things).

To calculate the mechanical advantage a screw produces, you can divide the circumference of the screw handle (you can think of this part of the screw as a lever—the longer it is the less force will be required to turn the screw) by the pitch of the screw.

Mechanical Advantage = Circumference ÷ Pitch

For example:

Question:
Firefighters are using the screw jack below to lift the back of a pickup truck. The length of the screw handle is 50 cm and the pitch of the screw pitch is .5 cm. What is the mechanical advantage the screw jack is producing?

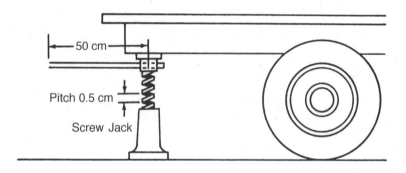

Answer:

Mechanical Advantage = circumference of screw handle ÷ pitch
Mechanical Advantage = 3.14 × 50 × 2 = 314 ÷ pitch
Mechanical Advantage = 314 ÷ .5 = 628
Mechanical Advantage = 628:1

Once you know the mechanical advantage that a screw produces, you can determine the amount of force that the screw can produce. Just use this formula:

Mechanical Advantage = Resistance ÷ Effort

For example:

Question:
You are using a screw jack with a mechanical advantage of 100:1. If you put 50 kilograms of force on the screw jack handle, how much weight can you lift?

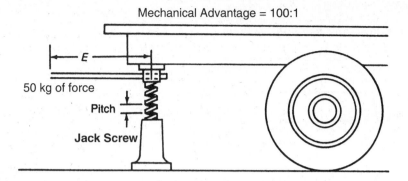

Mechanical Advantage = 100:1

E

50 kg of force

Pitch

Jack Screw

Answer:

Mechanical Advantage = Resistance ÷ Effort
100 = Resistance ÷ 50
5,000 = Resistance

Answer:
You can lift 5,000 kilograms with the screw jack if you exert 50 kilograms of force on the handle.

SPATIAL PERCEPTION

Orienting Shapes

Many exams ask questions regarding orienting shapes. These are true spatial perception questions and focus on gauging firefighter candidates' ability to orient themselves to their surroundings or their ability to orient the different parts of a machine to one another. This ability is crucial for a competent firefighter to have. Without the ability to orient themselves to their environment, firefighters could have difficulties in many aspects of their job and could end up getting hurt. With a good ability to orient the shapes in their environment firefighters will more easily be able to adjust themselves to find their way out of a smoky building, judge distance and space, and understand how machines work.

Orienting shapes questions on firefighter written tests will most frequently include a picture of a shape and the correct answer will be one of four corresponding shapes in a different orientation, view, or position. One of these corresponding shapes will be the same as the original shape except it will be in a different orientation or viewed from a different angle. These shapes could be anything from a picture of a building to a completely random shape. The key to selecting the correct answer is to carefully look over the options down to the smallest detail and be sure the answer you choose matches the original picture *exactly.* To choose the correct answer, you must visualize the original shape and transform it mentally into the position required to find the correct answer. You can practice orienting shapes during your daily life by simply looking at an object, visualizing it from another angle, and then moving to see if you were correct. Following are two common examples and their explanations.

Example 1- House and corresponding floor plan

Question:
What is the correct floor plan for this house?

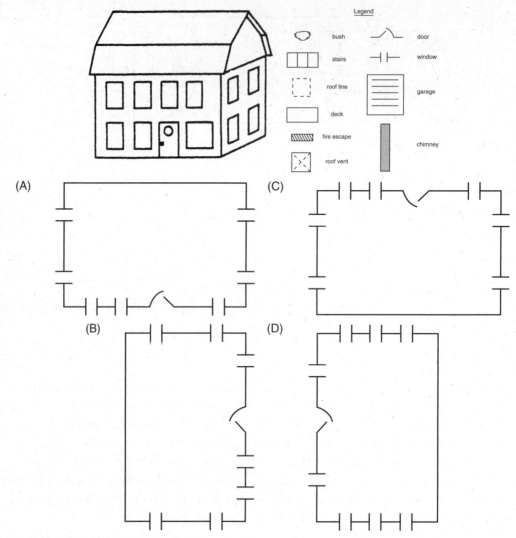

Legend

bush		door		
stairs		window		
roof line		garage		
deck				
fire escape		chimney		
roof vent				

(A)

(C)

(B)

(D)

Answer: The correct floor plan is (A).

Discussion: When you first look at the answers to determine which one is correct, you should notice that there are three details given about the house in the floor plan.

1. Its perimeter
2. Location of windows
3. Location of doors and their swing

You can now use these three pieces of information to begin to determine the correct answer.

Answer (B) is ruled out because the front door swings on the opposite side of the door frame compared to the original drawing (hinges are on the opposite side of the door).

Answer (D) is ruled out because the windows are not in the right spot (the windows from the front of the house are on the back of the house and the windows from the back of the house are on the front).

You are now left with answers (A) and (C). Answers (A) and (C) both look exactly the same except that they are a mirror image of each other. You must now look at the original picture to determine which floor plan mirror image matches the original.

If you look closely and visualize the house from above you can determine that (A) is the correct answer. Now look closely at all of the details included to double check your answer.

You should be able to see that (A) is clearly the correct answer.

Example 2- Positioning shapes in their correct orientation.

Question:

Which of the four answers shows the shapes below put together properly (match the numbers to each other)? The shapes cannot be flipped on their opposite sides.

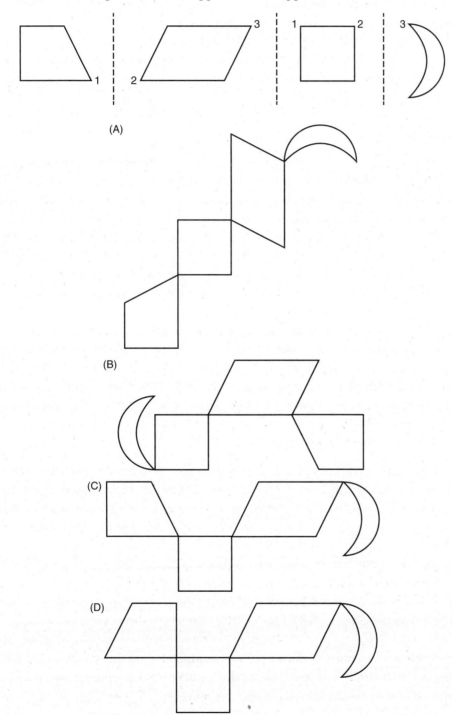

Answer: The correct answer is C.

Discussion: The best way to determine the answer to a question like this is to go through each answer and determine if it fits the parameters set out in the question. Be sure to visualize the shapes and how they should be oriented to each other.

Answer (A) is incorrect because the wrong corners of the parallelogram are touching the square and crescent.

Answer (B) is incorrect because the square and parallelogram are in the opposite position.

Answer (C) appears to be correct. Hold off on marking the answer down until you have thoroughly checked each possible answer.

Answer (D) is incorrect because the trapezium has been flipped. The instructions for the question state that no shapes can be flipped on their opposite sides.

Now that (A), (B) and (D) have been ruled out and you have looked closely at the details of (C) and visualized its orientation, you can determine that (C) is the correct answer.

Reading Maps

Reading maps is something that firefighters do constantly during the course of their shifts. It is crucial for firefighters to be able to quickly and efficiently read maps. Firefighters use maps for many things, including determining the best route to a call, reviewing buildings during pre-fire planning, and locating injured people. Questions on firefighter written tests that involve reading maps are very closely related to Orienting Shapes questions because you have to orient yourself to the shape and layout of the map. These questions are designed to truly test a firefighter candidate's sense of direction in relation to his surroundings, ability to follow directions to a location, and ability to get to places efficiently.

Map Reading questions come in many forms. Some may ask you for the best route to a location and then give you a selection of directions to choose the best option from. Others may give the firefighter candidate a set of directions and ask which route is the best (usually, the shortest route is the correct answer as long as it's safe). Whatever the question is the key to getting the correct answer is paying attention to the details of the instructions, question, potential answers, and the map.

Tips for reading maps successfully:

Orient the map in a direction that makes sense for you. Map reading questions can use a variety of different descriptions to direct the test takers to the correct location (and correct answer). These directions could use landmarks, up, down, left, right, North, South, East, West, etc. If turning or moving the test booklet improves your understanding of the directions, feel free to do it.

Follow the directions step by step. If the question or instructions have directions for you to follow, follow them carefully, one piece of information at a time.

Draw on the map. If the test provider allows it (and most do), draw your route on the map as you decide on the correct answer. This should help you visualize what you are doing.

Look closely at the details of the map. Pay attention to all of the details on the map. In particular, pay attention to the details of the route you are taking. For example, if a street is closed you will not be able to use that as part of your route.

Sample Map Reading Question

Question:

Using the map below, what is the best route from the fire hall to the fire on Hurley Ave. between Crouch Rd. and Roslyn Rd.?

(A) Left out of the fire hall onto Stewart Ave. Right on Lawrence Dr., Right on Henessey Rd., Right on Maxwell, Right onto Hurley.

(B) Right out of the fire hall onto Stewart Ave. Right on Crouch Rd., Right on Hurley.

(C) Right out of the fire hall onto Stewart Ave. Right on Spencer Rd., Left on Hurley.

(D) Left out of the fire hall onto Stewart Ave. Right on Grey St., Right on Henessey, Right on Roslyn, Left on Hurley.

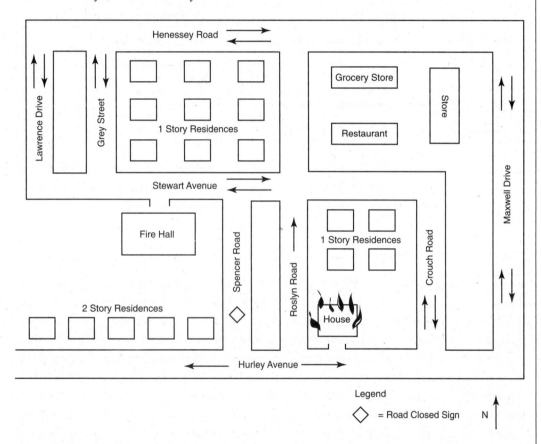

Answer: The correct answer is (B)

Discussion

Answer (A) is the longer route and is therefore incorrect.

Answer (B) is the shortest route without any safety concerns.

Answer (C) is through a closed road and is therefore incorrect because of safety concerns related to driving on a closed road.

Answer (D) travels the wrong way down a one-way street and is therefore incorrect due to safety concerns.

Reading Tables

Tables are a simple and effective way to present data and compare the relationship between that data. A table consists of two main parts: columns (up and down) and rows (left to right).

Following is an example of a common type of question you may encounter on a firefighter written test. Notice how you simply find the row and column related to the question and follow them until they meet at the correct answer.

Question:
Using the following table, what is the extinguishment method used for Class A fuels?

(A) cooling, water, foam
(B) oxygen exclusion, removal of fuel, foam
(C) de-energize, dry chemical, halon
(D) special agents

Class of Fire	Type of material	Extinguishment method
Class A fuels	wood, paper, cloth, plastic, etc.	cooling, water, foam
Class B fuels	liquid, grease, gas, oil, paint, etc.	oxygen exclusion, removal of fuel, foam
Class C fuels	energized electrical equipment	de-energize, dry chemical, halon
Class D fuels	magnesium, sodium, calcium, etc.	special agents

The answer is (A).

The answer can be found by following the Class A row over to the extinguishment method column. You should be able to see that the answer is (A): cooling, water, foam.

Reading Charts and Graphs

Charts and graphs are a very similar way to present numerical information using graphics or data points. Charts are more often used to represent data that is better understood when divided into categories (e.g., calls responded to per station). Graphs are more commonly used to represent data over time (e.g., calls per year over several years). This is because the data used in a graph is plotted along two axes during the graph's creation (e.g., time and frequency). There are several types of charts and graphs including pie charts, line graphs, histograms, and bar charts/graphs. Like tables, they are a simple and effective way to present data and compare the relationship between that data. Also similar to the information found in tables is that the answers to the questions relating to charts and graphs will always be fairly easy to find in the chart or graph.

Following is a common type of question you may see on a firefighter written exam involving a pie chart:

For example:

Question:
Using the chart, what was the most frequently attended type of call during the week of May 7–14?

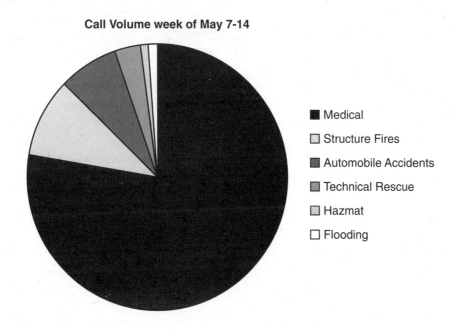

Call Volume week of May 7-14

■ Medical
□ Structure Fires
■ Automobile Accidents
▨ Technical Rescue
▨ Hazmat
□ Flooding

(A) Technical Rescue
(B) Structure Fires
(C) Medical
(D) Flooding

The answer is (C).

　　Discussion: The question asks for the most frequently attended type of call during the week of May 7-14. The colour representing Medical takes up the largest percentage of the pie chart. This indicates that the most frequently attended call during the week of May 7–14 were medical calls. Therefore, the answer is (C) Medical.

　　Following is a common type of question you may see on a firefighter written exam involving a line graph:

For example:

Using the graph, which year did Station 5 respond to the most calls?

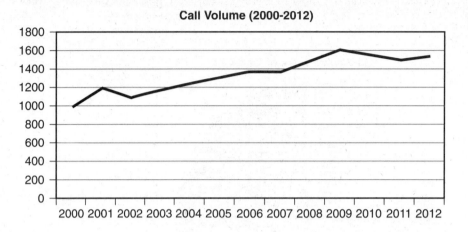

Call Volume (2000-2012)

(A) 2000

(B) 2002

(C) 2009

(D) 2011

The answer is (C)

   Discussion: The question asks for the year that Station 5 responded to the *most* calls. According to the graph, in 2009 Station 5 responded to 1,600 calls. This is the most of the years presented by the graph (it peaks in 2009). Therefore, the answer is (C) 2009.

Reading Gauges

Gauges are used for measurement. There are many different types of gauges used for many different things. Typically, firefighters use gauges that measure things such as pressure, speed, rpm, fluid level, etc., that are directly related to firefighting. These are the type of Reading Gauges questions you may see when you take an entry level firefighter written test.

   To answer questions involving gauges, it is important that you have a thorough understanding of fractions and numbers. When a gauge shows a reading that is less than a whole number, the most common way to answer is with a fraction. When a gauge shows a number between two numbers, the most common way to answer is by approximating a number that fits the situation.

For example:

What is the reading of the gauge on this firefighter's SCBA?

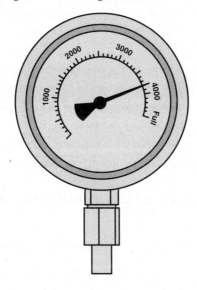

(A) 3,500 psi
(B) 3,750 bar
(C) 2,000 psi
(D) 3,750 psi

The answer is (D)

Discussion: the closest number to where the needle is pointing is 3,750. (D) is a more correct answer than (B) because it uses the correct units (psi).

Remember: It is very important to be sure you choose the answer with the correct units. Always read all the possible answers before selecting your answer.

SITUATIONAL JUDGMENT QUESTIONS

What Are They and Why Are They Used?

Assessing a situation and taking the appropriate action using sound reasoning and judgment is a major part of being a firefighter. Without this ability it is impossible for someone to become a successful, competent firefighter. Situational Judgment questions are designed to gauge this ability—a candidate's ability to identify the underlying logic of a problem. In short, they are intended to measure common sense and logic.

Situational Judgment questions are included on many of today's firefighter written tests. They are problem solving questions that usually present a firefighter-related scenario that asks firefighter candidates to choose the best solution to the problem from several possible answers (usually multiple choice). Some situational judgment questions will give a set of rules that the test taker will have to apply to the problem. Other questions may also involve inter-personal or relationship type issues (how to deal with another person in a certain situation). It is important to know that although these types of questions usually involve firefighting-related scenarios, test takers do not need to have any experience as a firefighter to answer these questions. The information provided will be enough to solve the problem using common sense.

Although the answers to some of these questions can often seem like they are a matter of opinion, correct answers are almost always based on research. Companies that design firefighter tests invest large amounts of time and money into validating test questions. Testing companies will often use firefighting job experts, the answers of successful firefighters, and research to determine correct answers.

How Can I Score Higher?

Situational Judgment questions are one of the most difficult types of questions to prepare for. Remember that you do not need to be a firefighter to answer these types of questions; all of your answers should be based on the information provided and your own common sense. Listed below is advice that will help you arrive at the correct answer. This advice should provide the "bones" of your reasoning. The solution needs to come from you and your common sense and instincts. Always be honest; never make the mistake of trying to fool, fake, or beat the test.

General rules for answering Situational Judgment Questions:

Identify problem to be solved.

Think of a solution (what would you do, be honest—this may not be exactly the same as the answers provided).

Find the answer that is most similar to your solution.

Before choosing your solution, make sure you eliminate any definitely wrong answers.

Make your final decision.

Try to think from the point of view of the person in the question. Put yourself in the position of the fictitious person in the question. This should help you determine the correct solution to the problem.

Pick the answer that most closely represents what you would do in that situation. Sometimes the answers will not be exactly the same as what you would do in that situation. Pick the closest answer. Remember to be honest with yourself; your first thought is usually the best answer.

Only use the information given in the question. Don't read into the question. Take the question at face value; the test designers are not trying to trick you.

Try to follow the most logical course of action. Think logically and use common sense.

Use situations from your life. Think about situations you have experienced during your life that are similar (if possible). Were your actions successful? Would you have the same solution if it happened again?

Answer the way you would in real life. Don't try to outsmart or beat the test.

Stick with your answer. When you have determined the course of action you think is best, stick with it.

Pay attention to the important details in the scenario. Separate important details in the question from the less important ones to help you reach a correct conclusion.

Teamwork. One of the most important aspects of firefighting is teamwork. Never forget this when answering questions during your exam (or during the course of your career as a firefighter). Firefighters need to be able to count on and trust each other. Good firefighters will be respectful to their fellow firefighters and be concerned for their well being. Always help other firefighters when they need it.

Chain of command. Remember and respect the chain of command if it comes up during testing. Following the chain of command is important to provide efficient and effective response to calls. When a superior gives an order to firefighters they are expected to carry it out.

Be safety conscious. When answering a question always put your safety and the safety of your fellow firefighters first.

Be accountable for your actions. Personal accountability is an important part of firefighting. Remember this when you are thinking of a solution to the problems presented during your test. You are responsible for the results of your actions.

Be efficient. If the question does not involve life or death or someone's feelings, the best answer is often the most efficient answer.

Be positive. Try to find positive solutions to the problems presented.

Be professional. Good firefighters should always be professional at calls and at work. If an answer involves a firefighter doing something unprofessional, it is probably incorrect.

Remember that most tests are written in the United States. If you have researched the test you are taking, you will know where the test has been designed. Test questions on U.S. tests were most likely designed and validated based on American firefighter responses, culture, and opinions (e.g., most fire department in the United States do not have a seniority system like most Canadian fire departments). When considering which answer to choose, look at the answers from your point of view as a firefighter, NOT as a rookie. It is usually best to just answer the questions from your "day to day life" point of view. Use your judgment.

Be consistent with your answers. Make sure you don't answer two similar questions with different solutions. Some tests contain several similar test questions and answers. Sometimes the pattern of your answers can be very important. Always be consistent and honest.

PERSONALITY PROFILING QUESTIONS
What Are They and Why Are They Used?

Fire departments choose written tests that contain Personality Profiling questions to try to identify candidates that have the "right" personality to be a successful firefighter. These tests can be seen as a tool that can help municipalities recruit the most suitable candidates for firefighter positions. They are intended to determine a candidate's "fit" in an organization based on his personality and attitude (e.g., Is the candidate motivated? Is the candidate conscientious?). Often, companies that provide personality profiling tests work with the fire department that is recruiting to identify the characteristics or personality types the fire department is looking for. This means that when the test is given firefighter candidates are often taking a "personalized" and therefore at least slightly different test for every fire department.

Personality Profiling questions attempt to a measure a firefighter candidate's personal values, life skills, and attributes. These are tests for non-cognitive ability. They attempt to calculate a firefighter candidate's personality by asking questions about his behavior, thoughts, and feelings in different situations. One of the aims of this type of test is to provide an insight into a candidate's ability to work well with others and handle the stress and intellectual demands of the job.

Generally, personality profiling tests attempt to gauge a candidate's personality in one of two ways: by personality trait or by personality type. Personality *trait* tests attempt to identify specific personality characteristics and match them to a particular job (in this case, firefighter). Personality *type* tests operate on the idea that everyone falls into a certain "personality type category" and tries to match firefighter candidates to their "category." Some of the personality profiling tests used for recruiting firefighter candidates are controversial because they are considered too short to get an accurate measure of an applicant's personality type or traits.

Most commonly used personality profiling tests and questions are presented separately from cognitive style tests as their own test booklet and answer sheet. Usually this type of test is presented in a multiple choice format.

How Can I Score Higher

Personality profiling questions (and tests) are by far the most difficult to prepare for. Because there are no right or wrong answers there is no definitive way to study. Personality profiling questions can also be considered the easiest to write because there is no specific knowledge needed to write them. Firefighter candidates who score the best on these tests are often the candidates who are the most relaxed and honest. Below are some general guidelines to follow when writing a Personality Profiling test.

Be as honest as possible. Do not try to answer the test in the way you think the test provider would like you to.

Be consistent. If you answer similar questions differently, this could result in an overall score that isn't ideal. Being honest as you are writing the test will keep your answers consistent.

Use the first answer that comes to mind. Remember, there are no right answers. Try not to read into questions or overthink the test.

Be confident in your answers. Firefighters have to be confident in their decisions, because in an emergency a firefighter will usually not get a chance to change his mind. Some tests have questions that ask the extent to which you agree or disagree with a statement. For example, the question may have ten options with one being disagree strongly and ten being agree strongly. Be as honest as possible with your answer. If you strongly agree with a statement, don't be afraid to put a nine or ten as your answer.

Be positive with your answers. Firefighters are often involved in stressful situations. The ability to maintain a positive attitude about these situations is a good personality trait to have.

Physical/Firefighting Abilities Testing Commonly Used in Canada

3

GENERAL ADVICE

To be an effective firefighter it is essential that you have the abilities to efficiently complete all of the physical aspects of the job. This is the main reason fire departments use physical abilities testing—to be sure they hire people who are physically capable of performing the duties of a firefighter. Firefighters are constantly using their bodies to achieve various tasks during their shifts. This could be anything from lifting a person onto a stretcher, performing a trail rescue, or extending a ladder to rescue someone from a fire. No matter how frequently or infrequently a physical task is completed, all firefighters must be capable of effectively completing that task at anytime during their shift.

There are many different physical tests used across Canada to identify firefighter candidates who have the ability to perform the firefighting tasks necessary to be a competent firefighter. The tests described in this chapter are four of the most commonly used tests used in Canada. Although these tests are common in Canada, they are not the only type of testing used. Some municipalities may use variations of these tests or their own test that is completely different from what is described. Municipalities often use different physical tests that are based on the needs of their community. For example, a municipality that has a large number of high rises may have a portion of their testing that involves carrying high rise firefighting equipment up several flights of stairs. This results in a large variety in the testing used across the country. Because of this variety, it is important that you fully understand the test you will be taking. Fire department websites will almost always have a description of their testing. Make sure you thoroughly review the information provided. If possible, you should take advantage of any practice sessions offered. Not only will this help you become more familiar with the test and improve your future performance, it will also expose you as a candidate to the people involved in the hiring process. If you are aware of what is involved in the physical abilities testing used by the municipality you are applying for, the testing will be much easier to prepare for and you will find it easier to reach your potential. It is very important to properly prepare for physical abilities testing; as discussed in earlier chapters of this book, preparation for every stage of the recruitment process is crucial.

This chapter is designed to provide readers with a basic understanding of what will most likely be included in their physical abilities test and how that test will most likely be scored. The more you know about the test you are taking, the better you can prepare for your test. A small difference in performance because of a lack of preparation could be the difference that prevents you from being successful in a recruitment process.

BASIC SCORING SYSTEMS

The common scoring systems for physical testing are very similar to the written test scoring systems described in Chapter 1. It is still very important to understand how you will be scored. Below are brief explanations of the two most frequently used scoring systems in Canada: pass/fail and banding (strict rank order is almost never used for physical testing).

Pass/Fail

A pass/fail scoring system means that a recruiting fire department will have determined a set time in which a firefighter candidate must complete a physical abilities test to move on to the next stage of the recruitment process. Basically, if the candidate exceeds the time allotted he or she will not progress further in the recruitment process.

When a fire department uses a pass/fail system for their physical abilities testing, it is important that the pass point is set correctly to accurately reflect the physical abilities required for candidates to be successful firefighters. If the pass point is too easy, the test will not be a very useful tool for the recruiting department to find effective firefighters and could lower physical standards. This can result in firefighters being hired who could jeopardize public safety. If the pass point is set at a point that is too difficult, candidates who may possess the skills to be effective firefighters could be excluded. A pass point that is too difficult can also put a fire department at risk for a lawsuit. For these reasons, firefighting experts, who use proven methods, usually determine pass/fail points.

Remember: strive to do your best regardless of the pass point. Although your actual time may not matter (as long as it's under the pass point), you are in a competitive process and those involved in the recruitment *may* note your performance and attitude.

Banding

As described in Chapter 1, essentially banding is separating candidates' scores into different groups (bands) based on standard error of difference. This means that a candidate's time on the physical abilities test will place them in a "band" with other candidates who have times that are considered reliably similar. This is usually done using the times of incumbent firefighters to find a mean (average) time and then using standard deviation to create the scoring bands. This type of scoring allows credit to be given to candidates for possessing higher levels of firefighting-related physical ability. Fire departments also use this type of scoring when they feel that small differences in times are not always representative of the best candidate (instead of strict rank order). If this type of scoring is used, your score may be weighted and combined with your scores from other portions of the recruitment process.

COMMON PHYSICAL ABILITIES TESTS USED IN CANADA

There are many different methods used across Canada to assess a firefighter candidate's job-related physical ability. What follows are the most common tests.

To be valid and useful tools for recruitment, the physical testing used by different municipalities should be linked to the job in some way. Generally, the physical ability of firefighter candidates is evaluated in one of two ways. The first method is to use tests that measure human physical ability. This can be tests such as VO_2 max, pushups, situps, grip strength, 1.5 mile run, etc. These tests are used less frequently in recent years because they are more difficult to link to firefighter job functions. The second and most common method is the work sample test. These are the tests that incorporate firefighting tasks such as forcible entry, advancing a hose, victim rescue, extending a ladder, and many other tasks that are described in this chapter. These tests typically measure skills and abilities that are necessary for firefighters to possess on their first day of work.

CPAT—CANDIDATE PHYSICAL ABILITY TEST

The Candidate Physical Ability Test was developed as part of the Fire Service Joint Labor Management Wellness/Fitness Initiative. The IAFF (International Association of Fire Fighters) and the IAFC (International Association of Fire Chiefs), along with ten North American fire departments, were involved in the process. The goal was to develop a fair and valid selection tool to ensure that firefighter candidates possess the physical abilities necessary to complete physical tasks safely and effectively. The CPAT was developed using a large amount of information, including surveys of over 1,000 firefighters, reviewing candidate performance tests, job surveys, and job analysis.

Candidates should be aware that there is only one official CPAT that will be the same department to department. Some municipalities may use a physical test called the CPAT, but this is not necessarily the official licensed CPAT test.

The Candidate Physical Ability Test (CPAT) is comprised of a series of eight events that continuously progress from one event to the next. Candidates are allotted 10 minutes and 20 seconds to complete this pass/fail exam.

The terms of this test require that all fire departments that administer this test must provide candidates with access to a CPAT orientation and practice program, which must begin at least eight weeks prior to the date of the actual CPAT exam. In the first phase of this program, the fire department must allow each candidate to complete at least two orientation sessions using actual CPAT test equipment. With the help of certified peer fitness trainers, fitness professionals, and/or CPAT-trained firefighters, candidates learn the specific conditioning techniques and procedures to prepare for the exam while also becoming familiarized with the equipment they will be using during the actual test. During the second phase of the program, candidates complete at least two timed practice runs of the CPAT, using CPAT equipment. This second phase takes place no more than thirty days prior to the beginning of CPAT test administrations. After completing these exercises, peer fitness trainers, fitness professionals, and/or CPAT-trained firefighters will be available to discuss the exam with candidates and review methods for improvement. Although these sessions are highly beneficial for potential candidates, individuals who feel they are already capable of passing may opt out of the orientation by completing a written and signed waiver from their fire department. This waiver acknowledges that these candidates are fully aware of the assistance available to them, but have knowingly and willingly decided not to participate in these sessions.

During the actual exam, candidates are equipped with a 50-pound (22.68 kg) vest that mirrors the weight of an actual self-contained breathing apparatus (SCBA) as well as protective firefighter attire. When completing the stair climb event, candidates are also required to wear an additional 25 pounds (11.34 kg), which is distributed as two 12.5 pound (5.67 kg) weights, acting as a high-rise pack, or hose bundle, across their shoulders. Candidates must always wear full length pants, work gloves, a hard hat equipped with a chin strip, and closed footwear for all eight events. It is not permissible for candidates to wear any accessories such as watches or jewelry.

Although course layouts are contingent upon each individual fire department's test area, the events and the distances between them remain consistent. Candidates need to walk 85 feet (25.91 m) between events, with approximately 20 seconds to rest between events. *Running is strictly prohibited* for safety reasons, and failure to adhere to this rule could result in a warning or even disqualification from the test if a second infraction is committed.

Potential candidates should be aware that two stopwatches will be used in order to accurately record their time. One stopwatch is official, while the other is a backup to account for any discrepancies or malfunctions with the official stopwatch. If a candidate successfully completes the test within 10 minutes and 20 seconds, he has passed. If time runs out prior to completion of all eight events, the candidate has failed the test.

Event 1: Stair Climb

Equipment

This event requires a StepMill stair-climbing machine, which will be faced against a wall on one side, while a proctor platform rests against the other open side. Candidates are provided with a single handrail on the wall side that they may use to mount and dismount the StepMill. There are also additional mounting steps at the base of the machine.

Purpose of Evaluation

The purpose of this event is for candidates to demonstrate that they can climb stairs in full protective clothing while carrying either a high-rise pack (hose bundle) or other firefighter equipment. A candidate's ability to balance, aerobic capacity, and lower body muscular endurance are assessed in this event. Candidates will use multiple muscle groups, including their calves, glutes, hamstrings, quadriceps, and lower back stabilizers, as well as their aerobic energy system.

Event

Before timing begins, candidates have 20 seconds to warm up on the StepMill at a 50 steps per minute (Level 3) set stepping pace. During this practice session, candidates can dismount if need be and grasp the rail or hold the wall to balance themselves. If the candidate falls during this warmup, he must remount the machine and begin the warmup again from the beginning. Only two restarts are allowed for this warmup period. There is no break between the practice session and the actual exam, and during both, candidates are equipped with two 12.5 pound (5.67 kg) weights on their shoulders, which reflect the weight of a high-rise pack (hose bundle). The actual test begins when the proctor says "START." During the timed event, candidates are given 3 minutes to walk at a set-stepping rate of 60 steps per minute (Level 4). After this event is completed, the weights are taken from the candidate's shoulders, and the candidate will begin an 85 feet (25.91 m) walk to the following event.

During this event, candidates are allowed to briefly touch the handrails or wall for balance as well as receive up to two warnings for gripping the handrails or resting their body weight on the wall or handrails. Candidates can also restart the warmup session up to two times if need be. Candidates who demonstrate poor balance or endurance are subject to failure. Furthermore, candidates who use the handrails in a way that gives them a mechanical advantage that they would not have on the fire ground will also fail the exam. Falling or voluntarily dismounting from the machine three times during warmup or after the start of the test, as well as receiving three infractions for gripping or resting against the wall or handrails, are also causes for failure.

Event 2: Hose Drag

Equipment

Candidates will pull an uncharged hose. The hose is marked 8 feet back from the nozzle to show candidates the maximum distance from the nozzle they may grasp the hose. The hoseline also contains a mark at 50 feet (15.24 m) past the coupling so candidates are aware of the amount of hoseline they must pull into the marked boundary box as a condition of finishing the exam.

Purpose of Evaluation

The purpose of this event is to allow candidates to demonstrate that they are capable of dragging an uncharged hoseline from the fire apparatus to the site of the fire as well as pulling an uncharged hoseline around objects while remaining stationary. Candidates will use their aerobic capacity, anaerobic endurance, grip strength and endurance, and lower body and upper back muscle strength and endurance. Candidates will use their biceps, calves, deltoids, glutes, hamstrings, lower back stabilizers, muscles of the forearm and hand (grip), quadriceps, and upper back muscles, as well as their aerobic and anaerobic energy systems.

Event

After grasping a nozzle attached to 200 feet (60 m) of 1 ¾ inch (44 mm) hose, candidates rest the hoseline either across the chest or over the shoulder without exceeding the 8 foot (2.44 m) mark. There is no penalty for running during this event. The candidate must then drag the hose across a distance of 75 feet (22.86 m) to the location of a drum setup, maneuver 90 degrees around the drum, and then proceed an additional 25 feet (7.62 m). After reaching the marked 5 feet by 7 feet (1.52 m by 2.13 m) marked box, the candidate drops to at least one knee and pulls the hoseline until the marked 50 foot (15.24 m) indicator has passed across the finish line. While pulling the hose, candidates must ensure that at least one knee is in contact with the ground and within the marked boundary lines. After the event is complete, the candidate must proceed 85 feet (25.91 m) to the following event.

During this event, candidates are allowed to run. Candidates are also permitted one warning for keeping their knees within boundary lines, keeping their knees down, and stepping outside of the marked box. If these three conditions are broken a second time, candidates will fail. Candidates will also fail if they travel outside of the marked path or forget to travel around the drum. This is because these infractions give candidates an unfair mechanical advantage that they would not have available to them on the ground. Furthermore, these infractions show that candidates have failed to demonstrate adequate upper body strength.

Event 3: Equipment Carry

Equipment

Candidates are equipped with two saws and a tool cabinet that mirrors an actual fire truck storage cabinet.

Purpose of Evaluation

The purpose of this event is for candidates to demonstrate removing tools from the fire apparatus, carrying them to the scene of the fire, and then returning them to their proper storage space. Candidates demonstrate their aerobic capacity, balance, grip endurance, and their lower and upper body muscle strength and endurance. Candidates will use their biceps, deltoids, glutes, hamstrings, muscles of the forearm and hand (grip), quadriceps, trapezius, and upper back muscles.

Event

After removing two saws, one at a time, from the tool cabinet, and placing them on the ground, candidates pick up one saw with each hand and transport them 75 feet (22.86 m) around the drum and back to the starting point. It is permissible for candidates to place the saws on the ground while they readjust their grip. After returning to the tool cabinet, candidates place both saws on the ground. Picking up the saws one at a time, the candidate returns each saw to its specific spot in the cabinet. After the event is complete, the candidate must proceed 85 feet (25.91 m) to the following event.

During this event, candidates may briefly place the saws on the ground to readjust their grip. There is also one warning for running. Candidates are not permitted, however, to run a second time with the saws or drop either saw during the event. Doing so will result in failure because these practices could cause injury or demonstrate insufficient muscle strength and endurance.

Event 4: Ladder Raise and Extension

Equipment

Candidates work with two 24-foot (7.32 m) fire department ladders. As a safety precaution, candidates are required to raise the retractable halyard attached to the ladder.

Purpose of Evaluation

The purpose of this event is to ensure the candidate can successfully place a ground ladder at the structure on fire and extend the ladder to the roof or appropriate window. Candidates will demonstrate their aerobic capacity, anaerobic endurance, balance, grip strength, and their lower and upper body muscle strength and endurance. Candidates use their biceps, deltoids, glutes, hamstrings, muscles of the forearm and hand (grip), quadriceps, trapezius, and upper back.

Event

After walking to the top rung of a 24 foot (7.32 m) aluminum extension ladder, candidates must lift the first rung that is located at the unhinged end from the ground and walk it up to the point where it becomes stationary against the wall. It is necessary for candidates to complete this using a hand over hand method, using each rung to the point where the ladder has successfully become stationary against the wall. It is not permissible for the ladder rails to be used as a tool to raise the ladder. From there, the candidate will move immediately to a secured and pre-positioned 24 foot (7.32 m) aluminum extension ladder. With both feet successfully planted in the 36 inch by 36 inch (91.44 cm by 91.44 cm) marked box, the candidate will extend the fly section, using the hand over hand method, until it hits the stop. Finally, the candidate will lower the fly section, using the hand over hand method, to the starting position. After the event is complete, the candidate must proceed 85 feet (25.91 m) to the next event.

During this event, candidates are allotted one warning for both a boundary violation during the ladder extension and for missing any rung during the raise. If the candidate commits either of these infractions for a second time, he will fail because skipping rungs gives taller candidates an unfair advantage. These practices may also allow candidates to throw the ladder in the air which is a safety risk. Candidates will also be failed if they allow the halyard to slip uncontrollably, fail to control the halyard using the hand over hand method, allow the ladder to fall to the ground while attempting to raise it, or release their grip on the ladder which will cause the safety lanyard to activate. These practices result in failure because they demonstrate poor muscle strength and grip and might unfairly allow candidates to walk the halyard backwards to compensate for this lack of upper body strength.

Event 5: Forcible Entry

Equipment

Candidates are equipped with a 10 pound (4.54 kg) sledgehammer and required to hit a mechanized device that is located 39 inches (1 m) off the ground. This device is designed to measure cumulative force.

Purpose of Evaluation

The purpose of this event is for candidates to demonstrate that they are able to open a locked door or breach a wall using force. Candidates demonstrate their aerobic capacity, anaerobic endurance, balance, grip strength and endurance, and their upper and lower body muscle strength and endurance. Candidates use their glutes, muscles of the forearm and hand (grip), quadriceps, trapezius, triceps, and upper back muscles in addition to the aerobic and anaerobic energy systems.

Event

Candidates use a 10 pound (4.54-kg) sledgehammer to strike a measuring device in the target area until a buzzer signal is activated, all the while keeping their feet outside of the toe box. Only after the buzzer is activated will the candidate be permitted to put the sledgehammer on the ground. After the event is complete, the candidate must proceed 85 feet (25.91 m) to the next event.

During this event, candidates are permitted one warning for stepping inside the toe box. A second infraction will result in failure. Candidates will also fail if they are unable to maintain control of the hammer while in the process of swinging it. Failing to maintain control of the hammer indicates poor muscle strength and creates the potential for injury.

Event 6: Search

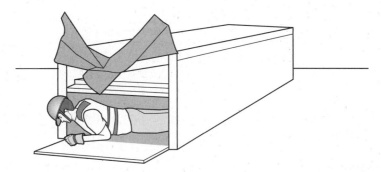

Equipment

This event consists of an enclosed search maze where candidates will encounter narrow spaces and other obstacles.

Purpose of Evaluation

The purpose of this event is to allow candidates to demonstrate that they can search for a fire victim in conditions with limited visibility in an unpredictable area. Candidates will demonstrate their aerobic capacity, agility, anaerobic endurance, balance, kinesthetic awareness, and upper body muscle strength and endurance. Candidates will use their abdominals, lower back, muscles of the chest, quadriceps, shoulder muscles, and triceps, in addition to the aerobic and anaerobic energy systems.

Event

Candidates crawl on their hands and knees through a tunnel maze that is approximately 3 fcct (91.44 cm) high, 4 feet (121.92 cm) wide, and 64 feet (19.51 m) in length. It contains two 90 degree turns. Throughout the tunnel, the candidate will encounter obstacles that must be navigated over, under, or around. At two locations, there will also be reduced tunnel dimensions. Candidates should be aware that their movement will be monitored throughout the event. If a candidate wants to end the event for any reason, assistance will be provided once the candidate calls out or knocks sharply on the ceiling or wall. After the event is complete, the candidate must proceed 85 feet (25.91 m) to the next event.

During this event, candidates can return into the tunnel if they have exited through the entrance space. If assistance from a proctor is required to open any escape hatches or entrance and exit covers, the candidate will fail because this indicates an inability to proceed confidently in a dark, confined space.

Event 7: Rescue

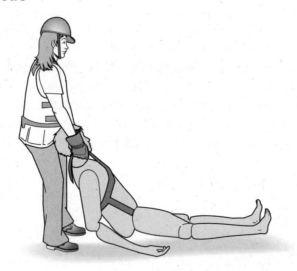

Equipment

Candidates are provided with a weighted mannequin that is wearing a harness which contains shoulder handles.

Purpose of Evaluation

The purpose of this event is to demonstrate that candidates are capable of removing a victim or injured fellow firefighter from the scene of the fire. Candidates will demonstrate their aerobic capacity, anaerobic endurance, grip strength and endurance, and upper and lower body muscular strength and endurance. Candidates will use their abdominals, biceps, deltoids, glutes, hamstrings, latissimus dorsi, lower back stabilizers, muscles of the forearm and hand (grip), quadriceps, trapezius, and torso rotators, as well as their aerobic and anaerobic energy systems.

Event

After grasping a 165 pound (74.84 kg) mannequin by the shoulder harness using one or both handles, the candidate must drag the mannequin 35 feet (10.67 m) to a pre-positioned drum, maneuver 180 degrees around the drum, and proceed an additional 35 feet (10.67 m) to the finish line. At no point may candidates grasp the drum or rest their own weight on it. It is acceptable, however, for the mannequin to touch the drum. In order to adjust their grip, candidates may also lower the mannequin to the ground if need be. The conclusion of this event is when the entire mannequin has been dragged past the marked finish line. After the event is complete, the candidate will proceed 85 feet (25.91 m) to the next event.

During this event, candidates are allowed to grab one or both of the shoulder handles while dragging the mannequin and lower the mannequin to the ground if the grip must be adjusted. There is also one warning permitted for resting on the drum or grabbing it in any way. In the event of a second infraction, however, candidates will fail because repeated instances of touching the drum demonstrate a lack of adequate muscular strength and endurance.

Event 8: Ceiling Breach and Pull

Equipment

Candidates will use a pike pole to push and pull an overhead mechanized device. The pike pole, which consists of a 6 foot long pole with a hook and point attached to one end of it, is a common piece of firefighter equipment.

Purpose of Evaluation

The purpose of this event is to allow candidates to demonstrate that they can breach and pull down a ceiling in order to check for fire extension. Candidates will demonstrate their aerobic capacity, anaerobic endurance, grip strength and endurance, and their lower and upper body muscular strength and endurance. Candidates will use their abdominals, biceps, deltoids, glutes, hamstrings, lower back stabilizers, muscles of the forearm and hand (grip), quadriceps, trapezius, torso rotators, triceps, as well as their aerobic and anaerobic energy systems.

Event

After removing the pike pole from its bracket, candidates must stand within the boundary of an equipment frame, placing the tip of their pole on the painted section of the hinged door that is located in the ceiling. The candidate must then fully push up the 60 lb (27 kg) hinged door in the ceiling with the pike pole for a total of three times. Next, the candidate will hook this pike pole to another 80 lb (36 kg) ceiling device, proceeding to pull the pole in a downward fashion for a total of five times. As described, each set requires three pushes followed by five pulls. The set must be repeated four times by each candidate. If need be, the candidate is allowed to momentarily stop to readjust the grip on the pole and then proceed with the event. For this particular event, slipping from the handle of the pike pole or releasing the grip does not result in a warning or failure, as long as the pike pole does not fall to the ground. In the event that the candidate is not able to maintain the up and down repetition motion, the proctor monitoring the event will yell out "MISS." The candidate will then have to pull or push the aforementioned apparatus again to complete the repetition motion. Only once the final pull stroke has been completed will the proctor yell out "TIME" and the event, as well as the total test time, ends.

During this event, candidates are allowed to pause to readjust their grip if need be. Furthermore, candidates are permitted one warning for either stepping outside of the designated boundaries or dropping the pike pole on the ground. A second infraction of either of these practices, however, will result in failure because the former provides an unfair advantage that is not available in real fire ground situations, and the latter indicates poor muscular strength and endurance.

TEST FORMS

Each candidate must bring a valid form of identification with him or her when preparing to take the CPAT. There are a number of forms that must be signed, including the sign-in form, which must be completed prior to the start of the CPAT. There is an opportunity before the exam begins to watch a video that will explains all the details of the CPAT, describing what constitutes failure points. This is the candidates' time to ask any remaining questions about how to complete these events. Candidates will then sign a waiver as well as a release form. Once the CPAT is complete, candidates will also sign the CPAT Evaluation form. Finally, prior to exiting the rehabilitation facility, candidates will complete and sign the Rehabilitation form. Failure to fully complete and sign any of these aforementioned forms will result in failing the CPAT.

COMBAT CHALLENGE TESTS

The Combat Challenge originated in 1975 as part of a research project at the Sports Medicine Center of the University of Maryland that was designed to link different physical performance constructs with essential functions for structural firefighters. Incumbent firefighters were randomly selected to perform lab-based aerobic and anaerobic tests. These tests were then compared to typically performed, non-skill-dependent fire ground evaluations to create a firefighter selection test. Aside from being used for pre-service testing, the Combat Challenge is also used as a race for incumbent firefighters. In Canada, the race is called the Scott FireFit Championships.

Many fire departments in Canada use physical testing that is based on the Firefighter Combat Challenge. This style of testing is considered by many to be an excellent measure of a candidate's firefighting-related fitness and ability, particularly when the amount of information that can be gathered in this shorter duration assessment is considered. This test can use either pass/fail or banded scoring.

Sometimes fire departments use the Combat Challenge events as individual stations (usually with other stations included) instead of the tasks being one continuous event. These stations are usually based on a pass/fail time that is derived from individual incumbent firefighter times.

The original Firefighter Combat Challenge consists of the six events that are described below completed continuously (weights and distances based on the Scott FireFit Championships). Many fire departments across Canada use this as their test, but many also use a modified version. It is important to remember that because many fire departments use a modified Combat Challenge, the events will often not be exactly as described below. Be sure to take advantage of all possible practice runs and test information provided by the municipality you are applying to. As always, the more prepared you are for a test, the better you will perform.

Stair Climb with High-Rise Pack

In this event, candidates carry a 42 lb. high-rise pack up six flights of stairs (60 steps). The 42 lb. hose is a 4 ft. bundle of 4 inch hose. Each of the six flights of stairs contains ten steps. The hose bundle must be placed in (or on) the box at the top of the stairs. Once the hose is placed in the box, the firefighter will complete the second event before descending the stairs. On the way down the stairs, the firefighter must touch every step.

Hose Hoist

The second event of the Combat Challenge is the hose hoist. This event takes place in the middle of the first event (at the top of the stairs). To complete this event, the candidate must raise a 45 pound hose roll using a 5/8 inch kernmantle rope. When the hose roll reaches the top, the candidate must place it in (or on) the box provided.

Forcible Entry

The third event simulates forcible entry using a Challenger Force Machine® or Keiser Force Machine®. To complete this event when using the Challenger Force Machine, the candidate must move the beam completely past the decal usually using a 9 pound sledgehammer (used by FireFit). To complete this event when using the Keiser Force Machine, the candidate must move the beam on the Keiser Machine five feet usually using a 9.5 pound sledgehammer. The sledgehammer must be placed in the designated area when the event is complete.

Run/Walk

To complete this event, candidates will run or walk (some fire departments may not allow running during their testing) 140 feet around cones (or hydrants in races) to the hose advance.

Hose Advance

The fifth event is the hose advance. The candidate will drag a 1.75 inch hoseline 75 ft. Once the nozzle enters a pre-determined area, the competitor can open the nozzle and hit the target. When the target is down, the candidate will shut the nozzle and drop it to the ground. The nozzle must be closed before it hits the ground.

Victim Rescue

The sixth and final event is the victim rescue. This event simulates a firefighter removing a victim from a fire. A 165 lb. (or sometimes 175 lb.) Rescue Randy mannequin must be dragged backwards a distance of 100 ft. The candidate must grasp the mannequin from behind with his or her arms beneath the mannequin's arms. Time stops when the candidate and the mannequin cross the finish.

YORK UNIVERSITY FIREFIGHTER APPLICANT FITNESS ASSESSMENT

The York University Firefighter Fitness Assessment is based at York University in Toronto. This firefighter fitness assessment was developed by Dr. Norman Gledhill. The York University Firefighter Fitness Assessment is widely used in Canada, particularly in Ontario. Testing takes approximately 4 hours to complete.

York requires candidates to complete a series of tests designed to evaluate their firefighting related physical abilities. This testing can be broken down into four main sections, listed below.

1. **SCREENING OF SELECTED HEALTH ITEMS**
   This portion of the testing involves:
   Visual Acuity (20/30—or NFPA standard at the decision of the municipality)
   Depth Perception (Steriopsis test)
   Colour Vision (Farnsworth D-15 test or City University test)
   Hearing (Audiometer, NFPA Standard)
   Normal resting lung function
2. **AEROBIC FITNESS TEST**
   During this test, the candidate's aerobic fitness is measured directly using expired air analysis while running on a treadmill. As the candidates run, the speed and incline on

the treadmill are increased until they reach their maximum capacity. This test measures a candidate's cardiorespiratory endurance ("work capacity").

This test measures VO_2 max. Basically this is a measurement of the millilitres of oxygen your body uses per kilogram of body weight per minute.

3. JOB SIMULATION PERFORMANCE TESTS

York uses eight job simulation tests to simulate the demands of a firefighter's job.

1. **Acrophobia—Ladder Climb. Pass/ Fail (not timed).**

Wearing an SCBA, candidates climb a 40 foot (12.2 metre) ladder. When they reach the top of the ladder, candidates couple and uncouple a hose before descending the ladder.

2. **Claustrophobia—Search a confined area. Pass/ Fail (not timed).**

Candidates are locked in a confined space wearing a blacked-out SCBA face piece. While confined, candidates are instructed by the evaluator to reach up to the top left-hand corner of the confined space and count the number of washers that are on a bolt protruding from the wall. The candidates are then instructed to call out the number of washers. This evaluates a candidate's fear of confined spaces.

3. **Hose Carry/ Stair Climb—85 lb. Pass/Fail (timed).**

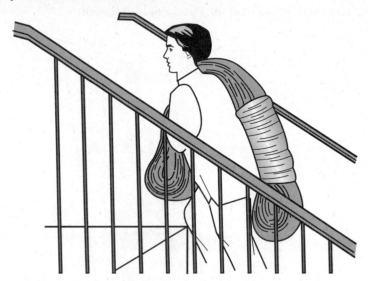

Candidates carry an 85 lb. bundle of hose up and down five flights of stairs. This test evaluates a candidate's ability to carry equipment to a high-rise fire. All candidates wear a 40 lb. vest and 4 lb. ankle weights.

4. **Rope pull—50 lb. Pass/ Fail (timed).**

Candidates raise and lower a section of 2½ inch hose 65 feet (20 metres) using a hand over hand motion. This simulates raising and lowering firefighting equipment to a window or roof. Candidates wear a 40 lb. vest and 4 lb. ankle weights.

5. Simulated Hose Advance—Pass/Fail (timed).

Candidates drag a weighted sled 50 feet (15 metres) requiring a force of 125 lbs. This test simulates advancing a charged hose. Candidates wear a 40 lb. vest and 4 lb. ankle weights.

6. Ladder lift—56 lb. Pass/Fail (not timed).

Candidates remove and replace a 24 ft extension ladder from wall-mounted brackets. This test assesses the ability of candidates to perform many firefighting tasks that involve lifting and working overhead. All candidates wear a 40 lb vest and 4 lb ankle weights.

7. Victim Drag—200 lb. Pass/ Fail (timed).

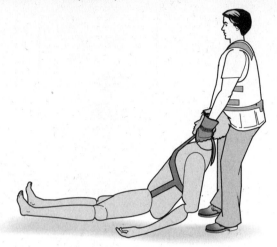

Candidates drag a rescue dummy through a 50 ft (15 metre) obstacle course. While dragging the dummy, the candidate weaves between cones that are placed every 10 feet (3 metres). This event simulates the rescue of a downed firefighter. The dummy is dragged using a harness attached to the dummy. All candidates wear a 40 lb. vest and 4 lb. ankle weights.

8. Forced Entry—Pass/Fail (timed).

Candidates strike a heavily weighted tire with a 10 lb. sledgehammer until it moves a distance of 12 inches (30.5 cm). The tire is positioned on a table at the approximate height of a doorknob. Candidates should be careful not to lose control of the sledgehammer, as it will rebound off the tire. This test simulates forcible entry. All candidates wear a 40 lb. vest and 4 lb. ankle weights.

4. SWIM TEST

During the swimming test, candidates are required to swim 8 lengths of the pool (200 metres) using any stroke or combination of strokes. A first infraction (standing up briefly on the bottom or holding onto the side or end) receives a warning. A second infraction results in a failure.

BROCK UNIVERSITY FIREFIGHTER SCREENING SERVICES

www.brockfirefighter.com

Brock University Firefighter Screening Services is located at Brock University in St. Catharines, Ontario. They offer five testing components that could be considered physical tests (they also offer the CPS test as a sixth option—this is a written test and is described in Chapter 1). Candidates should be aware that not all municipalities that require Brock screening services will require you to complete all of the testing available (for example, it's possible that a fire department may only require 3 of the 5 testing components). Therefore, it is important to know what the municipality you are applying for requires before registration.

> **NOTE:**
> All information contained in this section is the intellectual property of Brock University and may not be copied, reproduced, distributed or displayed without Brock University's written permission.

Testing Components (physical):

Clinical Assessment: *Valid for 6 months*
CPAT: *Valid for 1 year*
Medical Examination: *Valid for 1 year*
Hearing Examination
Visual Examination
Swim Test: *Valid for 1 year*
Acrophobia Test: *Valid for 1 year*

Fire Departments/Human Resource departments reserve the right to request different/shorter expiration lengths for all components.

Clinical Assessment

Make sure you read the following instructions prior to participating in the Firefighter Clinical Assessment. All candidates should be properly prepared by reviewing the purpose of the test, the associated warnings, how the test is evaluated, and have all questions answered before starting. Remember that all clinical assessment test protocols can only be conducted once. No applicant is allowed to observe another applicant perform during his or her tests. Finally, all candidates should be properly warmed up and stretched prior to any vigorous exercise.

The Clinical Assessment consists of five components:

1. **PRE-APPRAISAL SCREENING**

   The pre-appraisal screening procedures bring a measure of safety to the clinical assessment. After being greeted by one of the staff members at Brock, candidates will be required to complete a series of forms to ensure their safety. The PAR-Q questionnaire is a straightforward and simple, but essential, first step in the pre-appraisal screening procedure. It is designed to identify those candidates for whom certain physical activities might be inappropriate. Candidates with only "No" responses are cleared to participate in the clinical assessment, while those with one or more "Yes" responses should be instructed to see their physician along with the **PARmed-X** sheet before proceeding with the appraisal.

   It is the responsibility of the applicant to print and complete the **PAR-Q** and, if necessary, the PARmed-X prior to their scheduled appointment. Candidates are also required to read and sign a consent form prior to the administration of the clinical assessment. The consent form describes the nature of the appraisal items that will be undertaken and outlines the candidates' responsibilities.

Once again, it is the responsibility of the applicant to print and complete the **consent form** prior to their scheduled appointment. Once these two forms are completed, candidates will have their resting heart rate and blood pressure measured. For resting heart rate measurements, the candidate will sit for at least 5 minutes. The candidate's resting heart rate is measured using a polar heart rate monitor. Candidates will not be permitted to participate in the clinical assessment if their resting heart rate exceeds 100 beats per minute. The last component of the pre-appraisal screening involves measuring the candidate's resting blood pressure. Resting blood pressure will be measured using a sphygmomanometer and stethoscope.

Candidates will not be permitted to participate in the clinical assessment if their resting systolic blood pressure measurement is greater than 144 mm Hg and/or their resting diastolic blood pressure is greater than 94 mm Hg.

Once each component of the pre-appraisal screening is successfully completed, the candidate is cleared to participate in the remaining sections of the clinical assessment.

The candidate will receive a score for each component of the clinical assessment. The maximum cumulative score that a candidate can receive for the clinical assessment is 30 points. **The candidate must attain a score of at least 18 points out of 30 on the clinical assessment as well as successfully complete all 5 components in order to receive a "Pass" grade.**

2. BODY COMPOSITION

To determine a candidate's body composition, the candidate will be evaluated for both Waist to Hip Ratio (WHR) and body fat percentage.

It is recommended that candidates:

- Do not exercise within 12 hours of their appointment.
- Consume no alcohol within 48 hours of their appointment.
- Consume no diuretic medications within 7 days of their appointment.
- Consume no caffeine within 12 hours of their appointment.
- Empty their bladder within 30 minutes of their appointment.
- Do not consume food or drink within 4 hours of their appointment.

3. MAXIMAL AEROBIC FITNESS

The candidate will perform a graded exercise test on a motor-driven treadmill. The candidate's workload will be increased every 2 minutes by increasing the speed and elevation of the treadmill until the candidate is exhausted or until other symptoms dictate that the test should be terminated. Additionally, the candidate may voluntarily terminate the test at any time because of fatigue or discomfort.

The candidate will be instructed to wear a full-face mask for the purpose of collecting gases throughout the test. The maximal aerobic fitness test is measured in ml/kg 1-min-1 and is rated on a 10 point scale relative to the candidate's gender and age. For best results, candidates should dress in a short sleeve shirt, shorts, running shoes, and socks. The candidate is allowed one violation before the test is terminated.

Violations on this test include:

1. Holding onto the treadmill rails for extended periods (i.e., 2 seconds);

2. Talking while exercising (candidates will be instructed to communicate through hand gestures).

4. TRUNK FLEXIBILITY

Candidates will be required to stretch the related muscle groups before performing this test. Candidates will remove their shoes and sit down with their legs fully extended and the soles of their feet placed flat against the trunk flexometer. The candidate will place one hand on top of the other and extend their arms forward as far as possible along the measuring scale by pushing the measurement cursor.

The candidate will perform three trials. On the third trial, the candidate will hold the position for at least one second to determine maximum trunk flexion. Trunk flexibility will be measured in centimetres and rated on a 5 point scale relative to the candidate's gender and age. The candidate is allowed one violation before the test is terminated, except for on the fourth trial.

Violations on this test include:
1. Bending at the knees.
2. Holding the knees down.
3. Sliding the measurement cursor.

5. 60-SECOND SIT-UP TEST

Candidates will lie in a supine position and rest their head on a mat. With their arms folded across their chest, candidates will bend their knees at a 90° angle while a lab assessor anchors their feet. The candidate will move up and down in a continuous manner while bending at their hips. On each repetition the candidate's shoulder blades must touch the mat; then their elbows must touch their knees. Candidates will perform sit-ups at a maximal rate. This test will last 1 minute in duration. The 60-second sit-up test is rated on a 5 point scale relative to the candidate's gender and age.

Violations on this test include:
- Failure to touch the knees with elbows.
- Failure to return to the starting position (shoulder blades on the mat).

Medical Examination

The Brock Firefighter Screening Program vision and hearing standards follow the recommendations of the National Fire Protection Association (NFPA). These standards have been approved as the American National Standard since July 18, 2003. There is no comparable standard for Canada. Some fire departments in Canada set their own medical standards, which may be different. Brock University will test to the NFPA standard as stated below unless specifically requested to test to another standard by a specific fire department.

In these cases you will receive two certificates: the Brock Firefighter Screening Program and the one for the specific fire department that you are applying for. You may use the Brock certificate for any application to a fire department that uses the NFPA standard for 1 year from the date of issue. If you apply to a fire department that sets another standard, you will have to be retested to their standard to obtain their specific certificate.

Hearing Examination

Category A medical conditions shall include the following:

- Chronic vertigo or impaired balance as demonstrated by the inability to tandem gait walk.
- On audiometric testing, average hearing loss in the unaided better ear greater than 40 decibels (dB) at 500 Hz, 1,000 Hz, and 2,000 Hz when the audiometric device is calibrated to ANSI Z24.5.
- Any ear condition (or hearing impairment) that results in a person being unable to safely perform essential job tasks.

Category B medical conditions shall include the following:

- Unequal hearing loss
- Average uncorrected hearing deficit at the test frequencies 500 Hz, 1,000 Hz, 2,000 Hz, and 3,000 Hz greater than 40 dB in either ear
- Atresia, stenosis, or tumor of the auditory canal
- External otitis
- Agenesis or traumatic deformity of the auricle
- Mastoiditis or surgical deformity of the mastoid
- Meniere's syndrome, labyrinthitis, or tinnitus
- Otitis media

Visual Examination

Candidates wearing contact lenses must remove them prior to the visual examination. Please remember to bring your contact solution and case.

Category A Medical Condition—A medical condition that would preclude a person from performing as a member in a training or emergency operational environment by presenting a significant risk to the safety and health of the person or others.

Category A medical conditions should include the following:

- Far visual acuity. Far visual acuity less than 20/40 binocular, corrected with contact lenses or spectacles. Far visual acuity less than 20/100 binocular for wearers of hard contact or spectacles, uncorrected.
- Color perception. Monochromatic vision resulting in inability to use imaging devices.
- Monocular vision
- Any eye condition that results in a person not being able to safely perform essential job tasks.

Category B Medical Condition—A medical condition that, based on its severity or degree, could preclude a person from performing as a member in a training or emergency operational environment by presenting a significant risk to the safety and health of the person or others.

Category B medical conditions shall include the following:

- Diseases of the eye such as retinal detachment, progressive retinopathy, or optic neuritis.
- Ophthalmological procedures such as radial keratotomy, Lasik procedure, or repair of retinal detachment.

- Peripheral vision in the horizontal meridian of less than 110 degrees in the better eye or any condition that significantly affects peripheral vision in both eyes.

Swim Test

The Brock University Firefighter Screening Services swim test is a 15 minute treading water test where candidates must remain free of the pool wall, lane ropes, and other candidates for the duration of the test. Also, candidates must remain vertical (i.e., no floating on their backs) and keep their heads completely above water. Please bring a bathing suit and towel for this test.

Acrophobia Test

The acrophobia test requires candidates to climb a 40-foot ladder, wearing a harness for safety purposes. Once at the top of the ladder candidates will be asked to anchor themselves with one leg over and through the rung.

They will then be required to uncouple and couple a hose. Before returning to the ground, candidates will be asked to lean backwards on the ladder and look down at an X on the floor for 10 seconds.

NOTE:

NFPA standard for eyes and vision include in their category A medical conditions Colour Perception: "monochromatic vision resulting in inability to use imaging devices." Applicants are screened using colour plates on an Ishihara test for colour blindness. If the applicant fails this test, the Farnsworth D-15 test is used. An applicant who fails the Ishihara can still pass the Farnsworth D-15 demonstrating they are not monochromatic—thus demonstrating they can operate imaging devices. A severe failure of the D-15 would indicate monochromatic colour vision and a failure of the eye and vision section of the NFPA.

Physical/Firefighting Abilities Testing Preparation

4

GENERAL ADVICE

This chapter is designed to help you prepare for any firefighter physical testing that you will encounter in Canada. The training principles described will assist you in training successfully and help you reach your full potential during any firefighter physical testing. It

> Always remember to seek the advice of a physician before starting any exercise program. Some of the prep covered in this section is strenuous, and therefore you should consider your personal fitness level before getting started.

is your responsibility to take the information provided and use it effectively. Your preparation for the physical testing portion of a recruitment process is just as important as your preparation for any other stage of the process. Becoming a firefighter is very competitive. There are many firefighter candidates training hard for the same physical tests as you. It is essential that you take your training seriously.

Firefighting is a very physically demanding career. It is crucial that all firefighters have the physical ability to successfully and efficiently perform at any type of call they are involved in. For most firefighters, fitness is part of their lifestyle. Proper physical training will not only help you prepare for your physical/firefighting abilities entry testing but also for your career as a firefighter. To do well on any firefighter physical test it is very important that you are fully committed to training. To be properly prepared for your physical testing, your level of fitness should exceed the demands of the physical abilities test you are taking.

The difficulty, type, style, and skills involved in firefighter physical ability testing vary extensively across the country. It is important to make sure you learn as much as possible about the testing you will be participating in. The more you know about the test, the more prepared you will be on the day of your physical abilities testing. For example, if you have the opportunity to take part in a practice run of the physical testing or have done it before, be sure to identify your weaknesses and work on them. Training specifically for your test can be very helpful.

When taking part in any type of physical abilities testing, it is important to remember that this step of the recruitment process, like any other step, can be considered part of an interview. Have respect for the position you are applying for and do everything you can to show fire department personnel that you are an excellent candidate. Dress appropriately and respectfully for your test. Remember: You are being watched during all stages of the recruitment. If you are remembered from the testing, it is better to be remembered in a positive light rather than a negative one.

It is your responsibility to properly prepare for all aspects of the recruitment process if you expect to be hired. Physical testing is no exception. An extra day or hour of preparation could be the difference that gets you a job as a firefighter.

EVALUATING YOUR PHYSICAL ABILITIES TEST

It is very important that you have a thorough understanding of the physical abilities testing you will be taking part in. Learn everything you can about the test (the most common Canadian tests were described in Chapter 3). Some tests are run at your body's maximum capacity for the duration of the test, while others require that you meet a predetermined pass point that may not challenge your body to its maximum capacity. Whatever type of testing you are involved in, it is important that you perform to the best of your ability. To do this you should have a firm grasp of how your personal strengths and weaknesses relate to the testing. Firefighter physical abilities testing challenges a wide range of firefighter-related physical abilities. These include muscular endurance, cardiovascular endurance, upper body strength, and lower body strength. A complete understanding of the test you are taking will help you train effectively. If you know what is involved in the test you will be taking, you can tailor your training for that test.

Muscular Endurance

It is important that candidates understand the muscular endurance demands of the physical test they will be taking. It is very uncommon for a candidate to be required to produce a maximal effort during a firefighting test. The ability to produce force for an extended period of time will often be the biggest contributing factor for good performance.

Cardiovascular Endurance

Cardiovascular endurance is essential for good performance on almost all physical abilities testing. Firefighter candidates should make sure they are aware of the cardiovascular demands of any physical test they participate in. Effective cardiovascular endurance will allow for faster recovery between events and will provide a conditioning base for longer testing.

Upper Body Strength and Lower Body Strength

Strength is an important part of any firefighting physical ability test. Often, strength training is overlooked because many physical abilities tests appear to be largely endurance based. Strength training should never be disregarded because all physical qualities depend in some way on strength levels. The stronger people are the more power they can produce, and the less energy they will expend. For example, if the heaviest object a firefighter candidate can pick up is 200 pounds, he will expend a huge amount of energy lifting a 175 pound dummy and will most likely be exhausted. On the other hand, if the heaviest object the firefighter candidate can lift is 375 pounds, lifting a 175 pound dummy will require less energy. This is an example of a case where exhaustion may be indicative of low strength levels and poor economy rather than low levels of cardiovascular fitness.

It is important that candidates are aware that hypertrophy can be a disadvantage. Any muscle gain without a significant gain in strength is unwanted. This muscle mass can just be excess weight to carry and will use more oxygen during the test.

Body Composition—Eliminating excess body fat prior to your firefighter physical abilities testing will make you quicker and more energy efficient. Make sure that any weight gain comes with improved performance.

Overall Advice/Tips

Wearing turnout gear. Many physical tests will require candidates to wear turnout gear. There has been much debate in recent years surrounding proper turnout gear fit and its effect on firefighter performance. Although fit is important it is almost never perfect. Even the fitted turnout gear used by professional firefighters is almost never ideal. As with many aspects of firefighting, you will have to adapt and find what works best.

TIP

Although there are many different physical tests used by fire departments across Canada, many of the events within the tests are similar or the same. These events may be placed in a different order or excluded from some testing. This chapter highlights some of the most common events that you may encounter during the physical assessment portion of a recruitment process. Remember: Researching the test you will be completing is crucially important! Some events may be slightly different than described or not part of your testing at all.

Finding what works best for you. Usually candidates will be allowed to select their own gear from a variety of turnout gear. Make sure you take the time to find the gear that works best for you. Remember not to be concerned about how the gear looks—performance is far more important. Make sure you don't pick any turnout gear that will inhibit movement.

Hike up the turnout pants using the suspenders. If the crotch on the turnout pants is high, it will be easier to move your legs. If the pant legs are too short, don't be concerned—it's just less weight to carry during the test.

Loosen airpack shoulder straps. Loose air pack shoulder straps will allow your arms to move more freely. Many firefighters prefer to have the waist strap of their air pack very tight so they can have slightly loose shoulder straps on their air pack. This is a personal choice—as always do what works best for you.

Pacing. This does not refer to just one particular event but to the test overall. It is very important to be aware of your personal strengths and weaknesses and use that knowledge to your advantage. Your extensive training for your testing should have made you well aware of your own unique abilities—use this to your advantage. This is where proper research and if possible practice runs of the physical testing are essential. The more knowledge and experience you have with the test you are taking, the more likely you will be able to perform at your personal best.

Individual Event Advice/Tips

Stair Climb with High-rise Pack/Hose Bundle

Pick up the high-rise pack/hose bundle properly. It is important to pick up and carry the hose bundle effectively. If possible, practice with the equipment provided and find the way that works best for you. Most people find the most efficient way to carry a high-rise pack/ hose bundle is on their shoulder (usually their outside shoulder—explained below). When you start make sure that you place the high-rise pack/hose bundle so that it is balanced on your shoulder (or other position that works best for you). This will ensure that you don't overuse muscles that you don't need to use yet (arm, hand, core). It is worth taking a few seconds to do this as it will save energy for other portions of your test.

Pace yourself properly. You should know your level of fitness from the training you have put in preparing for your test. If you have had an opportunity to try a practice run before your test date, you should have an idea of how fast you should go up the stairs. It is very important not to go so fast that you adversely affect your performance on the rest of the test. Know your fitness level. Many people find it most efficient to take two steps at a time while climbing (if permitted).

Use the railings (if permitted). People often underestimate how much help the railings can be when climbing stairs with a high-rise pack/hose bundle. Pulling on the railings as you climb the stairs can help you reach the top faster and more efficiently. Often, candidates will carry the high-rise pack/hose bundle on their outside shoulder so that they can pull on the railings around corners as well. The railings can also be an asset on your way down the stairs; they can assist you around corners and when descending each flight.

StepMill Stairclimb (CPAT Style)

Stay centered and balanced. Many candidates find that holding onto the shoulder weights helps them keep their body weight in a neutral position and maintain their balance. Many candidates also find that swinging their arms can throw them off balance. Keeping your eyes on one spot may also help you find your balance.

Note: Many Stairmaster brand StepMills have the CPAT program built into them and can be used for training.

Hose Hoist/Donut Roll Raise

These tips apply for both the Combat Challenge style hose hoist and the York-style pulley hose hoist and lower.

Pull as much rope as possible with each pull. The farther you reach and the farther you pull the faster the load will be raised. If you have to lower the load as part of your assessment, the same principle applies.

Manage the rope properly (applies more to a Combat Challenge style hose hoist). If possible, try to throw the rope behind you as you go. This way you will not have to worry about grasping the correct piece of rope. If throwing the rope behind you does not work best for you, try to keep your eye on the rope so you don't accidently grab the wrong piece. Some people pull the rope through the thumb and pointer finger of the hand they aren't pulling with. This allows them to immediately grasp the correct piece of rope for their next pull.

Momentum. Keep a steady pace. If you can keep the hose (load) moving upwards (not pausing or going down each pull), you maintain some momentum that will assist you in raising the load.

Forcible Entry (Keiser Force Machine® or Challenger Force Machine®)

Choke up. Choke up on the sledgehammer (see picture). This will allow your strikes to be faster and more accurate.

Make proper contact. Make sure the face of the sledgehammer contacts the ram/beam as flush/flat as possible. This will help ensure that the force of your swing is driving the ram/beam backwards not downwards.

Keep your feet in the right spot. Try to keep the face of the ram/beam behind your feet (heels). This will help you strike the beam flush and in the correct portion of your swing driving the ram/beam backwards.

Hit the center of the beam. Hit the ram/beam in the center of the face (part you are striking). This will allow it to slide smoothly.

Forcible Entry (CPAT Style)

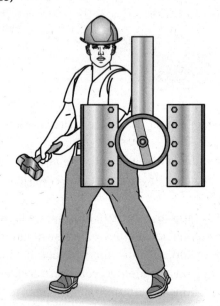

Swing like a baseball bat. The best way to strike this type of force machine is similar to the way a person would swing a baseball bat. Don't choke up on the sledgehammer; hold the handle near the end and try to swing through the target area. Be sure not to drop the sledgehammer.

Hose Drag (Charged, Uncharged, or When Dragging a Sled)

Use friction. Pull the hose over your shoulder so the nozzle is down closer to your waist. This will create some friction on your shoulder and allow you to use less energy when dragging the hose. If you hold the nozzle at your shoulder you will tire out muscle groups that you may need later in the test.

Change the nozzle pattern while dragging the hose. Some tests will require you to hit a target at the end of a charged hose drag. If the nozzle pattern is not set at a straight stream you can change it as you are dragging the hose. Remember: A straight stream is all the way to the right on a fog nozzle (left for life, right to fight).

Lean into it. Lean forward while pulling the hose.

Dummy Carry/Drag (No Harness)

Get the dummy set. When you reach the dummy, pick up its head and push it forward to get the dummy in a seated position. Make sure the dummy's arms are cleared out of the way; if they are not, push them forward and out. This can be done very quickly and will put the dummy in an ideal position to be picked up.

Get yourself set. When picking up the dummy, crouch down behind the dummy and make sure you are set before you lift. Always lift with your legs (similar to performing a deadlift).

Make sure you have a good grip. Before you pick up the dummy, make sure you have a secure grip. It is recommended that you interlock your fingers before you pick up the dummy. This technique provides the most friction and will allow you to rest the dummy on your body's structure more than other techniques. If you can't reach around the dummy, another option is to grasp the lapels of the clothing on the dummy (make sure this is permitted before the test). Another option if you can't reach around the dummy is to put one arm over the dummy's shoulder and one under (see illustration—this is recommended as a last resort). Often during firefighter Combat Challenge races the professional firefighters competing will pick up the dummy without interlocking their fingers. This takes a lot of practice and knowledge of the course and how their body will react. As always, do what works best for you.

Do everything you can not to drop the dummy. You will expend a very large amount of energy if you drop the dummy and have to pick it up. If you do drop the dummy, take the time to go through the steps to pick it up properly. Do not try to rush picking up the dummy if you have dropped it. If you do not pick it up properly you will raise your chances of dropping it again. If you need to rest briefly before picking up the dummy again, do it; this is better than dropping the dummy again.

Have good posture. While dragging the dummy maintain good posture—this will allow your body to most effectively support the weight of the dummy.

Dummy Carry/Drag (with Harness)

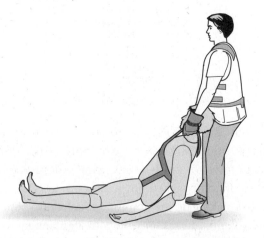

Have good posture. When you pick up a dummy using a harness lean back slightly and use good posture. The harness can put many people in a poor anatomical position; be sure you drag the dummy in a way that is safe for your body.

Important: **Drag the dummy in the way that is most efficient for you.**

Some municipalities will allow you to drag the dummy using one hand and facing forward (see previous illustration). This works particularly well if the surface that the dummy is being dragged on is smooth. Knowledge of the course and your body will help you decide if this is the best option for you.

Some municipalities' physical testing will provide candidates with the option of picking up the dummy or using the harness. In some cases it may be more efficient or even easier to pick up the dummy. (E.g., You are dragging the dummy over rough concrete). If this is the best option for you, follow the advice above regarding picking up dummies. Once again, the more knowledge you have of the testing you will be doing, the easier it will be to make an informed decision on what will work best for you.

Ceiling Breach and Pull (CPAT Style)

Breach (upward pushes). Using your legs to push up is more efficient than using only your arms. Some candidates prefer to put one hand on the bottom of the pike pole.

Pull. Using your body weight while pulling will make this event easier.

Ladder Extension/Retraction

Make sure you have adequate grip strength. Work on your grip strength before testing. Most candidates who have difficulty with this portion of testing have problems because of grip strength. If grip strength is an issue for you, be sure to address it through proper training.

Grasp the halyard properly. When extending the ladder there are two common ways candidates can grasp the halyard—with their thumb facing up and with their thumb facing down (see illustrations). When the halyard is grasped with the thumb facing down this creates a bight in the rope and may make ladder extension easier for some people. As always, use the technique that works best for you.

Move as much halyard as possible with each pull. When extending and retracting the ladder make sure your pulling and lowering motions move the most halyard possible (without being in danger of losing control of the ladder—safety is the first priority). When extending the ladder, reach as high as possible before each pull and pull as low as you can when finishing. When retracting the ladder start your motion as low as possible and finish as high as possible. The more halyard you move, the more efficient your ladder extension/retraction will be.

Pay attention to where the dogs lock. If part of this event involves locking the ladder dogs on a rung (usually when fully extended and when fully retracted), pay attention to which rung the ladder will lock on (the ladder used in the CPAT has the dogs removed). Not going past the correct rung will save you time and energy.

Take a rest if you need to (if allowed by testing department). If you have difficulty during this event and the testing allows you to lock the ladder, take a break. This is better than losing control of the ladder and not completing the event.

Swim Tests

Research the test and try it beforehand. If you have any difficulty, take the time to get some advice on your technique (swim lessons, etc.) and then practice. Swimming is much easier with proper technique—the more efficient your stroke is the less effort it will take to move through the water.

If the test involves treading water, the most efficient way is to use the "eggbeater style" as opposed to the "whip kick style."

EVALUATING YOUR PERSONAL PHYSICAL ABILITIES

To train effectively for any firefighter physical abilities testing, it is important that candidates honestly and accurately evaluate their own strengths and weaknesses. People often focus on what they are good at when they are training. To be successful and perform to the best of their abilities, it is important that candidates identify and train their weaknesses as well.

To identify your strengths and weaknesses as a firefighter candidate, you should definitely take advantage of any practice runs of the physical testing that are offered. If a practice run is not an option, it is recommended that you use your knowledge of the test to create a simulation (to the best of your abilities). Once you have run through the practice test or simulation, you should be able to identify any weaknesses that are related to muscular endurance, cardiovascular endurance, and/or upper/lower body strength. For example, if loads feel light during the test but your arms and legs fatigue quickly and adversely affect your performance, a more muscular endurance-based program may be beneficial. If your heart and lungs feel like they are working at maximum capacity, a focus on a cardiovascular-based program may be beneficial. If you find lifting or pulling objects during the test difficult, you may want a program that is strength focused.

PROGRAM DESIGN

Once you understand the physical test you will be taking and your own strengths and weaknesses, you can design a program that will best suit your needs. Several samples are provided in this chapter to help guide your planning. Similar parts of one training day can be interchanged with others as long as you follow the principles described in this chapter. If you are unsure about any of the training principles or exercises provided, consult a personal trainer or fitness expert. This is especially true if injuries or equipment restrictions limit your training options. In simple terms to ensure positive results a program should follow three basic principles: specificity, overload, and progression.

Specificity. Your program should have carryover to the testing you are preparing for.

Overload. For the best gains your program should subject you to stimulus your body has not yet adapted to. This can be volume, load, frequency, etc.

Progression. Your program should progress as your body begins to adapt to the stresses it is being put through.

When training for your physical abilities testing, it is important that you resist the temptation to just constantly repeat the test itself or imitate the motions seen during the test. Rarely will this be the best approach. Instead, if you focus on building a solid base of strength and conditioning you will have more physical potential to use to your advantage. This will provide a larger pool of strength and conditioning to tap into when you are focusing on a particular event.

Training Template

When following an existing program or building your own, each training session should include some work from each of the following four stages (in order). As you get closer to your testing date, your training should begin to focus more on skill and strategy.

Stage 1—Movement Preparation. This stage will prepare you physically and mentally for your workout by serving as a transition from your normal daily activities to a higher stress activity (training). This stage will also raise body temperature and improve movement quality prior to training. For example, this can include any or all of the following, depending on your needs:

- Light aerobic activity. E.g., jogging, biking, rowing.
- Soft tissue work. E.g., foam rolling or trigger point work.
- Dynamic mobility drills to increase range of motion. E.g., walking lunges, body weight squats.
- Any prescribed rehabilitation exercises.
- Core exercises. E.g., planks, bird dogs, palloff presses, glute bridges.
- Practicing techniques to be used later in the session. E.g., Olympic lifts with a dowel, overhead squat with a dowel.

Stage 2—Nervous System. The goal of this stage is to prime the nervous system and train the body to be quick and explosive. For example, this can involve:

- Lower body plyometrics
- Skipping and bounding
- Medicine ball tosses
- Reactive training
- Kettlebell swings and snatches
- Olympic lifts

These should not be heavy or grinding exercises and should not be done to exhaustion. Remember: The purpose of this stage is to train the central nervous system and work on speed. This stage is not for conditioning purposes.

Stage 3—Structural System. The goal of this stage is to train the muscles and connective tissues of the body. This will not only help you become stronger, it will also make your body more resilient and protect you from injury. This stage should focus on strengthening compound, fundamental movements and balancing strength levels around your joints. Examples of these types of exercises can range from a heavy deadlift to a light bicep curl.

Stage 4—Energy System. This stage aims to build or maintain your conditioning base. This is the stage where you could include activities that closely resemble the test you are training for. For example, this can include:

- Complexes (covered below)
- Circuits
- Sprints/ interval training
- Some strongman style training (weighted carries, pulls, drags, etc.)

Remember. Time spent on each stage can vary. Equal time can be spent on each stage or up to 45 minutes can be spent on one stage and only minutes on others. This will depend on your goals. For example, a strong, pain-free person may use stages 1–3 as a way to maintain baseline levels of strength and movement while focusing almost entirely on stage 4 to condition themselves.

Reasons for using this system

1. This system helps ensure that a candidate is not lacking in any of the four areas and serves as a continuing self assessment. For example, if your strength starts to drop below an acceptable level while you are focusing on your cardiovascular endurance, this type of program will bring attention to it and provide an opportunity for you to make adjustments. If you were solely focusing on cardiovascular improvement, you may not have noticed any drop in strength.
2. This program takes advantage of the effects of different types of training. For example: there are positive effects to doing strength training prior to energy system training but not necessarily in reverse.

KEY TRAINING PRINCIPLES

Do not train in pain. Training while you are in pain will alter the way your body uses and sequences muscles. This will cause inefficient movement. Take the time to see a clinical practitioner to find ways to find alternative non-painful movements. Do not risk injuring yourself further.

Quality over quantity. Take the time to build the volume or intensity of your workout. Stop the second your form deteriorates. Part of training is learning to move well and efficiently. It is better to do more rounds of high power, perfect form sets than just one round to complete exhaustion followed by several poor attempts with reduced form. You may feel like you are working harder but this only serves to create inefficient motor patterns and could possibly result in injury.

Periodization. This can be a complicated topic. Knowing your body and tracking your performance is one way to be sure that you are progressing without overtraining. If you begin to notice that your performance is declining, it is a sign that you may require less work, not more. Some general guidelines for periodizing your training:

- Try to move forward in your training for three weeks and then lighten up for one. During the lightening up phase, reduce the frequency of your training by half but keep the weights the same.
- Vary training loads throughout the week. For example: Mondays could be a heavy day. On this day you would choose a weight that would require all of your effort to finish the required reps. Wednesdays could be a light day. On this day you would use a weight that is about 80% of the weight used on Monday. Friday could be a medium day. On Friday you would use a weight that is about 90% of the weight used on Monday. On the following Monday you would exert yourself fully again and use those weights to set the loads that would be used for the rest of the week. Always focus on perfect form and make sure to complete all of the work.
- Start training with a higher volume and lighter loads and progress towards lower volume with heavier loads.
- As you approach your firefighter physical abilities test date, begin training at speeds similar to the testing (without sacrificing form).

Grip strength. Grip strength is a common and very important quality seen in firefighter physical abilities testing. A lack of grip strength can often be a limiting factor in many upper body strength exercises. Possessing appropriate levels of grip strength will have a positive effect on your performance during firefighter physical testing. When possible, train using thick handled instruments to improve your grip strength (e.g., kettlebells, thick barbells, thick gripped dumbbells).

SAMPLE FIREFIGHTER PHYSICAL ABILITIES TEST TRAINING PROGRAMS

Warm Up!

It is very important that you do a proper warm up before you participate in any physical testing. An effective warmup will increase body temperature and excite your nervous system. This will help prepare your body for testing and have a positive effect on your performance. To prepare properly use a warm up that includes movements from stage 1 (movement preparation) and 2 (nervous system) of the training template described earlier. Below is a sample warm up that includes activities from these stages.

Side lying T spine rotations with reach—6× each side
Knee hug to forward lunge—8×
Reverse lunge with twist—8× each side
Walking heel to glute with reach—8×
Squat to stand—8×
Lateral squat—8× each side
Marching glute bridge—6× each
Palloff presses—12× each side
Bounds or split squat jumps—1–2 sets of 5–10 reps

FIREFIGHTER FITNESS PROGRAMS

The firefighter physical testing focused sample programs at the end of this chapter focus on either general training, strength focused training, or conditioning focused training. If you are unsure about any part of the fitness programs below, consult a personal trainer or other fitness professional.

Understanding the Firefighter Physical Testing Focused Sample Programs

Perform "A" exercises before "B" exercises, etc. All sets of "A" exercises are performed before "B" exercises and so on. For example, if a program calls for three sets of "A1" and three sets of "A2" they should be performed in this order: A1, A2, A1, A2, A1, A2 before doing the same with the "B" exercises, then the "C" exercises, etc.

Reps denoted as (1,2,3). Reps denoted as (1,2,3) means that only 1 rep of each exercise is done in the first round, then 2 reps, then 3 reps before starting over at 1 again. For example, in "Strength Focused Program 1" you would perform 1 rep of a kettlebell overhead press, 1 rep of a chinup, then 2 reps of a kettlebell overhead press, 2 reps of a chinup and then 3 reps of a kettlebell overhead press, 3 reps of a chinup for a complete set. You would complete this cycle three times. Rest as needed between sets.

Complexes. Complexes are exercises performed one after the other without ever putting down the weight you are using. Be sure that you choose a load that can be done on all exercises involved when performing a complex. These are conditioning drills and therefore the loads chosen should be light enough that you can perform the entire complex without failure, loss of form, or a notable power decrease.

Tabata protocol. The tabata protocol starts with a 2 minute warmup. It is then followed by a 20 second all-out exertion with a 10 second rest. This is repeated 8 consecutive times (20 seconds all-out exertion, 10 second rest 8×). You would then finish with a 2 minute cooldown.

How frequently you should train. It is recommended that you perform one of these sessions 2–3 times per week.

What to do between firefighter fitness program training days. Your level of activity on your off days will depend on your level of conditioning and how far you are from the date of your firefighter physical abilities test. Aside from proper recovery (mentioned below), your off days can be used for cross training, aerobic based training, sports, etc. It is important to remember that your focus should be to perform well during the training days that are specifically built to prepare you for your firefighter physical abilities testing. If your cross training negatively affects your performance during your training days, it is recommended that you lower the volume of work you are doing on your off days.

Recovery. Recovering properly from training is just as important as the actual training. Quality recovery requires proper nutrition and rest. Remember that rest does not mean doing absolutely nothing. Often, light activity will allow you to recover faster and more effectively than doing nothing. Some examples of recovery activities include yoga, massage, light aerobic activity, wading in a pool, light weight training, and stretching.

Firefighter Fitness

Strength and Conditioning

Sample Training Programs

General Training Program 1	Kettlebells			
	Exercise	Sets	Reps	Rest
Nervous System	A1) Double Kettlebell Swing	2	5	2 min
Strength	B1) Kettlebell Front Squat	3	5	3-5 min
Muscular Endurance	C1) Travelling Kettlebell Lunges	2	12	0-30 s
	C2) Kettlebell Renegade Row	2	12	0-30 s
	C3) Kettlebell Goblet Squat	2		0-30 s
	C4) Seasaw Kettlebell Press	2	12	0-30 s
Conditioning	D1) Kettlebell swing	2	20	0 s
	D2) Kettlebell Farmers Walk	2	75'	1 min

General Training Program 2	Barbell & Dumbell	Sets	Reps	Rest
Nervous System	A1) Power Cleans	2	3	2 min
Strength	B1) Thick Bar Sumo Deadlift	3	5	3–5 min
Muscular Endurance	C1) Dumbell Bulgarian Split Squat	2	12	0–30 s
	C2) Inverted Row	2	12	0–30 s
	C3) Dumbell Goblet Squat	2	12	0–30 s
	C4) Weighted Pushup	2	12	0–30 s
Conditioning (complex)	D1) Clean, Press, Front Squat, Deadlift, Row	2	8,8,8,8,8	2 min

General Training Program 3	Mixed Equipment	Sets	Reps	Rest
Nervous System	A1) Double Kettlebell Swing	2	5	2 min
Strength	B1) Thick Bar Deadlift	3	5	3–5 min
Muscular Endurance	C1) Low Box Weighted Step Up	2	12	0–30 s
	C2) 1 Arm Cable Row	2	12	0–30 s
	C3) Cable Pull Throughs	2	12	0–30 s
	C4) Alligator Pushup	2	12	0–30 s
Conditioning	D1) Sled Sprint	3	100'	0 s
	D2) Hand Over Hand Sled Pull	3	50'	0 s
	D3) Backward Sled Drag	3	75'	3 min

Strength Focused Program 1	Exercise	Sets	Reps	Rest
Nervous System	A1) Power Cleans	2	3	2 min
Strength	B1) Thick Bar Deadlift	5	5	3–5 min
	C1) Overhead Kettlebell Press	3	(1,2,3)	as needed*
	C2) PullUp	3	(1,2,3)	as needed*
Conditioning	D1) Kettlebell Swing	3	20	0 s
	D2) Farmers Walk	3	75'	3 min

Strength Focused Program 2	Exercise	Sets	Reps	Rest
Nervous System	A1) Double Kettlebell Swing	2	5	2 min
Strength	B1) Barbell Front Squat	5	5	3-5 min
	C1) Barbell Overhead Press	3	(1,2,3)	as needed*
	C2) Inverted Row	3	(1,2,3)	as needed*
Conditioning	D1) Tabata Protocol on Airdyne Bike	8	20 s	10 s

Conditioning Focused Program 1	Exercise	Sets	Reps	Rest
Nervous System	A1) Double Kettlebell Swing	2	5	2 min
Strength	B1) Thick Bar Sumo Deadlift	2	5	3-5 min
Conditioning (Complex)	C1) Clean, Press, Front Squat, Deadlift, Row	3	8,8,8,8,8	3-5 min
Conditioning (Timed Sets)	D1) Pullup	AMAP	5	0 s
10 Minutes Continous	D2) Pushup	AMAP	10	0 s
As Many Rounds as Possible	D3) Bodyweight Squat	AMAP	15	0 s

Conditioning Focused Program 2	Exercise	Sets	Reps	Rest
Nervous System	A1) Box Jumps	2	10	2 min
Strength	B1) Front Squat	2	5	3-5 min
Conditioning (Kettlebell Complex)	C1) Clean, Press, Front Squat, Deadlift, Swing	3	8,8,8,8,8	3-5 min
Conditioning	D1) Sled Sprint	3	100'	0 s
	D2) Hand Over Hand Sled Pull	3	50'	0 s
	D3) Backward Sled Drag	3	75'	3 min

Notes:

Interview Preparation

5

GENERAL ADVICE

If you have reached the interview stage of the recruitment process, you should be proud of your accomplishment. You have made it further down the path to being hired as a firefighter than hundreds or even thousands of other applicants. To be one of the few offered a job, it is critical that you prepare for your interview as effectively as possible.

The interview is often one of the last chances for a recruiting fire department to evaluate potential candidates. Interviewers take this portion of the process very seriously. Not only are their decisions affecting the people being interviewed, they will also have a long term effect on the fire department. A poor decision could result in a candidate being hired who could have a negative effect on the fire department for decades.

When you are interviewed by a fire department, the most important thing to remember is to be yourself. Always give answers that you believe in and can support. Never lie during your interview. Keep in mind that the interviewers are trying to get to know you so they can make the most effective decision possible regarding your abilities to be a competent firefighter. There is very little chance that you will be asked any trick questions.

Although interviewers for every type of job are looking to hire the best person for the job, almost every interviewer has his own ideas regarding who that ideal person is. These ideas can be formed based on opinions and ideas related to experiences from the interviewer's life (on and off the job), the culture of the particular job, and many other factors. This can also be true for fire department interviewers. While many of the people who conduct fire department interviews may have similar opinions of what an ideal firefighter is, rarely will these ideas be exactly the same. This does not mean that these interviewers will hold a negative bias because of something not related to firefighting (for example bias related to culture, appearance, stereotypes, etc.), as most fire department interviewers will be very experienced and have the training to eliminate this issue. What this does mean is that interviewers may be looking for slightly different things in your answers that are based on their impression of who is the best candidate for the job. This is why it is impossible to predict a perfect answer for any type of question in a firefighter interview and, because of this, it is very important to thoroughly prepare for your interview in the areas outlined in this chapter.

This chapter will focus on how to plan for your interview. Instead of giving the answers to certain questions that may or may not be included in your interview, the aim of this chapter is to help you gather the information necessary to answer any interview question to the best of your ability. The four sections that will be covered include fire department related life experience, fire department specifics, hall tours, and practicing for your interview. If you spend the time to learn as much as possible about the fire department you are applying for and prepare examples from your life experiences that you can use to support your answers, you will be well prepared to answer any question.

WHAT YOU CAN DO TO PREPARE FOR YOUR INTERVIEW
Fire Department–related Life Experience

Try to think of examples from your life involving:

Stress. Have you ever dealt with a stressful situation? When? Why? How did you handle it?

Past work environments. What was the work like? Did you enjoy it/not enjoy it? Have you had any difficult situations at work?

Danger. Have you experienced any dangerous situations? Have you put yourself in danger? What were the circumstances?

Teamwork. Have you ever been part of a team? What was your experience like? Do you like working with other people?

Authority. How do you deal with authority? Have you ever disobeyed an order? Why?

Safety. Have you done anything unsafe? Why?

Anger. How do you deal with anger? When have you experienced anger in your life?

Leadership/follower roles. Have you been a leader? Have you been a follower?

Conflict resolution. Have you experienced a lot of conflict in your life? When? How do you deal with conflict?

Problem solving ability. Can you think on your feet? Are you good at solving problems? Does anything affect your ability to solve problems? Are you adaptable? Are you a flexible thinker?

Confidence. Are you a confident person? Have you ever had your confidence challenged? Can you remain confident in spite of a setback?

Community experience. Do you care about your community? What experience do you have in your community? Do you consider the fire department part of the community?

Initiative/motivation. Are you a motivated person? When have you shown initiative in your past?

Attention to detail. Are you thorough when completing tasks?

Ability to deal with pressure. Have you worked under pressure? Have you ever been in a high-pressure situation?

Integrity. Are you honest, reliable, and truthful? What are some examples of these traits?

Communication. Have you ever experienced any communication issues in the past? When has communication been important in your life? Do you communicate effectively? Have you ever had problems communicating?

Judgment. Do you have good judgment? When has your judgment let you down? Did you learn from your mistake? Do you understand the impact of your actions on others?

Reasoning ability. Do you complete tasks logically? Are you good at prioritizing?

Experience with the fire department. What experience have you had with the fire department in the past? What made you want to become a firefighter? Do you understand the role of a rookie firefighter?

Fire Department Specifics

Learn everything you can about the fire department and municipality you are interviewing for.

Number of stations. Find out how many fire stations the department has. Learn as much as you can about each station. This can include the number of firefighters at each station, the number of trucks at each station and their uses, and what type of calls the station frequently gets. Are there any unique hazards that this station responds to?

Overall size of the fire department. Find out the number of firefighters in the fire department, number of chiefs and officers, and number of other people working in the fire department (mechanics, fire prevention, etc.).

Chiefs. Research the names of the fire chiefs and their positions. This is particularly true for smaller departments. For a larger fire department, learn the names of the fire chief, the deputies, and the other higher-ranking chiefs, within reason.

Major hazard areas. Learn about the main hazard areas in the municipality. For example: major industry, hospitals, airports, highways, rivers, ocean, canyons and mountains, etc.

Municipal borders. Find out the borders of the municipality. Does the municipality border other municipalities? Where are the borders? Does the fire department have mutual aid agreements with neighboring municipalities?

Location of industrial, commercial, residential areas. Where are these areas located?

Population. Find out the population of the municipality.

Specialized teams/trucks. Find out about any specialized teams the fire department might have (e.g., high angle rescue, hazmat, etc). How many people are on the team? What station do they operate out of?

Fire department history. Find out as much as possible about the history of the fire department.

Understand shift patterns. Make sure you have a thorough grasp of the type of shifts and shift patterns of the fire department.

Mayor's name. Find out the mayor's name.

Hall Tours

Many fire departments expect that candidates will complete hall tours to learn more about the fire department that they are applying to. This is an excellent way to network and prepare for your interview. It can be one of your best opportunities to learn about your interview and gain an understanding of the fire department, its firefighters, and culture. When participating in hall tours, it is important to be respectful and conscious of your actions. Below are some tips to use when organizing and taking part in a hall tour.

Organize the hall tour ahead of time. Call the station at the start of shift (usually just after 8 A.M. is best) and ask for the captain (or officer in charge). Explain to the captain that you have an interview coming up and ask if there is any time that you could come by the fire hall. Do not just show up at a fire hall without calling first.

Dress appropriately. When you go to a fire hall for a hall tour, dress in a way that shows your respect for the position you are trying to attain. A good rule of thumb is to never be underdressed when compared to the firefighters on duty. Usually, this means wearing leather dress shoes, dress pants with belt, and a collared shirt (a golf shirt is acceptable). Be sure to be properly groomed.

Be humble and respectful, but be yourself. While at the fire hall, respect where you are and mentally acknowledge that you are applying to be a probationary firefighter. As with any stage of the recruitment process be humble and respect the position you are trying to attain but always be yourself.

Have questions prepared. Be prepared with intelligent questions for the firefighters on duty. These should be questions related to the fire department. This is an excellent time to learn about the fire department so take advantage of it.

Make your visit short but effective. Make your visit effective but don't overstay your welcome.

Practicing for Your Interview

Think about the types of questions you may be asked and get someone to practice a mock interview with you. Use the things you have learned in this chapter to create questions and answers. This way your answers will be informed, supported, and your own, which will help you avoid answers that may come across to the interviewers as coached and repetitive.

Sometimes you will be asked a question that will have to do with a hypothetical situation. These questions will require your answer to be based on what you might do in that situation. If possible, use a similar situation from your life to answer the question. When answering these types of questions, take into account safety, teamwork, and the chain of command.

Remember, you made it to the interview based on your past accomplishments (résumé), aptitude, and physical ability. The interview is to assess your intangible qualities. The more you practice, the more prepared and confident you will be during the interview.

TIPS FOR A SUCCESSFUL INTERVIEW
Before the Interview

Dress appropriately. Wear a suit. Your interviewers will most likely be wearing their dress uniforms (and civilian interviewers will wear suits). You should dress in a way that reflects your respect for the job.

Groom appropriately. Almost all fire departments have a grooming policy. The best idea is to follow traditional firefighter grooming. Basically this means that you are clean shaven (mustache is acceptable); if you have long hair it is worn up, and you are clean in general.

Public image and professionalism are very important to fire departments. How candidates dress for each stage of the recruitment can be an indicator of how seriously they will take the job and how they will represent the department in the future. Some say that an untrained interviewer can make a decision regarding a candidate in the first few minutes of an interview. Do not let something as simple as not dressing or grooming yourself respectfully affect your interview.

Go over your notes. Make sure you go over everything you have done to prepare for the interview.

Eat and drink properly. Be properly hydrated and nourished for your interview.

Be well-rested. Make sure you get enough rest to function at your highest level during the interview.

Arrive early. Make sure you preplan the route to the location of the interview. Never be late.

During the Interview

Be respectful. Respect the position you are working toward.

Be honest. Be honest when answering questions. Rarely will there be any trick questions in a fire department interview. Remember, the interviewers are trying to get to know you. Never lie for any reason. If you lie and get caught, chances are you have ruined any possibility of ever being hired by that fire department. Do not lose your credibility.

Be positive. Whatever happens in the interview, remain positive.

Be competent. If you have prepared properly it will show. Proper preparation will help you be seen as more capable and knowledgeable.

Be confident. The better your preparation for the interview is, the more confident you will be. Remember that you can be confident and yet still be nervous. A lot is at stake and the interviewers expect you to be nervous.

Answer questions succinctly. Don't spend too much time answering questions. Be concise. Answer the question and support your answer. Some people have been known to talk themselves out of a job—don't do this.

Support your answers. A yes or no answer is often not the best option. Support your answers with valid points. This can be brief. If you don't have an example that's okay—do not make something up or exaggerate. Remember to always be honest.

If you do not know the answer, don't worry. If you are unsure of the answer to a question, ask to come back to it. If the question is asked again in the interview, you will have had some time to prepare for it. Almost all fire departments will allow this during their interviews. Remember, interviewers expect you to be nervous.

After the Interview

No matter how good you feel after an interview, never assume that you got the job. After the interview, go home and go over it in your mind. Review every question that you were asked. Think about your answers and how they could be improved. The point of this post-interview assessment is not to worry and overthink your answers, but to help you prepare if you have another interview in the future.

You have made it this far, but don't slow down. If you truly want to be a firefighter, you have to be determined and put in the work. It will show.

SECTION TWO
SAMPLE TESTS

This section contains five practice tests that are similar in format and content to the firefighter exams you are likely to find throughout Canada, including two CPS-style tests, one IPMA-style test, and two generalized firefighter tests.

IMPORTANT NOTE

The following two sample CPS-style tests are NOT actual CPS exams. These tests were created to give you an idea of what to expect on the CPS. The actual CPS is subject to change, so for the most recent information available, please go to *www.cps.ca.gov*

All actual CPS tests contain 100 questions. However, sample CPS test 2 in this book (starting on page 188) contains only 80 questions due to the difficulty of reproducing teamwork/public relations/community relations questions. Please refer to Chapter 1 for details on these types of questions.

ANSWER SHEET
Test 1

SECTION 1

1. Ⓐ Ⓑ Ⓒ Ⓓ   6. Ⓐ Ⓑ Ⓒ Ⓓ   11. Ⓐ Ⓑ Ⓒ Ⓓ   16. Ⓐ Ⓑ Ⓒ Ⓓ
2. Ⓐ Ⓑ Ⓒ Ⓓ   7. Ⓐ Ⓑ Ⓒ Ⓓ   12. Ⓐ Ⓑ Ⓒ Ⓓ   17. Ⓐ Ⓑ Ⓒ Ⓓ
3. Ⓐ Ⓑ Ⓒ Ⓓ   8. Ⓐ Ⓑ Ⓒ Ⓓ   13. Ⓐ Ⓑ Ⓒ Ⓓ   18. Ⓐ Ⓑ Ⓒ Ⓓ
4. Ⓐ Ⓑ Ⓒ Ⓓ   9. Ⓐ Ⓑ Ⓒ Ⓓ   14. Ⓐ Ⓑ Ⓒ Ⓓ   19. Ⓐ Ⓑ Ⓒ Ⓓ
5. Ⓐ Ⓑ Ⓒ Ⓓ   10. Ⓐ Ⓑ Ⓒ Ⓓ   15. Ⓐ Ⓑ Ⓒ Ⓓ   20. Ⓐ Ⓑ Ⓒ Ⓓ

SECTION 2

21. Ⓐ Ⓑ Ⓒ Ⓓ   29. Ⓐ Ⓑ Ⓒ Ⓓ   37. Ⓐ Ⓑ Ⓒ Ⓓ   45. Ⓐ Ⓑ Ⓒ Ⓓ
22. Ⓐ Ⓑ Ⓒ Ⓓ   30. Ⓐ Ⓑ Ⓒ Ⓓ   38. Ⓐ Ⓑ Ⓒ Ⓓ   46. Ⓐ Ⓑ Ⓒ Ⓓ
23. Ⓐ Ⓑ Ⓒ Ⓓ   31. Ⓐ Ⓑ Ⓒ Ⓓ   39. Ⓐ Ⓑ Ⓒ Ⓓ   47. Ⓐ Ⓑ Ⓒ Ⓓ
24. Ⓐ Ⓑ Ⓒ Ⓓ   32. Ⓐ Ⓑ Ⓒ Ⓓ   40. Ⓐ Ⓑ Ⓒ Ⓓ   48. Ⓐ Ⓑ Ⓒ Ⓓ
25. Ⓐ Ⓑ Ⓒ Ⓓ   33. Ⓐ Ⓑ Ⓒ Ⓓ   41. Ⓐ Ⓑ Ⓒ Ⓓ   49. Ⓐ Ⓑ Ⓒ Ⓓ
26. Ⓐ Ⓑ Ⓒ Ⓓ   34. Ⓐ Ⓑ Ⓒ Ⓓ   42. Ⓐ Ⓑ Ⓒ Ⓓ   50. Ⓐ Ⓑ Ⓒ Ⓓ
27. Ⓐ Ⓑ Ⓒ Ⓓ   35. Ⓐ Ⓑ Ⓒ Ⓓ   43. Ⓐ Ⓑ Ⓒ Ⓓ
28. Ⓐ Ⓑ Ⓒ Ⓓ   36. Ⓐ Ⓑ Ⓒ Ⓓ   44. Ⓐ Ⓑ Ⓒ Ⓓ

SECTION 3

51. Ⓐ Ⓑ Ⓒ Ⓓ   58. Ⓐ Ⓑ Ⓒ Ⓓ   65. Ⓐ Ⓑ Ⓒ Ⓓ   72. Ⓐ Ⓑ Ⓒ Ⓓ
52. Ⓐ Ⓑ Ⓒ Ⓓ   59. Ⓐ Ⓑ Ⓒ Ⓓ   66. Ⓐ Ⓑ Ⓒ Ⓓ   73. Ⓐ Ⓑ Ⓒ Ⓓ
53. Ⓐ Ⓑ Ⓒ Ⓓ   60. Ⓐ Ⓑ Ⓒ Ⓓ   67. Ⓐ Ⓑ Ⓒ Ⓓ   74. Ⓐ Ⓑ Ⓒ Ⓓ
54. Ⓐ Ⓑ Ⓒ Ⓓ   61. Ⓐ Ⓑ Ⓒ Ⓓ   68. Ⓐ Ⓑ Ⓒ Ⓓ   75. Ⓐ Ⓑ Ⓒ Ⓓ
55. Ⓐ Ⓑ Ⓒ Ⓓ   62. Ⓐ Ⓑ Ⓒ Ⓓ   69. Ⓐ Ⓑ Ⓒ Ⓓ
56. Ⓐ Ⓑ Ⓒ Ⓓ   63. Ⓐ Ⓑ Ⓒ Ⓓ   70. Ⓐ Ⓑ Ⓒ Ⓓ
57. Ⓐ Ⓑ Ⓒ Ⓓ   64. Ⓐ Ⓑ Ⓒ Ⓓ   71. Ⓐ Ⓑ Ⓒ Ⓓ

SECTION 4

76. Ⓐ Ⓑ Ⓒ Ⓓ   83. Ⓐ Ⓑ Ⓒ Ⓓ   90. Ⓐ Ⓑ Ⓒ Ⓓ   97. Ⓐ Ⓑ Ⓒ Ⓓ
77. Ⓐ Ⓑ Ⓒ Ⓓ   84. Ⓐ Ⓑ Ⓒ Ⓓ   91. Ⓐ Ⓑ Ⓒ Ⓓ   98. Ⓐ Ⓑ Ⓒ Ⓓ
78. Ⓐ Ⓑ Ⓒ Ⓓ   85. Ⓐ Ⓑ Ⓒ Ⓓ   92. Ⓐ Ⓑ Ⓒ Ⓓ   99. Ⓐ Ⓑ Ⓒ Ⓓ
79. Ⓐ Ⓑ Ⓒ Ⓓ   86. Ⓐ Ⓑ Ⓒ Ⓓ   93. Ⓐ Ⓑ Ⓒ Ⓓ   100. Ⓐ Ⓑ Ⓒ Ⓓ
80. Ⓐ Ⓑ Ⓒ Ⓓ   87. Ⓐ Ⓑ Ⓒ Ⓓ   94. Ⓐ Ⓑ Ⓒ Ⓓ
81. Ⓐ Ⓑ Ⓒ Ⓓ   88. Ⓐ Ⓑ Ⓒ Ⓓ   95. Ⓐ Ⓑ Ⓒ Ⓓ
82. Ⓐ Ⓑ Ⓒ Ⓓ   89. Ⓐ Ⓑ Ⓒ Ⓓ   96. Ⓐ Ⓑ Ⓒ Ⓓ

CPS STYLE TEST 1

Section 1—Understanding Oral Information

Oral Passage:

When extinguishing a fire, there are three extinguishing and fire control methods commonly used by firefighters. These methods are direct, indirect, and gas cooling. Each method has its own strengths and weaknesses and because of this some methods are better suited to certain situations than others. No single method is best for all situations. As firefighters gain experience and knowledge they will be better able to identify which method is best suited for the firefighting situation they are involved in. Often, firefighters may use a combination of these methods when fighting a fire.

A direct fire attack is the application of water to the seat of the fire using a straight stream or solid stream. This can be achieved using a combination nozzle or a solid bore nozzle. Direct application of water to the seat of the fire cools the burning fuels to below their ignition temperature. A direct attack can be used offensively or defensively. For example, if the fire is in one of its early stages of growth, an offensive direct attack will work well to extinguish the fire quickly. If the fire is well involved, a defensive direct attack may be the best way to control the fire if firefighters can't enter the structure. Direct attack is well suited for these types of situations. A disadvantage of direct attack is that it can disrupt the thermal balance if it is overapplied.

An indirect fire attack is the application of water to the superheated surfaces of the fire compartment in order to create a large amount of steam. The intent is for the steam to smother the flames and sometimes even extinguish the seat of the fire. Indirect attack can be performed using a straight stream, solid stream, or narrow fog pattern. Usually, indirect fire attack is used for defensive operations and works particularly well when backdraft conditions are present. When using an indirect attack it is important not to overapply water to any one surface in the fire compartment. Overapplication of water tends to overcool that area and stop the production of steam. To produce steam the portion of wall or ceiling coming in contact with water must be over 100 degrees Celsius. This type of extinguishment method is not ideal when victims may still be in the fire compartment.

Gas cooling is an extinguishment method that uses short pulses of water fog. The main purpose of gas cooling is to control the fire gas layers by reducing their temperature. This is done by applying short or medium pulses of water from a combination nozzle in a fog pattern into the fire gas layers. When using gas cooling, it is important to control the droplet size produced by the nozzle. If the proper droplet size is maintained when the water droplets enter the fire gas layers, they will be vaporized and some of the heat energy from the fire gasses will be transferred to the water. This can help maintain visibility and improve thermal conditions. The gas cooling extinguishment method can also be used to cool the linings in the room. Gas cooling is often used to reach the seat of the fire where the fire will be extinguished using a direct attack.

Water droplet size is much more critical when gas cooling than when using an indirect attack. This is because gas cooling seeks to cool overhead layers of fire gas while an indirect attack seeks to create steam in order to smother the flames.

DIRECTIONS: Answer the following twenty questions based on the information that was just read to you.

1. How many methods are commonly used by firefighters to extinguish or control a fire?

   (A) 1
   (B) 5
   (C) 3
   (D) 8

2. Which of these methods is not an extinguishment or fire control method commonly used by firefighters?

   (A) indirect
   (B) direct
   (C) multi direct
   (D) gas cooling

3. Direct fire attack is

   (A) the application of water to the seat of the fire
   (B) going straight to the fire
   (C) trying to bounce water off a wall to hit the fire
   (D) extinguishing a fire outside of the building

4. What type of nozzle can be used for a direct attack?

   (A) combination
   (B) bresden
   (C) solid bore
   (D) both A and C

5. The direct application of water to the seat of the fire

   (A) smothers the fire
   (B) creates steam which excludes oxygen from the environment
   (C) is an indirect attack
   (D) cools the burning fuels to below their ignition temperature

6. A direct fire attack can be used offensively or _____

   (A) indirectly
   (B) structurally
   (C) independently
   (D) defensively

7. If it is overapplied direct attack can

(A) disrupt the thermal balance
(B) interfere with a firefighter's ability to cool burning material
(C) both A and B
(D) none of the above

8. The seat of the fire can best be defined as

(A) the room the fire is in.
(B) the source of the flames.
(C) the floor the fire is on.
(D) a fire attack method.

9. What is an indirect attack?

(A) A method of extinguishment where firefighters in a compartment bounce water off the ceiling onto the seat of the fire.
(B) The application of water to the superheated surfaces of the fire compartment in order to create a large amount of steam.
(C) The application of water to the seat of the fire.
(D) All of the above.

10. What type of nozzle pattern is used to perform an indirect attack?

(A) straight stream
(B) solid stream
(C) narrow fog
(D) any of the above will work

11. Why would a firefighter want to create steam when performing an indirect fire attack?

(A) A firefighter does not want to create steam when performing an indirect attack.
(B) To push down the neutral plane.
(C) To smother the flames.
(D) To improve visibility.

12. Does an indirect extinguishing method work well when backdraft conditions are present?

(A) No, an indirect extinguishing method only makes backdraft conditions worse.
(B) No, an indirect extinguishing method can only be used from inside a structure.
(C) Yes, an indirect extinguishing method works well when dealing with backdraft conditions.
(D) None of the above.

13. Why should firefighters be careful not to overapply water when using an indirect attack?

(A) It will make the fire burn hotter.
(B) It can cause a flashover.
(C) It will cause a backdraft.
(D) It can overcool the area and stop the production of steam.

14. To produce steam the portion of wall or ceiling coming in contact with water must be over _____ degrees Celsius.

    (A) 100
    (B) 115
    (C) 200
    (D) 45

15. When performing gas cooling as an extinguishment method, what type of nozzle will a firefighter use?

    (A) solid bore
    (B) bresden
    (C) combination nozzle
    (D) any of the above will work

16. Gas cooling uses

    (A) water fog
    (B) straight stream
    (C) solid stream
    (D) any of the above

17. Sometimes firefighters use gas cooling to reach the seat of the fire and then switch to a _____ to extinguish the fire.

    (A) water fog
    (B) direct attack
    (C) indirect attack
    (D) positive pressure fan

18. Water droplet size is

    (A) more critical when gas cooling than when using an indirect attack.
    (B) less critical when gas cooling than when using an indirect attack.
    (C) never critical during fire attack.
    (D) none of the above.

19. In general, this passage intends to inform the listener of

    (A) what firefighters do at work.
    (B) the three most commonly used fire extinguishing/control methods.
    (C) the types of nozzles used by firefighters.
    (D) the best type of hose to use during a fire.

20. What type of extinguishment method is best?

    (A) direct
    (B) indirect
    (C) gas cooling
    (D) No method is best; some methods are better suited to certain situations than others.

Section 2—Understanding Written Information

DIRECTIONS: The questions below measure your ability to understand written information. Base your answers on the information provided by the questions, not on any previous knowledge. Fill in the bubble on the answer sheet that corresponds to your answer.

DIRECTIONS: Questions 21 and 22 refer to the following passage.

Frostbite is a serious condition that requires immediate medical attention. Frostbite is the freezing of the body's tissues. Cells in the frozen area can be damaged or destroyed when their fluid freezes and swells. Frostbite can be superficial or deep depending on if just the skin is frozen or if the skin and the tissues below are frozen. Signs of frostbite include skin that is cold to the touch and discolored skin (flushed, white, yellow, or blue depending on the length of exposure).

21. According to the passage, signs of frostbite include

    (A) cold skin
    (B) discolored skin that can be blue
    (C) a strong odor
    (D) both A and B

22. Frostbite is the _____ of the body's tissues.

    (A) serious condition
    (B) freezing
    (C) shivering
    (D) ice

DIRECTIONS: Questions 23 and 24 refer to the following passage.

The fire department uses the SSSAGE protocol when dealing with motor vehicle accidents. SSSAGE is an acronym for the steps used in extricating victims after a motor vehicle accident. It stands for scene assessment, staging, stabilization, access patient, glass management, extrication.

23. According to the passage, what is the third step used in extricating victims from a motor vehicle accident?

    (A) scene assessment
    (B) stabilization
    (C) glass management
    (D) extrication

24. As it is used in the passage, what is the meaning of the word acronym?

(A) short form
(B) lesson
(C) math equation
(D) short video

> **DIRECTIONS: Questions 25 through 27 refer to the following passage.**

An important law when dealing with fire department facilities is the Occupiers Liability Act. This act imposes high standards of care on any person (including cities and municipalities) who occupies a premise that is open to the public. Essentially, when members of the public are in the fire hall, every practical precaution must be taken to prevent them from being injured. For example, if the bay floor is wet and no warning signs are up or barriers are erected, then if the bay door is open and a member of the public walks in, slips, and breaks their arm they can sue under the Occupiers Liability Act.

25. What should firefighters do to avoid issues involving the Occupiers Liability Act?

(A) Take every practical precaution to prevent the public from being injured while on fire department property.
(B) Mop the bay floor thoroughly.
(C) Keep the fire hall locked.
(D) Keep the public out of the fire hall.

26. What does the word "practical" mean as it is used in the passage?

(A) inconvenient
(B) easy
(C) realistic, reasonable
(D) none of the above

27. The passage is describing a

(A) operational guideline
(B) rule
(C) firefighting principal
(D) law

> **DIRECTIONS: Questions 28 through 32 refer to the following passage.**

There are basically three types of near drownings. They are dry drowning, wet drowning, and secondary drowning. These are called near drownings because usually when people drown, their lungs are not completely filled with water; therefore, the victims are referred to as near drowned.

A dry drowning is a drowning in which no water enters the lungs. Death is caused by suffocation. When the victim takes a breath, the sudden intake of water causes a reflex called laryngospasm (this is the reflex closure of the epiglottis). This closes the trachea so no air can enter the lungs and causes the suffocation. Most victims who are successfully resuscitated after a near drowning are victims of a dry drowning.

A wet drowning is a drowning in which water has entered the lungs. Asphyxia is due to fluid in the lungs. Laryngospasm can happen during a wet drowning but subsides and water enters the lungs. This water causes pulmonary edema (excessive fluid in the membranes which cause the lungs to separate from the blood vessels). This can present problems if the victim is rescued.

Secondary drowning can occur minutes or even weeks after the victim is rescued or resuscitated. Essentially, death is caused by the complications due to inspired water or vomit that occurred during the immersion episode. Some of these complications include pulmonary edema, pneumonia, and atelectasis.

28. Using the information provided in the passage, what is the difference between a dry drowning and a wet drowning?

   (A) A dry drowning takes place only outside the water while a wet drowning takes place in the water.
   (B) A dry drowning involves virtually no water entering the lungs while a wet drowning involves water entering the lungs.
   (C) There is no difference.
   (D) Laryngospasm takes place during a dry drowning but not during a wet drowning.

29. Why are the three types of drownings called near drownings?

   (A) Because they almost happened.
   (B) Because they happen near other people.
   (C) Because their definitions are so near to each other.
   (D) Because usually when a person drowns, his lungs are not completely filled with water.

30. What is a laryngospasm?

   (A) Another name for dry drowning.
   (B) The dilution of the surfactant in the alveoli.
   (C) The reflex closure of the epiglottis.
   (D) It is the same as expiration.

31. According to the passage, which of these options is not a cause of death related to secondary drowning?

   (A) pneumonia
   (B) atelectasis
   (C) melanoma
   (D) pulmonary edema

32. According to the passage, most victims that are successfully resuscitated after a near drowning are victims of

   (A) wet drowning
   (B) dry drowning
   (C) secondary drowning
   (D) water drowning

In technical rescue applications, a pulley is a free running metal wheel. The pulley(s) is held between two metal side plates that a carabiner can be attached to. Technical rescue pulleys have removable side plates. Pulleys reduce friction at turns in rope (compared to other methods of turning a rope). They can also be used to create a mechanical advantage. There are several different kinds of pulleys that can be used for different things during a technical rescue. Some examples of these types of pulleys are prusik minding pulleys, knot passing pulleys, double pulleys, and pulleys with a built-in cam. Because a rope weakens when it is turned, the structure of a pulley can also increase the strength of the rope at the turn. The strength of a rope is returned fully when the turn in the rope is at least four times its diameter.

33. A pulley contains two _____ side plates.

(A) plastic

(B) metal

(C) plexiglass

(D) silver

34. Which one of the following pulleys is not used for technical rescues?

(A) Prusik minding pulleys.

(B) Tensionless friction pulleys.

(C) Knot passing pulleys.

(D) Pulleys with a built-in cam.

35. How much bigger than the diameter of the rope does the turn around the pulley have to be to fully return the strength of the rope?

(A) A minimum of 4 times bigger.

(B) A minimum of 6 times bigger.

(C) This information is not contained in the passage.

(D) None of the above.

36. According to the passage, what are two things that technical rescue pulleys are used for?

(A) Reducing friction and anchoring.

(B) Creating a mechanical advantage and anchoring.

(C) Reducing friction and creating a mechanical advantage.

(D) Anchoring and creating a mechanical advantage.

DIRECTIONS: Questions 37 through 40 refer to the following passage.

The shade of smoke can often be an indicator of fire conditions. These shades and various densities can vary significantly, depending on what is burning and the ventilation profile of the fire. Smoke that is a lighter shade is produced when the oxygen levels in the fire are low (under 14%), or when the temperature in the fire is too low to support flames. This is because when the fuel in the fire breaks down without flame most of the carbon remains on the material that is pyrolysing. Flaming or smoldering fires produce smoke that is a darker shade. This is because when the combustion of the burning material is significant enough, a greater percentage of the carbon in the product is released. Synthetic products often create dark smoke.

37. The shade of smoke can often be an indicator of _____ conditions.

    (A) smoke
    (B) fire
    (C) attack
    (D) atmospheric

38. According to the passage, what are some things that do not affect the shade of smoke?

    (A) the material that is burning
    (B) ventilation profile
    (C) low oxygen levels
    (D) time of day

39. According to the passage, what are considered low oxygen levels that may not support a fire?

    (A) under 21%
    (B) under 18%
    (C) under 14%
    (D) This is not mentioned in the passage.

40. What does this passage indicate as a cause of darker smoke?

    (A) more carbon release
    (B) the type of material burning
    (C) less carbon release
    (D) both A and B

DIRECTIONS: Questions 41 through 45 refer to the following passage.

Many fire stations have truck bays that require the fire truck to be backed into them. There is a procedure used for this process that starts as the truck approaches the fire station. As the truck is nearing the station, the two tailgaters put on traffic vests and retrieve stop/slow signs from their storage positions. Next, the driver pulls the truck up to the curb outside the station and activates the emergency lights. At this time the junior tailgater opens the bay door remotely. When the truck has come to a complete stop the tailgaters both exit the truck. The tailgater on the curb side of the truck goes to the front of the truck and stops traffic. The tailgater on the traffic side of the truck goes to the rear of the truck and stops traffic. When traffic has been completely stopped the tailgater at the front of the truck will indicate to the driver that they can turn into the street and begin to back up. When the fire truck is perpendicular to the street the tailgater at the front of the truck will move to the front of the truck and control traffic in both directions as the truck is backing onto the tarmac. The tailgater at the rear of the truck will back the truck up making sure the driver doesn't hit anything. When the fire truck is completely on the tarmac the tailgater backing up the truck will stop the truck. The senior tailgater will go into the bay and back the truck the rest of the way in. The junior tailgater will connect the exhaust extractor as the fire truck backs in. When the fire truck is completely in the bay the senior tailgater will stop the truck. The driver will then apply the spring brake, turn off the truck, and get out to plug the truck into shore power.

41. According to the passage, when the fire truck is preparing to pull out into the street, will the junior tailgater always stop traffic at the front of the fire truck?

    (A) Yes
    (B) No
    (C) Not necessarily; the tailgater on the curbside of the truck stops traffic at the front of the truck.
    (D) No, they are in charge of the exhaust fan.

42. What is one of the driver's jobs as they pull the fire truck up to the curb next to the fire hall?

    (A) Open the bay door.
    (B) Tell the captain to open the bay door.
    (C) Turn into traffic.
    (D) Turn on the emergency lights for the fire truck.

43. According to the passage, what do the tailgaters need to wear while they direct traffic?

    (A) turnout gear
    (B) helmets
    (C) traffic vests
    (D) gloves

44. Who backs the driver and fire truck into the fire station?

    (A) the captain
    (B) the senior tailgater
    (C) the tailgater that sat curbside
    (D) it doesn't matter

45. What does the driver do as his or her last step in backing the truck into the fire station?

    (A) Turn the truck off.
    (B) Plug the truck in.
    (C) Stop the truck.
    (D) Apply the spring break.

DIRECTIONS: Following are the steps for connecting to a hydrant with a 4-inch hose. Use these steps to answer Questions 46–50.

1. Firefighter follows company officer's direction to "take hydrant," "lay in," or "grab the hydrant."

2. Firefighter waits for apparatus to come to a complete stop, removes seatbelt, and exits.

3. Firefighter removes several cones from the apparatus and places them on the roadway.

4. Firefighter grasps hydrant bag attached to 4″ hose and steps off tailboard pulling hose.

5. Firefighter places a bite of hose (with minimum 10′ of slack) against base of hydrant furthest from the fire. Stands on hose.

6. Firefighter signals the driver to "GO" using an appropriate means of communication (radio, verbal, or hand signal).

7. Firefighter opens the hydrant bag:
   1. Removes hydrant key and loosens the large cap, and the small cap pointing toward the fire.
   2. Removes the caps by hand standing behind the ports.

8. Firefighter makes hose connections:
   1. Attaches 4″ hose to large port using "Stortz / hydrant" adapter ensuring a minimum of 10′ hose laid straight out from port.
   2. Attaches 2½″ gate valve to small port (2½″ / Stortz adapter can stay in hydrant bag for "single lay").
   3. Makes sure the 2½″ gate valve is closed.

9. Firefighter advises pump operator by radio when ready to charge hydrant line (unless command to open hydrant has already been given).

10. Firefighter does not open hydrant until (one of the following):
    - Pump operator's command for water via radio to open hydrant or,
    - hearing the air horn signal to open hydrant. Two 3-second blasts. Used in the event of a radio problem. Radio is preferred method.

11. Firefighter opens hydrant fully until stem stops turning then backs off ¼ turn.

12. Firefighter positions traffic cones to:
    1. Protect the hose.
    2. Block traffic on street.
    3. Protect pedestrians from hose hazards.

13. Firefighter follows hose back to pumping apparatus checking for:
    1. Kinks
    2. Leaks
    3. Position of hose impeding access for other apparatus.

46. In what order should the firefighter remove the cones and the hydrant bag from the apparatus?

(A) Remove the cones, then the hydrant bag.
(B) Remove the hydrant bag, then the cones.
(C) Remove both at the same time.
(D) The cones always stay on the truck.

47. According to the passage, what is the minimum amount of slack that should be in the bite of hose that is placed at the base of the fire hydrant?

(A) 100′
(B) 11′
(C) 10′
(D) 12′

48. When can the firefighter open the hydrant?

(A) As soon as the hose is connected.
(B) When the pump operator asks the firefighter for water over the radio.
(C) When the firefighter hears the air horn signal for water.
(D) B or C.

49. Which of the following is the firefighter not looking for as he follows the hose back to the truck?

(A) kinks
(B) loops
(C) the hose impeding access for other apparatus
(D) both A and C

50. According to the passage, how far does the firefighter open the hydrant?

(A) three turns
(B) fully
(C) fully, then backs off ¼ turn
(D) fully, then backs of 1 turn

Section 3—Mathematical Ability

DIRECTIONS: Answer Questions 51 through 75 by choosing the best answer for each question and filling in the corresponding bubble on the answer sheet.

51. 324.1 minus 235.22 equals?

    (A) 88.88
    (B) 87.88
    (C) 76.86
    (D) 86.67

52. 100 divided by 20 equals?

    (A) 4
    (B) 5
    (C) 25
    (D) 6

53. 625 divided by 25 equals?

    (A) 23
    (B) 24
    (C) 25
    (D) 21

54. 43.98 multiplied by 34.3 equals?

    (A) 1,508.514
    (B) 1,508.524
    (C) 1,509.524
    (D) 1,509.514

55. 5/8 plus 3/4 plus 7/16 equals?

    (A) 1 13/16
    (B) 1 7/8
    (C) 28/16
    (D) 13/4

56. 6/8 minus 4/32 equals?

    (A) 5/4
    (B) 3/5
    (C) 5/8
    (D) 3/4

57. 1/5 plus 3/15 plus 7/25 plus 4/20 equals?

    (A) 22/25
    (B) 21/25
    (C) 4/5
    (D) 4/6

58. 3/5 multiplied by 6/8 equals?

   (A) 15/12
   (B) 3/4
   (C) 4/5
   (D) 9/20

59. 4/8 divided by 6/7 equals?

   (A) 7/12
   (B) 3/6
   (C) 8/12
   (D) 2/3

60. 15 is what percentage of 30?

   (A) 50%
   (B) 60%
   (C) 70%
   (D) 40%

61. When expressed as a fraction 25% is the same as _____

   (A) 1/6
   (B) 2/6
   (C) 1/5
   (D) 1/4

62. A fire truck takes 2 minutes to travel 6 kilometres. How many minutes will it take the fire truck to travel the remaining 9 kilometres to the fire hall?

   (A) 4 minutes
   (B) 6 minutes
   (C) 3 minutes
   (D) 2 minutes

63. There are 20 firefighters on 5 fire trucks. What is the ratio of firefighters to trucks?

   (A) 5:1
   (B) 4:1
   (A) 6:2
   (A) 6:1

64. A fire truck has travelled 45 miles in the last 15 minutes. How far will it travel in the next 5 minutes if it travels at the same speed?

   (A) 15 miles
   (B) 10 miles
   (C) 5 miles
   (D) 8 miles

65. Engine 4 has been to 12 structure fires in the past 16 shifts. If they keep going at the same rate, how many structure fires can they expect to go to in the next 8 shifts?

   (A) 2 fires
   (B) 8 fires
   (C) 6 fires
   (D) 4 fires

66. Quint 2 has pumped 40,300 gallons of water in the past hour. If Quint 2 keeps pumping at the same rate, how many gallons of water will Quint 2 pump in the next 30 minutes?

   (A) 30,100 gallons
   (B) 30,200 gallons
   (C) 40,300 gallons
   (D) 20,150 gallons

67. Firefighters Johnson and Smith have travelled 1,200 metres in the past 5 minutes on their way to a technical rescue. If they keep travelling at the same speed, how far will they travel in 2 minutes?

   (A) 500 metres
   (B) 520 metres
   (C) 1,000 metres
   (D) 480 metres

68. Five exposure lines are flowing 14,770 gallons of water each every hour. How much water are the exposure lines flowing combined per hour?

   (A) 15,000 gallons
   (B) 73,850 gallons
   (C) 75,000 gallons
   (D) 73,840 gallons

69. If a firefighter attends 3,487 of a possible 3,860 calls, what percentage of calls did they attend?

   (A) about 90%
   (B) about 94%
   (C) about 85%
   (D) about 70%

70. A firefighting course is presented in eight sections. The first 5 sections have been completed in 6 hours. If every section takes the same amount of time to teach, how long will it take to teach the last three sections?

   (A) 4.5 hours
   (B) 3.7 hours
   (C) 3.6 hours
   (D) 3 hours

71. Ladder 8 is at a structure fire. 1,250 feet of hose are off Ladder 8 and being used on the fire. If each length of hose is 50 feet long, how many lengths of hose are off the truck?

   (A) 24
   (B) 25
   (C) 20
   (D) 26

72. There is about .946 of a litre in one quart. How many litres are there in 60 quarts?

   (A) 56.76
   (B) 57.76
   (C) 46.77
   (D) 48.98

73. Five of the firefighters at Station 2 have been firefighters for less than 3 years. There are 90 total firefighters working at Station 2. What percent of firefighters at Station 2 have been firefighters for less than 3 years?

   (A) 6%
   (B) 5.5%
   (C) 7%
   (D) 8%

74. If you cut 850 feet of rescue rope in 4 equal pieces, how long will those pieces be?

   (A) 214.5 ft.
   (B) 212.5 ft.
   (C) 210 ft.
   (D) 205.5 ft.

75. The chainsaw on Engine 3 will run out of fuel after 30 minutes if it is run consistently on a full tank of 4 litres of fuel. How much fuel will be used if the chainsaw is run for 15 minutes?

   (A) 3.75 litres
   (B) 1.25 litres
   (C) 2 litres
   (D) 1.75 litres

Section 4—Mechanical Aptitude

> **DIRECTIONS:** Answer Questions 76 through 100 based on the information presented. Choose the best answer for each question and fill in the corresponding bubble on the answer sheet.

76. If gear B is turning counterclockwise, which gears will turn in the same direction?

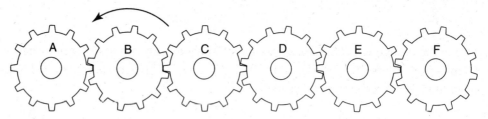

    (A) B, D, F
    (B) B, C, A
    (C) B, C, D
    (D) B, A, C

77. If the drive gear is turning clockwise, what direction will gear B turn?

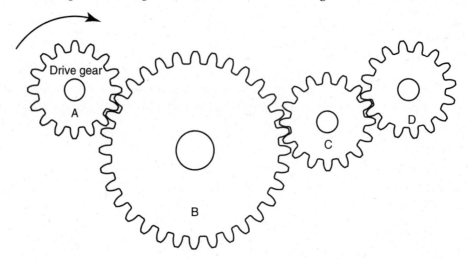

    (A) Clockwise
    (B) Counterclockwise
    (C) Faster
    (D) Slower

78. The gear being driven in the picture below will have _____

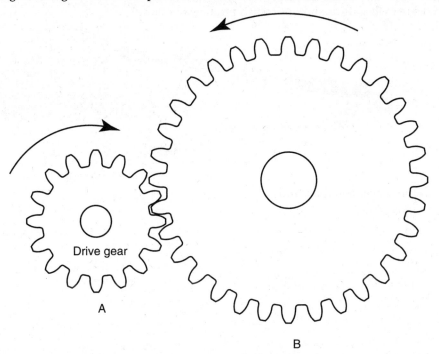

(A) twice the torque and twice the speed as the drive gear.
(B) twice the torque and half the speed as the drive gear.
(C) half the torque and twice the speed as the drive gear.
(D) half the torque and half the speed as the drive gear.

79. Wheel A will turn _____ and Wheel D will turn _____.

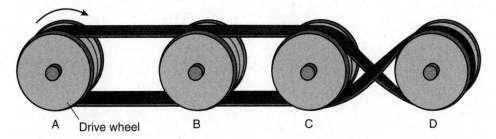

(A) clockwise, clockwise
(B) counterclockwise, clockwise
(C) clockwise, counterclockwise
(D) counterclockwise, counterclockwise

80. If a belt drive has a drive wheel that is 1/4 the size of the second wheel, how fast will the second wheel turn and how much torque will it have?

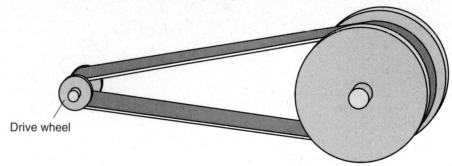

Drive wheel

(A) ¼ the speed, half the torque
(B) ¼ the speed, 4 times the torque
(C) ½ the speed, 3 times the torque
(D) ⅓ the speed, 4 times the torque

81. Which load will be easiest to lift?

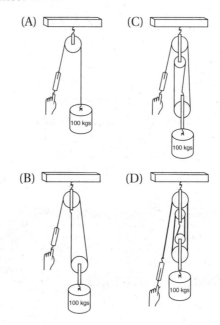

(A) 100 kgs

(C) 100 kgs

(B) 100 kgs

(D) 100 kgs

82. How much faster does load A move than Load B if the rope is pulled at the same speed?

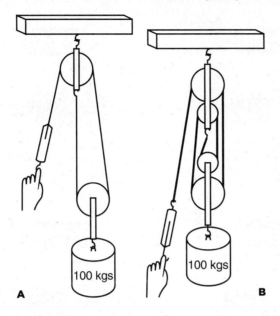

A   B

(A) 4 times as fast
(B) 2 times as fast
(C) 3 times as fast
(D) They will move at the same speed

83. Which shape when added to the shape below forms a square?

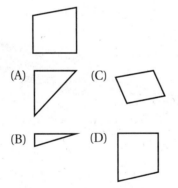

(A)   (C)

(B)   (D)

84. Which circle is tallest?

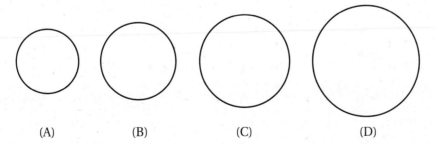

(A)   (B)   (C)   (D)

85. The buckets in the well all weigh the same amount. Which will be easiest to raise?

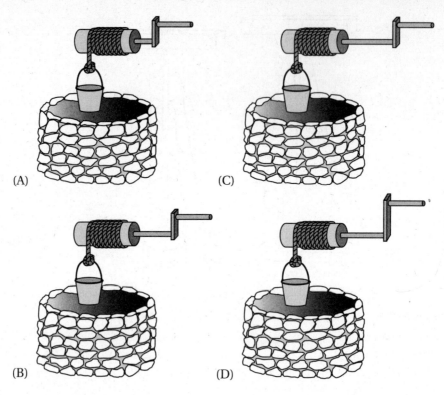

86. What type of simple machine is the screwdriver below?

(A) wheel and axle
(B) gear
(C) pulley
(D) inclined plane

87. Which wheel turns faster?

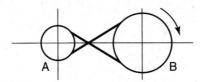

(A) wheel A
(B) wheel B
(C) they turn at the same speed
(D) cannot be determined

88. Firefighters are loading foam into a truck to take to an industrial fire. Which ramp would be the hardest to roll the foam barrels up?

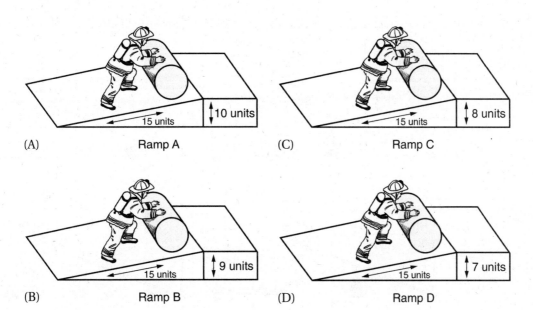

(A)   Ramp A   (C)   Ramp C

15 units   10 units   15 units   8 units

(B)   Ramp B   (D)   Ramp D

15 units   9 units   15 units   7 units

89. For the hour hand on this clock to be pointed at the number 9, how many degrees would it have to move?

(A) 360 degrees

(B) 90 degrees

(C) 180 degrees

(D) 30 degrees

90. In which picture will it be easiest for the firefighter to move the load?

(A)

(C)

(B)

(D)

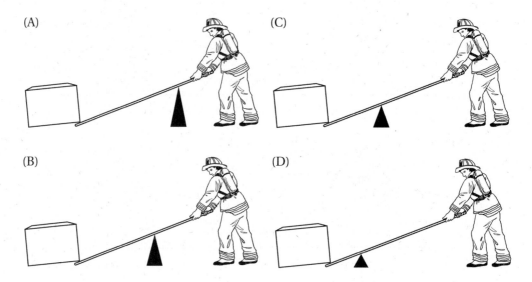

91. Which wheelbarrow will be easiest to use?

(A)

(C)

(B)

(D)

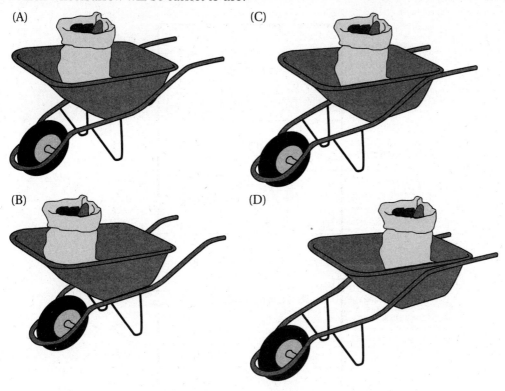

92. What does this gauge read?

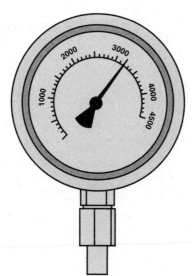

(A) 3,100
(B) 3,200
(C) 3,400
(D) 2,200

93. How long is this house from north to south?

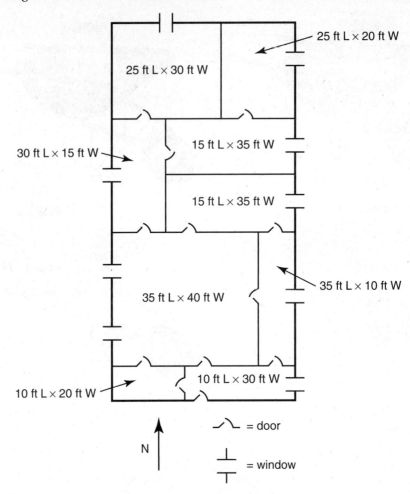

25 ft L × 30 ft W

25 ft L × 20 ft W

30 ft L × 15 ft W

15 ft L × 35 ft W

15 ft L × 35 ft W

35 ft L × 40 ft W

35 ft L × 10 ft W

10 ft L × 30 ft W

10 ft L × 20 ft W

N

= door

= window

(A) 90 ft.
(B) 100 ft.
(C) 95 ft.
(D) 50 ft.

94. How wide is this house from west to east?

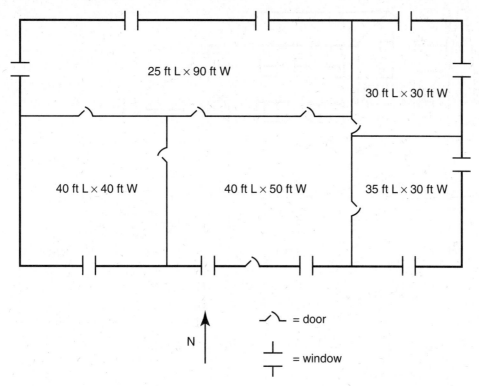

25 ft L × 90 ft W

30 ft L × 30 ft W

40 ft L × 40 ft W

40 ft L × 50 ft W

35 ft L × 30 ft W

N

⌒ = door

⊥ = window

(A) 60 ft.
(B) 70 ft.
(C) 115 ft.
(D) 120 ft.

95. Which of the floor plans below matches the house?

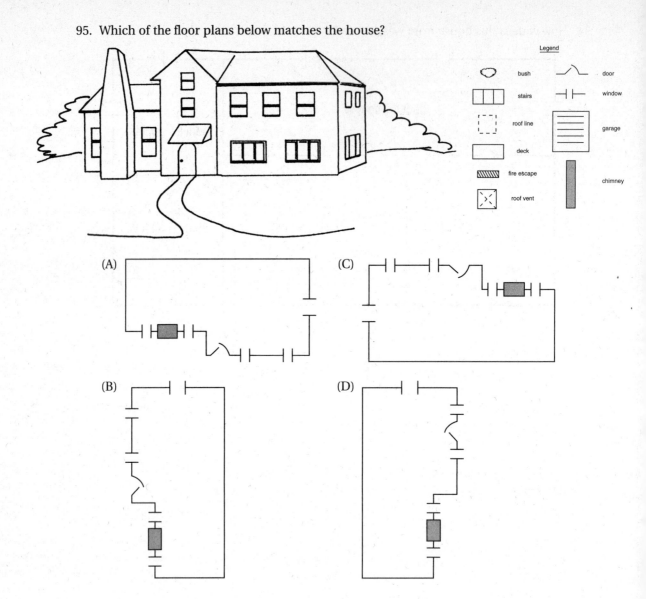

Legend

bush

stairs

roof line

deck

fire escape

roof vent

door

window

garage

chimney

(A)

(B)

(C)

(D)

96. Which of the floor plans below matches the house?

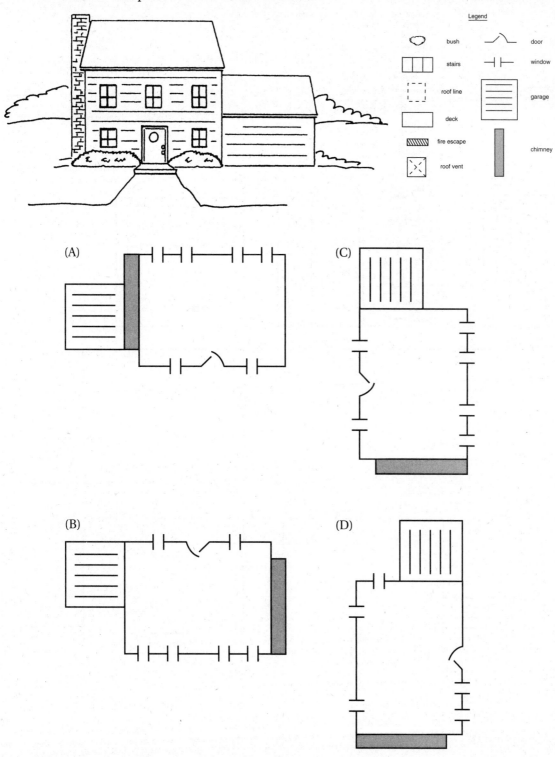

97. Which of the floor plans below matches the house?

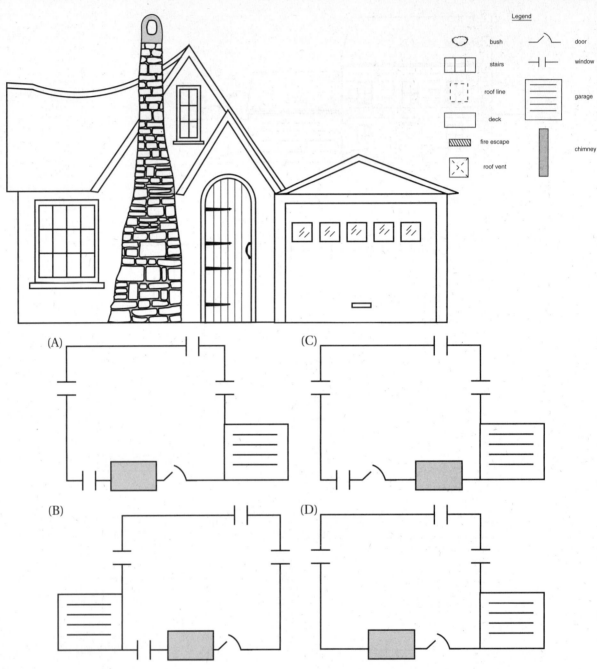

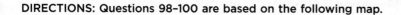

DIRECTIONS: Questions 98–100 are based on the following map.

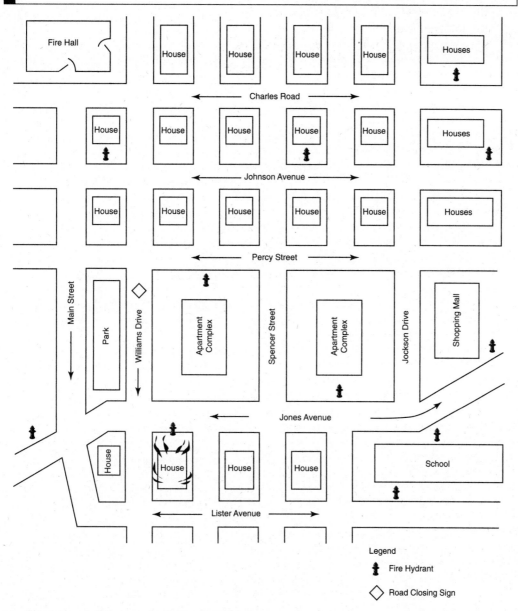

98. What is parallel to and north of Johnson Avenue?

    (A) Williams Drive
    (B) Percy Street
    (C) Charles Road
    (D) Lister Avenue

99. How many fire hydrants are on Jones Avenue?

    (A) 4
    (B) 5
    (C) 6
    (D) 3

100. Williams Drive is closed. Which street is the next most efficient route to take from the fire hall to get to the fire at Lister Avenue and Williams Drive?

(A) Charles Road

(B) Percy Street

(C) Johnson Avenue

(D) Main Street

ANSWER KEY
Test 1

SECTION 1

1. C	5. D	9. B	13. D	17. B
2. C	6. D	10. D	14. A	18. A
3. A	7. A	11. C	15. C	19. B
4. D	8. B	12. C	16. A	20. D

SECTION 2

21. D	27. D	33. B	39. C	45. B
22. B	28. B	34. B	40. D	46. A
23. B	29. D	35. A	41. C	47. C
24. A	30. C	36. C	42. D	48. D
25. A	31. C	37. B	43. C	49. B
26. C	32. B	38. D	44. B	50. C

SECTION 3

51. A	56. C	61. D	66. D	71. B
52. B	57. A	62. C	67. D	72. A
53. C	58. D	63. B	68. B	73. B
54. A	59. A	64. A	69. A	74. B
55. A	60. A	65. C	70. C	75. C

SECTION 4

76. A	81. D	86. A	91. B	96. B
77. B	82. B	87. A	92. B	97. A
78. B	83. B	88. A	93. B	98. C
79. C	84. D	89. C	94. D	99. B
80. B	85. D	90. D	95. C	100. D

ANSWER EXPLANATIONS
Section 1:

> NOTE: All answers to Oral Comprehension questions can be found in the text that was read for this section. The portions of the explanations that are in quotes are taken directly from the passage.

1. **(C)** 3. "When extinguishing a fire, there are three extinguishing methods commonly used by firefighters."

2. **(C)** Multi Direct. This technique is not mentioned during the oral passage.

3. **(A)** The application of water to the seat of the fire. "A direct fire attack is the application of water to the seat of the fire using a straight stream or solid stream."

4. **(D)** Both A and C. "A direct fire attack is the application of water to the seat of the fire using a straight stream or solid stream. This can be achieved using a combination nozzle or a solid bore nozzle."

5. **(D)** Cools the burning fuels to below their ignition temperature. "Direct application of water to the seat of the fire cools the burning fuels to below their ignition temperature."

6. **(D)** Defensively. "A direct attack can be used offensively or defensively."

7. **(A)** Disrupt the thermal balance. "A disadvantage of direct attack is that it can disrupt the thermal balance if it is overapplied."

8. **(B)** The source of the flames. The reader can come to this conclusion because the seat of the fire is mentioned in this context many times. For example: "Direct application of water to the seat of the fire cools the burning fuels to below their ignition temperature" or "The intent is for the steam to smother the flames and sometimes even extinguish the seat of the fire."

9. **(B)** The application of water to the superheated surfaces of the fire compartment in order to create a large amount of steam. "An indirect fire attack is the application of water to the superheated surfaces of the fire compartment in order to create a large amount of steam." Notice that this question provides a hint for Question 11.

10. (D) Any of the above will work. "Indirect attack can be performed using a straight stream, solid stream, or narrow fog pattern."

11. (C) To smother the flames. Smothering the flames is a positive benefit of indirect attack and its main purpose. "The intent is for the steam to smother the flames . . .". Notice that this question provides a hint for Question 9.

12. (C) Yes, an indirect extinguishing method works well when dealing with backdraft conditions. This is implied by the portion of the passage that states ". . . indirect fire attack is used for defensive operations and works particularly well when backdraft conditions are present."

13. (D) It can overcool the area and stop the production of steam. This is the only one of the answer options mentioned in the passage. "When using an indirect attack, it is important to not overapply water to any one spot in the fire compartment. Overapplication of water tends to overcool that area and stop the production of steam."

14. (A) 100. "To produce steam, the portion of wall or ceiling coming in contact with water must be over 100 degrees Celsius."

15. (C) Combination Nozzle. "This is done by applying short or medium pulses of water from a combination nozzle . . ."

16. (A) Water fog. "Gas cooling is an extinguishment method that uses short pulses of water fog."

17. (B) Direct attack. This is the best answer. It is mentioned in the passage "Gas cooling is often used to reach the seat of the fire where the fire will be extinguished using a direct attack." Notice that indirect attack does not fit grammatically as an answer.

18. (A) More critical when gas cooling than when using an indirect attack. This statement is mentioned in the last portion of the passage. "Water droplet size is much more critical when gas cooling than when using an indirect attack."

19. (B) The three most commonly used fire extinguishing/control methods. This is mentioned in the beginning of the passage and enforced throughout when all three methods are explained.

20. (D) No method is best; some methods are better suited to certain situations than others. "Each method has its own strengths and weaknesses and because of this some methods are better suited to certain situations than others. No single method is best for all situations."

Section 2:

21. (D) Both A and B. The information needed to answer this question is found in the last sentence of the passage. "Signs of frostbite include skin that is cold to the touch and discolored skin (flushed, white, yellow, or blue depending on the length of exposure)."

22. (B) Freezing. This information is contained in the second sentence of the passage. "Frostbite is the freezing of the body's tissues."

23. (B) Stabilization. This is the type of reading comprehension question that asks you to order information (find the steps involved in doing something). If you look at the third sentence in the paragraph, you will see that the steps of SSSAGE are given: "It stands for scene assessment, staging, stabilization, access patient, glass management, extrication." You can use this information and count to the third step and find that the correct answer to the question is stabilization.

24. (A) Short form. This is a vocabulary question. Look for the answer that is closest to the meaning to find the answer. If you need further help with a question like this, try to substitute the possible answers into the sentence that the unknown word is in. Do not worry about grammar. If we substitute "short form" for acronym in the sentence "SSSAGE is an acronym for the steps used in extricating victims after a motor vehicle accident" you can see that "short form" is the best answer.

25. (A) Take every practical precaution to prevent the public from being injured while on fire department property. This question asks the reader to figure out what firefighters should do to avoid issues involving the Occupiers Liability Act. The best answer is (A) because answer (B) only addresses one issue and answers (C) and (D) are not practical.

26. (C) Realistic, reasonable. This is a vocabulary question. Look for the answer that is closest to the meaning to find the answer. If you need further help with a question like this, try to substitute the possible answers into the sentence that the unknown word is in. Do not worry about grammar. Realistic, reasonable is the best answer for this question as it is closest to the meaning of practical.

27. (D) Law. This passage is describing a law entitled the Occupiers Liability Act. This is noted in the first sentence of the passage.

28. (B) A dry drowning involves virtually no water entering the lungs while a wet drowning involves water entering the lungs. The information required to answer this question is in the second and third paragraphs. If both paragraphs are read closely, (B) is the only correct answer. All other options mentioned are incorrect.

29. (D) Because usually when a person drowns, his lungs are not completely filled with water. This answer is found in the second sentence of the first paragraph. "These are called near drownings because usually when people drown, their lungs are not completely filled with water; therefore, the victims are referred to as near drowned."

30. (C) The reflex closure of the epiglottis. This answer is found in the second sentence of the second paragraph, "When the victim takes a breath, the sudden intake of water causes a reflex called laryngospasm (this is the reflex closure of the epiglottis)."

31. (C) Melanoma. This is not mentioned as a cause of death related to secondary drowning. From the fourth paragraph: ". . . death is caused by the complications due to inspired water or vomit that occurred during the immersion episode. Some of these complications include pulmonary edema, pneumonia, and atelectasis."

32. (B) Dry Drowning. This is mentioned in the last sentence of the second paragraph. "Most victims who are successfully resuscitated after a near drowning are victims of a dry drowning."

33. (B) Metal. This information is found in the second sentence "The pulley(s) is held between two metal side plates . . ." To answer this question correctly, test takers are required to reorder or interpret the information contained in the applicable sentence.

34. (B) Tensionless friction pulleys. This type of pulley is not mentioned anywhere in the passage. Therefore it is incorrect because the test is asking test takers to use the information in the passage to answer the questions.

35. (A) A minimum of 4 times bigger. This answer requires the test taker to reorder some information. The answer is contained in the last sentence of the passage: "The strength of a rope is returned fully when the turn in the rope is at least four times its diameter."

36. (C) Reducing friction and creating a mechanical advantage. The answer is found in the fourth and fifth sentences: "Pulleys reduce friction at turns in rope (compared to other methods of turning a rope)." They can also be used to create a mechanical advantage. The passage does not mention pullies being used for anchors.

37. (B) Fire. This is the best answer and is mentioned in the first sentence. "The shade of smoke can often be an indicator of fire conditions."

38. (D) Time of day. This is not mentioned in the passage.

39. (C) Under 14%. This is mentioned in the third sentence ". . . when the oxygen levels in the fire are low (under 14%) . . .".

40. (D) Both A and B. This question asks you to find and interpret information found in the passage. The information is found in the last three sentences of the passage. "Flaming or smoldering fires produce smoke that is a darker shade. This is because when the combustion of the material burning is significant enough a greater percentage of the carbon in the product is released. Synthetic products often create dark smoke."

41. (C) Not necessarily. The tailgater on the curbside of the truck stops traffic at the front of the truck. This is indicated in the seventh sentence "The tailgater on the curb side of the truck goes to the front of the truck and stops traffic."

42. (D) Turn on the emergency lights for the fire truck. This answer is found in the fourth sentence of the passage, "Next, the driver pulls the truck up to the curb outside the station and activates the emergency lights." To answer this question correctly, test takers are required to reorder or interpret the information contained in the applicable sentence.

43. (C) Traffic vests. This question requires the test taker to find the meaning of the applicable sentence. The answer is found in the third sentence of the passage: "As the truck is nearing the station, the two tailgaters put on traffic vests and retrieve stop/ slow signs from their storage positions." Tesk takers should be able to identify that "put on" means the same as wear in this situation.

44. (B) The senior tailgater. This question requires the information to be interpreted from the paragraph. The answer is found in this portion of the passage: "When the fire truck is completely on the tarmac, the tailgater backing up the truck will stop the truck. The senior tailgater will go into the bay and back the truck the rest of the way in."

45. (B) Plug the truck in. In the last sentence of the passage "plug the truck into shore power" is the last step mentioned. Therefore the answer is (B), plug the truck in. Notice that this sentence shows the driver doing several things, but he has to get out of the truck to plug it in.

46. (A) Remove the cones, then the hydrant bag. Removing the cones is part of step 3. Removing the hydrant bag is part of step 4. Therefore, the cones should be removed first.

47. (C) 10′. This question can be answered by finding information contained in step 5: "Firefighter places a bite of hose (with minimum 10′ of slack) against base of hydrant furthest from the fire."

48. (D) B or C. Some words have to be reordered and their meaning considered. This answer can be found in step 10. "10- Firefighter does not open hydrant until (one of the following):

- Pump operator's command for water via radio to open hydrant or,
- hearing the air horn signal to open hydrant . . ."

49. (B) Loops. Notice that the question asks for what the firefighter would NOT be looking for. Always be careful to fully read and comprehend the question and what it is asking, not just the passage and answers. The answer is found in step 13: "13- Firefighter follows hose back to pumping apparatus checking for:

1. Kinks
2. Leaks
3. Position of hose impeding access for other apparatus."

50. (C) Fully, then backs off ¼ turn. This information is found in step 11: "Firefighter opens hydrant fully until stem stops turning, then backs off ¼ turn."

Section 3:

51. (A) 88.88. This is a subtraction question. Remember to use subtraction with regrouping.

Here is how the answer is found:

```
 | |  | |
324.10
235.22
088.88
```

52. (B) 5. This is a division question. You can check your answer by using multiplication ($5 \times 20 = 100$). See Chapter 2 for an expanded explanation of division.

CANADIAN FIREFIGHTER EXAMS 179

53. (C) 25. This is a division question. You can check your answer by using multiplication ($25 \times 25 = 625$). See Chapter 2 for an expanded explanation of division. You can use long division to find the answer.

Here is how the answer is found:

$$
\begin{array}{r}
025 \\
25\overline{)625} \\
0 \\
62 \\
\underline{50} \\
125 \\
\underline{125} \\
0
\end{array}
$$

54. (A) 1,508.514. This is a multiplication question. You should use long multiplication to answer this question. Don't forget about the decimal (you can add it after if you want). See Chapter 2 for further explanation of this type of question.

Here is how the answer is found:

$$
\begin{array}{r}
4398 \\
\times\, 343 \\
\hline
13194 \\
175920 \\
\underline{1319400} \\
1508514
\end{array}
$$

55. (A) 1 13/16. This question involves adding fractions. Remember to make the denominator the same, then add the numerator. See Chapter 2 for further explanation of this type of question.

Here is how the answer is found:

5/8 + 3/4 + 7/16 =
10/16 + 12/16 + 7/16 = 29/16

Simplify: 1 13/16

56. (C) 5/8. This question involves subtracting fractions. Remember to make the denominator the same, then subtract the numerator. Don't forget to simplify the answer. See Chapter 2 for further explanation of this type of question.

Here is how the answer is found:

6/8 – 4/32 =
24/32 – 4/32 = 20/32

Simplify—5/8

57. (A) 22/25. This question involves adding equivalent fractions. Remember to make the denominator the same and then add the numerators. See Chapter 2 for further explanation of this type of question.

Here is how the answer is found:

$1/5 + 3/15 + 7/25 + 4/20 =$
$5/25 + 5/25 + 7/25 + 5/25 = 22/25$

58. (D) 9/20. This question involves multiplying fractions. See Chapter 2 for further explanation of how to multiply fractions.

Here is how the answer is found:
$3/5 \times 6/8 = 18/40$
Simplify—9/20

59. (A) 7/12. This question involves dividing fractions. Don't forget to simplify the fraction if possible. See Chapter 2 for further explanation of how to divide fractions.

Here is how the answer is found:

$4/8$ divided by $6/7 =$
$4/8 \times 7/6 = 28/48$

Simplify—7/12

60. (A) 50%. This question asks for a percentage. To find the answer, first realize you have a fraction (15/30). The next step is to simply divide the top number by the bottom number, then multiply by 100.

Here is how the answer is found:

$15 \div 30 = .5$
$.5 \times 100 = 50$ (just add the %)

61. (D) 1/4. This question asks for a percentage to be converted into a fraction. To find the answer, convert the percentage to a fraction. Don't forget to simplify the fraction.

Here is how the answer is found:

$25\% = 25/100$
$25/100 = 1/4$

62. (C) 3 minutes. This question involves a proportion. Because one ratio (2 minutes to travel 6 kilometres) is known, the equation can be solved. See the algebra, ratios, and proportions sections in Chapter 2 for additional explanation.

Here is how the answer is found:

$$\frac{2 \text{ minutes}}{6 \text{ kilometres}} = \frac{x \text{ minutes}}{9 \text{ kilometres}}$$
$$18 = 6x$$
$$18 \div 6 = 6 \div 6x$$
$$3 = x$$

63. (B) 4:1 This question asks for a ratio. The ratio is 20:5. Like a fraction this ratio can be simplified further to 4:1.

64. (A) 15 miles. This can be considered a proportion or ratio question. To find the answer you first need to find the ratio. For this question, the truck will travel 45 miles every 15 minutes. The ratio is 45 to 15. To correctly answer this question you will need to simplify the ratio the same way you would simplify a fraction (this is the easiest way, although the answer can be found using algebra). See the algebra, ratios, and proportions sections in Chapter 2 for additional explanation.

Here is how the answer is found:
The ratio:

$$\frac{45 \text{ miles}}{15 \text{ minutes}}$$

Simplified (top and bottom divided by 3)

$$\frac{15 \text{ miles}}{5 \text{ minutes}}$$

65. (C) 6 fires. This can be considered a proportion or ratio question. To find the answer you first need to find the ratio. Engine 4 had 12 fires in 16 shifts. The ratio is 12 to 16. To correctly answer this question, you will need to simplify the ratio the same way you would simplify a fraction (this is the easiest way; algebra can also be used to solve this question). See the algebra, ratios, and proportions sections in Chapter 2 for additional explanation.

Here is how the answer is found:
The ratio:

$$\frac{12 \text{ fires}}{16 \text{ shifts}}$$

Simplified (top and bottom divided by 2)

$$\frac{6 \text{ fires}}{8 \text{ shifts}}$$

66. **(D)** 20,150 gallons. This can be considered a proportion or ratio question. To find the answer you first need to find the ratio. It is important to know that there are 60 minutes in an hour. Quint 2 pumped 40,300 gallons in the past hour. The ratio is 40,300 gallons to 60 minutes. To correctly answer this question, you will need to simplify the ratio the same way you would simplify a fraction (this is the easiest way). Use the algebra, ratios, and proportions sections in Chapter 2 for additional explanation.

Here is how the answer is found:
The ratio:

$$\frac{40,300\,\text{gallons}}{60\,\text{minutes}}$$

Simplified (top and bottom divided by 2 because 30 minutes is half of one hour)

$$\frac{20,150}{30\,\text{minutes}}$$

67. **(D)** 480 metres. The ratio in this question is 1,200 metres travelled to 5 minutes. To find the answer use algebra and cross multiply. The algebra, ratios, and proportions sections in Chapter 2 provide additional explanation.

Here is how the answer is found:

$$\frac{5\,\text{minutes}}{1200\,\text{metres}} = \frac{2\,\text{minutes}}{x}$$

$5x = 2400$

$2400 \div 5 = 5 \div 5x$

$480 = x$

68. **(B)** 73,850. This is a multiplication question. Multiply the gallons per hour by the exposure lines. $14,770 \times 5 = 73,850$.

Here is how the answer is found:

$$\begin{array}{r} {\scriptstyle 233} \\ 14,770 \\ \times\ \ \ \ 5 \\ \hline 73850 \end{array}$$

69. **(A)** About 90%. This question asks for a percentage. To find the answer, first realize you have a fraction (3,487/3,860). The next step is to simply divide the top number by the bottom number, then multiply by 100.

Here is how the answer is found:

$3487 \div 3860 = .9033$

$.9033 \times 100 = 90.33$ (just add the %)

The best answer is about 90%.

70. (C) 3.6 hours. This is a proportion question. The ratio is 6 hours to 5 sections. 6:5. To find the answer use algebra and cross multiply. You can check your answer by checking to see if the equation is equal. The algebra, ratios, and proportions sections in Chapter 2 provide additional explanation.

Here is how the answer is found:

$$\frac{6 \text{ hours.}}{5 \text{ sections}} = \frac{x}{3 \text{ sections}}$$

$5x = 18$

$5x \div 5 = 18 \div 5$

$x = 3.6 \text{ hours}$

71. (B) 25. This is a division question. To find the correct answer, divide 1,250 (total hose) by 50 (length of hose). To learn more about division, see Chapter 2.

72. (A) 56.76. This is a multiplication question. To find the answer, multiply 60 quarts by .946. Chapter 2 contains more information on multiplication.

73. (B) 5.5%. This is a percentage question. To find the answer, first realize you have a fraction (5/90). The next step is to simply divide the top number by the bottom number, then multiply by 100. $5 \div 90 = 0.055$. $0.055 \times 100 = 5.5$.

74. (B) 212.5 ft. To find the correct answer to this question, use division. $850 \div 4 = 212.5$. See Chapter 2 for more information on division.

75. (C) 2 litres. You could find the answer to this question using proportions. But, it is easier to notice that 15 minutes is half of 30 minutes and 2 litres is half of 4 litres. Therefore, it is known that about 2 litres of fuel will be used in 15 minutes. The best answer is 2.

Section 4:

76. (A) B, D, F. When two gears meet, they turn in opposing directions.

77. (B) Counterclockwise. When two gears meet, they turn in opposing directions.

78. (B) Twice the torque and half the speed as the drive gear. This answer has to do with gear ratio. Refer to the Gears section of Chapter 2 for further explanation.

79. (C) Clockwise, counterclockwise. All of the pulleys turn the same direction until the twist in the pulley. Refer to the Belt Drives section of Chapter 2 for further explanation.

80. (B) ¼ the speed, 4 times the torque. This answer focuses on gear ratio and belt drives. Refer to the Gears and Belt Drive sections of Chapter 2 for further explanation.

81. (D) D. This is a 4 : 1 mechanical advantage system. It will be easiest to pull because it has the most mechanical advantage. See the pulleys section of Chapter 2 for more information.

82. (B) 2 times as fast. The load shown in diagram A will move 2 times as fast (or faster) as the load shown in diagram B for any amount of rope that is pulled. See the Pulleys section of Chapter 2 for more information on mechanical advantage.

83. (B) This shape completes the square.

84. (D) Circle D has the greatest diameter, making it the widest, and therefore tallest, circle.

85. (D) This is a wheel and axle question. D has the longest handle (wheel) and therefore offers the most mechanical advantage. See Chapter 2 for more information regarding the wheel and axle.

86. (A) Wheel and axle. The handle of the screwdriver is the wheel, the bit/shaft is the axle. See Chapter 2 for more information regarding the wheel and axle.

87. (A) Wheel A. The smaller wheel will turn faster. See the Belt Drive section of Chapter 2 for more information.

88. (A) Ramp A. This is an inclined plane. The higher the ramp, the more difficult it will be to roll the foam up (assuming all ramps are the same length). See the inclined plane section of Chapter 2 for more information on inclined planes.

89. (C) 180 degrees.

90. (D) This is a leverage question. The closer the fulcrum is to the weight, the easier it will be to lift the weight. Information regarding levers is contained in Chapter 2.

91. (B) A wheelbarrow is a second class lever. The further the load is from the wheel the closer it is to the hands. This requires more effort to use. Think of the wheel as the fulcrum. Information regarding levers is contained in Chapter 2.

92. (B) 3200. The gauge points closest to 3200 psi.

93. (B) 100 ft. The answer to this question is found by adding up the lengths of each room in a north/south direction.

94. (D) 120 ft. The answer to this question is found by adding up the lengths of each room in an east/west direction.

95. (C) This floor plan most closely matches the house. The other options are incorrect. Option A shows the door swinging the wrong direction. Option B is a mirror image of the correct floor plan. Option D shows the front door in the wrong place.

96. (B) This floor plan most closely matches the house. The other options are incorrect. Option A shows the garage door in the wrong place. Option B is correct. Option C is a mirror image (reversed). Option D shows windows in the wrong place.

97. (A) This floor plan most closely matches the house. The other options are incorrect. Option B shows the garage in the wrong place. Option C shows the chimney in the wrong place. Option D is missing a front window.

98. (C) Charles Road. See the Map reading section of Chapter 2 for more information.

99. (B) 5. See the Map reading section of Chapter 2 for more information.

100. (D) Main Street. See the Map reading section of Chapter 2 for more information.

ANSWER SHEET
Test 2

SECTION 1

1. (A) (B) (C) (D)
2. (A) (B) (C) (D)
3. (A) (B) (C) (D)
4. (A) (B) (C) (D)
5. (A) (B) (C) (D)
6. (A) (B) (C) (D)
7. (A) (B) (C) (D)
8. (A) (B) (C) (D)

9. (A) (B) (C) (D)
10. (A) (B) (C) (D)
11. (A) (B) (C) (D)
12. (A) (B) (C) (D)
13. (A) (B) (C) (D)
14. (A) (B) (C) (D)
15. (A) (B) (C) (D)
16. (A) (B) (C) (D)

17. (A) (B) (C) (D)
18. (A) (B) (C) (D)
19. (A) (B) (C) (D)
20. (A) (B) (C) (D)
21. (A) (B) (C) (D)
22. (A) (B) (C) (D)
23. (A) (B) (C) (D)
24. (A) (B) (C) (D)

25. (A) (B) (C) (D)
26. (A) (B) (C) (D)
27. (A) (B) (C) (D)
28. (A) (B) (C) (D)
29. (A) (B) (C) (D)
30. (A) (B) (C) (D)

SECTION 2

31. (A) (B) (C) (D)
32. (A) (B) (C) (D)
33. (A) (B) (C) (D)
34. (A) (B) (C) (D)
35. (A) (B) (C) (D)
36. (A) (B) (C) (D)
37. (A) (B) (C) (D)
38. (A) (B) (C) (D)

39. (A) (B) (C) (D)
40. (A) (B) (C) (D)
41. (A) (B) (C) (D)
42. (A) (B) (C) (D)
43. (A) (B) (C) (D)
44. (A) (B) (C) (D)
45. (A) (B) (C) (D)
46. (A) (B) (C) (D)

47. (A) (B) (C) (D)
48. (A) (B) (C) (D)
49. (A) (B) (C) (D)
50. (A) (B) (C) (D)
51. (A) (B) (C) (D)
52. (A) (B) (C) (D)
53. (A) (B) (C) (D)
54. (A) (B) (C) (D)

55. (A) (B) (C) (D)
56. (A) (B) (C) (D)
57. (A) (B) (C) (D)
58. (A) (B) (C) (D)
59. (A) (B) (C) (D)
60. (A) (B) (C) (D)

SECTION 3

61. (A) (B) (C) (D)
62. (A) (B) (C) (D)
63. (A) (B) (C) (D)
64. (A) (B) (C) (D)
65. (A) (B) (C) (D)

66. (A) (B) (C) (D)
67. (A) (B) (C) (D)
68. (A) (B) (C) (D)
69. (A) (B) (C) (D)
70. (A) (B) (C) (D)

71. (A) (B) (C) (D)
72. (A) (B) (C) (D)
73. (A) (B) (C) (D)
74. (A) (B) (C) (D)
75. (A) (B) (C) (D)

76. (A) (B) (C) (D)
77. (A) (B) (C) (D)
78. (A) (B) (C) (D)
79. (A) (B) (C) (D)
80. (A) (B) (C) (D)

CPS STYLE TEST 2

Section 1—Understanding Written Information

> DIRECTIONS: Questions 1 through 30 below measure your ability to understand written information. Base your answers on the information provided by the questions, not on any previous knowledge. Fill in the bubble on the answer sheet that corresponds to your answer.

*See important note about the length of this test on page 140.

1. Usually, rookie firefighters are the first to answer the phone at the fire hall. When they answer the phone, they will identify themselves correctly and then immediately ask how they can help the caller. If the caller is a member of the public who has a question or problem that the rookie firefighter can't immediately help with, then the firefighter should pass the call on to the captain. If the person calling is another member of the fire department, the firefighter should help to the best of his abilities. If the rookie firefighter can resolve the call without help from other members of the crew, he should be sure to pass the information on to the rest of the crew.

   A member of the public calls and asks a question that the firefighter who has answered the phone can't answer. What should the firefighter do?

   (A) Get the captain to take the phone call.
   (B) Use a best educated guess to answer the question.
   (C) Help to the best of his abilities.
   (D) Put the person on hold and go ask another firefighter for the answer.

2. Water keys are available to the public at any of the fire halls in the area. When a member of the public comes to the fire hall to get a water key, it is the responsibility of one of the firefighters on shift to sign the water key out properly. Firefighters should always remember that it is very important to treat the public with respect and dignity. When a water key is signed out, the firefighter will use form 27-C and ensure that the member of the public presents a piece of identification to verify the information on the form. The firefighter will inform the member of the public that he can have the water key for a maximum of seven days. The firefighter will then give the member of the public a copy of the form and the water key.

   What is the last step when providing a water key to the public?

   (A) Fill out form 27-C.
   (B) Take a piece of photo identification from the member of public.
   (C) Give the member of the public a copy of form 27-C and the water key.
   (D) Inform the member of the public that he or she can have the water key for a maximum of seven days.

3. Atelectasis is the collapse of lung tissue. Drowning can cause atelectasis. It can happen when the alveoli are filled with fluid, lose their elasticity, and collapse. This happens because the surfactant present in the alveoli is diluted and loses its ability to prevent the walls of the alveoli from sticking together during expiration. This can make breathing very difficult.

   What does "expiration" mean as it is used in the passage?

   (A) death
   (B) atelectasis
   (C) alveoli
   (D) exhalation

4. When a firefighter is responsible for driving the fire truck, it is part of the job to do a truck check at the start of each shift. A truck check should be very thorough and cover everything on the truck including the engine, the firefighting equipment, and fire pump. As the firefighter is checking the truck, he should be filling out his daily truck check form and the air brake check sheet. If the firefighter finds a problem with the truck, he should fill out a maintenance repair form and send it to fire maintenance. The firefighter should also write the problem on the back of the daily truck check sheet and the board next to the truck. Drivers must not be complacent when doing truck checks, because it is very important that everything on the truck functions properly at all times.

   According to the passage, what forms does a firefighter fill out as part of the daily truck check?

   (A) Maintenance repair form.
   (B) Maintenance repair form and daily truck check form.
   (C) Air brake check sheet and daily truck check form.
   (D) Maintenance repair form and air brake check sheet.

5. Carabiners are used for many applications by fire departments. Most frequently they are used for rescues. Usually the strength of a carabiner is marked on the spine. Carabiners' strength is measured along its spine (carabiners should never be side loaded). Common strengths are between 1,500–6,000 kgs. Carabiners are made from either steel or aluminum. Steel carabiners have better locking mechanisms, greater strength, and hold up better to shock loads than aluminum carabiners. Aluminum carabiners are lighter than steel carabiners and do not rust.

   According to the passage, which statement is true?

   (A) Aluminum carabiners are subject to rust.
   (B) Carabiners function well when side loaded.
   (C) Aluminum carabiners do not hold up as well to shock loads as steel carabiners.
   (D) Aluminum carabiners have greater strength than steel carabiners.

6. Critical flow rate is the minimum amount of water flow needed to suppress a fire at any stage of involvement. The phase a fire is in will have an influence on critical flow rate. When a fire is in its growth phase, it will produce a lot more heat than a fire in its incipient phase or decay phase. Because a fire in its growth phase produces more heat, it will need more water to be fully suppressed. Therefore, the critical flow rate may be higher or lower depending on the amount of heat being produced by a fire at a given time. Critical flow rate can also be influenced by the style of firefighting attack and the ventilation profile of the fire.

According to the passage, what influences critical flow rate?

(A) The phase the fire is in.
(B) The style of firefighting attack.
(C) The ventilation profile of the fire.
(D) All of the above.

7. The rules and regulations state that firefighters cannot carry their personal cell phones while on shift. Firefighters may use their cell phones during their designated break times only, as long as they are not involved in an incident. Cell phones must be left in the firehall at all times. Under no circumstances will they be allowed away from the firehall (including on the fire truck) during shift hours. If special circumstances exist, the battalion chief shall be consulted and will have the final decision.

Where and when can firefighters use their cell phones while on shift?

(A) During designated break times and on the fire truck.
(B) During designated break times, when not involved in an incident, and when inside the firehall.
(C) During designated break times, when not involved in an incident, and in the fire truck.
(D) Anytime as long as they are not involved in an incident.

8. A stored pressure extinguisher is used for extinguishing Class A material. This type of extinguisher is sometimes referred to as a P can. Class A extinguishers usually contain water mixed with a small amount of foam that is under compressed air pressure. A gauge on the top of the extinguisher shows that the extinguisher is properly pressurized. When a firefighter uses the extinguisher, the water is forced up a siphon tube and out of the extinguisher by the air pressure.

When inspecting a stored pressure extinguisher, how does a firefighter know if there is enough compressed air in the extinguisher?

(A) He will check weight of the extinguisher.
(B) He hopes the firefighter who filled the extinguisher did it properly.
(C) There is a gauge that shows the pressure.
(D) He will check the siphon tube.

9. A hydraulic is a feature formed in a river. It can also be called hole or a keeper. Hydraulics are formed when water picks up speed as it flows over an object. This could be a log, rock, dam, or other river feature. When the water drops off the object and hits the water below, it rolls back (reverses or flows back upstream) on itself. This roll back is dangerous because it can hold an object (e.g., a person) and cause it to be recirculated or "kept" in the hydraulic.

According to the passage, why is a hydraulic sometimes called a keeper?

(A) There is no specific reason for this.
(B) They are worth keeping an eye on.
(C) In a hydraulic, the water rolls back and can keep objects.
(D) None of the above.

10. A carcinogen is a substance that can cause cancer. Firefighters get many types of cancers at a much higher rate than the general public. Carcinogens are commonly found in firefighting environments and firefighters must be aware of their dangers. Cancer is a disease caused by the uncontrolled division of abnormal cells (a malignant tumor) and its invasive spread into surrounding tissues. A malignant tumor is composed of cells that can break off and spread to other locations in the body. This process is called metastasis.

According to the passage, what is metastasis?

(A) The spread of a malignant tumor to other tissues in the body away from the original tumor.
(B) A type of cancer.
(C) A type of carcinogen.
(D) All of the above.

DIRECTIONS: Questions 11 through 15 refer to the following passage.

Combustion is a self sustaining oxidization process accompanied by the release of energy. For combustion to occur, four elements are needed. Those elements are heat, fuel, oxygen, and self sustained chemical reaction. These four components together are sometimes called the fire tetrahedron. Combustion is an exothermic reaction (a reaction that produces energy) between fuel and oxygen. The production or release of energy during combustion is usually in the form of heat and light. This is a flame. There are several types of flames produced by combustion. Essentially these flames are either premixed or diffused. A premixed flame occurs when fuel and air have been mixed before combustion occurs. A diffusion flame happens when fuel and air mix in the region where combustion takes place. Most structure fires contain diffusion flames because the fuel (structure and contents) and air mix as the fire grows.

11. Four elements are needed for combustion to occur; those four components together are sometimes called _____.

   (A) fuel, oxygen, and heat
   (B) the fire tetrahedron
   (C) the fire triangle
   (D) self sustained chemical reaction

12. According to the passage, what is an exothermic reaction?

   (A) A reaction that absorbs energy
   (B) A premixed flame
   (C) A reaction that produces energy
   (D) None of the above.

13. Some forms of energy released by combustion are:

   (A) heat
   (B) light
   (C) kinetic
   (D) both A and B

14. What is the difference between a premixed flame and a diffusion flame?

   (A) A premixed flame is only found in structure fires.
   (B) A premixed flame is bigger.
   (C) In a premixed flame, fuel and air have been mixed before combustion, while in a diffusion flame fuel and air are mixed at the site of combustion.
   (D) In a premixed flame, fuel and air have been mixed at the area of combustion, while in a diffusion flame fuel and air are mixed before combustion.

15. What type of flame is most common in a structure fire?

   (A) diffusion flames
   (B) non-diffusion flames
   (C) premixed
   (D) countermixed

DIRECTIONS: Questions 16 through 20 refer to the following passage.

There are several different conscious victim types that firefighters may have to deal with during a swiftwater rescue. It is important for firefighters to be able to recognize the different types of victims to determine the most appropriate form of rescue. Some of these are:

Normal. These victims are very aware of their situation and are doing everything in their power to help themselves (including attempting to swim to safety). They are often very vocal.

Drowning non-swimmer (DNS). This type of victim displays the common characteristics of a person who is drowning. Usually, these victims appear as though they are climbing a ladder (may be slapping the surface, cycling their legs and attempting to raise their mouth out of the water to breathe). Usually, drowning non-swimmers will not call out for help because any time their mouth is out of the water they are gasping for air.

Injured. This type of victim is holding the injured part of their body and shouting for help. If the injury is severe, the victim may be submerged.

Panic. This type of victim displays the typical signs of panic. Their movement is often counterproductive due to their panic because it does not contribute to self rescue. They are usually shouting and active in the water.

Counterpanic. The most obvious feature of this victim type is that they seem to have completely given up. They may appear detached and very unconcerned about the situation they are in. They are not vocal.

Weak or tired swimmer. This type of victim is often near vertical in the water and very sluggish with wide eyes looking in the direction of safety. They usually will not be able to call for help.

16. How many types of conscious victims are described in the passage?

 (A) 2
 (B) 5
 (C) 4
 (D) 6

17. Why is it important for firefighters to understand the different types of conscious victims they may have to rescue?

 (A) It's not an important part of rescue.
 (B) To properly fill out post-incident reports.
 (C) To help them determine the most appropriate form of rescue.
 (D) So they can tell if the person is pretending to be in trouble.

18. Which types of conscious victims will usually not be able to call for help?

 (A) Normal and weak or tired swimmers.
 (B) Counterpanic, injured, and weak or tired simmers.
 (C) Drowning non-swimmers, counterpanic, and weak or tired swimmers.
 (D) Drowning non-swimmers, counterpanic, and normal swimmers.

19. According to the passage, drowning non-swimmers appear as though they are

 (A) climbing a ladder
 (B) doing flips
 (C) jumping
 (D) dancing

20. According to the passage, weak or tired swimmers' bodies are often

 (A) horizontal in the water
 (B) vertical in the water
 (C) looking with wide eyes in the direction of safety
 (D) both B and C

Sometimes at a motor vehicle accident, firefighters will have to remove the roof of a vehicle in order to remove the patient safely. Because this is part of the SSSAGE protocol and roof removal is part of extrication, we can start the steps for this procedure at door removal. We can assume that things such as patient protection, glass removal, and seatbelt removal have already been completed.

1. Open and remove all doors. If doors cannot be opened by hand, pop them hydraulically. Doors and other parts should be placed in the parts dump after removal.

2. Peel and peak. Make sure before step three that there are no hidden dangers in the posts that will be cut.

3. Cut the required posts. Usually the cuts should be made low for ease of patient removal. The posts nearest to the patient(s) should be cut last.

4. Lift the roof off. If possible, the roof should be removed over the front of the car (in an effort not to pass the windshield over the patient). A minimum of four rescuers should be used to remove the roof and should keep it supported at all times.

5. Place protection on any sharp edges that were made during roof removal.

6. Remove patient.

21. According to the passage, what should be done if the doors cannot be opened by hand?

    (A) Cut them off with a reciprocating saw.
    (B) Make sure there are no hidden dangers.
    (C) Pop them hydraulically.
    (D) Place them in the parts dump.

22. According to these steps, why should firefighters peel and peak?

    (A) To remove plastic before cutting
    (B) To check for hidden dangers in the posts
    (C) To remove seatbelts
    (D) All of the above.

23. Why isn't glass removal included in these steps?

    (A) The windows are all rolled down.
    (B) Glass is ignored during auto extrication.
    (C) This car must be a convertible.
    (D) Glass removal has been completed.

24. When the roof is removed, why would firefighters elect to remove it over the front of the car?

    (A) It's easier.
    (B) For patient safety.
    (C) It's faster.
    (D) It's closer to the parts dump.

25. Where will firefighters put the roof after it is removed?

(A) On the hood of the car.

(B) In the parts dump.

(C) On the trunk of the car.

(D) In the fire truck.

DIRECTIONS: Questions 26 through 30 refer to the following passage.

Heat exhaustion and heat stroke are serious conditions caused by overexposure to heat.

Heat Exhaustion (Heat Prostration)

Definition—A disturbance of the circulatory system due to a large loss of salt and fluid due to sweating. This is an early indicator that the body's temperature regulating mechanism is becoming overwhelmed. As a person loses fluid through sweating, it will decrease blood volume. Blood flow to the skin increases, causing less blood to flow to vital internal organs. The person can go into mild shock.

History—Exposure to a hot, humid environment or extreme heat. Overactivity under hot sun.

Symptoms—Nausea, dizziness, weakness, headache. May have cramps in legs or abdomen.

Pulse—Weak and rapid.

Respiration—Shallow.

Skin—Pale, cool, sweaty.

Temperature (by thermometer)—Normal, slightly lowered, slightly elevated.

Heat Stroke (Sun Stroke)

Definition—A failure of the body's heat regulating mechanism that renders the body unable to cool itself. Sweating stops when fluid levels in the body are low. When the body can't sweat, it can't cool itself and body temperature will rise rapidly. This condition is more serious than heat exhaustion.

History—Exposure to a hot, humid environment or extreme heat. Overactivity under hot sun.

Symptoms—Nausea, dizziness, weakness, headache. Convulsions may occur.

Pulse—Strong and fast.

Respiration—Deep and fast.

Skin—Hot, dry, red.

Temperature (by thermometer)—Very high (can be 41 °C and higher).

26. Why would a patient with heat stroke have dry skin?

(A) The hot sun evaporated all the sweat.

(B) He hasn't been exercising.

(C) His body has stopped sweating.

(D) A person with heat stroke will have very sweaty skin.

27. According to the information in the passage, what is the difference between the history of a patient with heat exhaustion and a patient with heat stroke?

(A) There is none.

(B) The skin of a patient with heat stroke is drier than the skin of a patient with heat exhaustion.

(C) Body temperature is higher in a patient with heat stroke.

(D) Respiration is more shallow in a patient with heat exhaustion.

28. What is another name for heat exhaustion?

(A) heat stroke

(B) sun stroke

(C) heat cramps

(D) heat prostration

29. According to the information provided, what is the difference between the symptoms of heat exhaustion and heat stroke?

(A) Patients with heat exhaustion feel nauseous.

(B) Patients with heat stroke may have convulsions.

(C) Patients with heat exhaustion and heat stroke have a headache.

(D) All of the above.

30. Heat exhaustion and heat stroke are both caused by

(A) overexertion

(B) extreme cold temperatures

(C) running

(D) overexposure to heat

Section 2—Mathematical Ability

DIRECTIONS: Answer Questions 31 through 60 by choosing the best answer for each question and filling in the corresponding bubble on the answer sheet.

31. 42.1567 plus 63.876 plus 546.4 plus 67.1 equals?

(A) 719.6327

(B) 720.5327

(C) 719.5327

(D) 719.5338

32. 3.456 plus 7.345 plus 856.1 equals?

(A) 866.901

(B) 867.901

(C) 867.911

(D) 868.011

33. 546.98 minus 324.2 minus 45.678 equals?

(A) 177.106

(B) 176.102

(C) 177.102

(D) 177.202

34. 100 divided by .20 equals?

   (A) 5
   (B) 6
   (C) 500
   (D) 100

35. 4,562 multiplied by 318 equals?

   (A) 1,460,717
   (B) 1,470,617
   (C) 1,451,716
   (D) 1,450,716

36. 3/5 plus 3/15 equals?

   (A) 7/8
   (B) 7/7
   (C) 12/15
   (D) 14/5

37. 7/7 plus 6/7 plus 2/3 plus 1/3 equals?

   (A) 1 6/7
   (B) 2 6/7
   (C) 2 5/7
   (D) 1/5

38. 3/12 minus 6/24 minus 4/48 equals?

   (A) –1/12
   (B) 3/6
   (C) 4/3
   (D) 8/12

39. 2/5 multiplied by 4/7 equals?

   (A) 12/35
   (B) 8/35
   (C) 4/5
   (D) 2/5

40. 5/8 multiplied by 3/4 equals?

   (A) 15/34
   (B) 15/24
   (C) 15/32
   (D) 10/33

41. 20/2 is the same as _____

   (A) 20
   (B) 10
   (C) 5
   (D) 40

42. 2/5 divided by 2/4 equals?

   (A) 3/5
   (B) 1/5
   (C) 4/5
   (D) 10/20

43. 236 plus (–176) equals?

   (A) 50
   (B) 60
   (C) 412
   (D) 422

44. 642 minus (–543) equals?

   (A) 1,185
   (B) 99
   (C) 98
   (D) 1,195

45. The fire department has 3,000 ft. of rescue rope. How much is 30% of that rope?

   (A) 300 ft.
   (B) 600 ft.
   (C) 900 ft.
   (D) 1,000 ft.

46. The rescue bag has 16 carabiners and 8 utility belts. What is the ratio of carabiners to utility belts?

   (A) 12:4
   (B) 2:1
   (C) 4:1
   (D) 3:1

47. Ladder 4 has pumped 60,660 gallons of water in the past hour. If Ladder 4 keeps pumping at the same rate, how many gallons of water will Ladder 4 pump in the next minute?

   (A) 1,011 gallons
   (B) 1,000 gallons
   (C) 1,101 gallons
   (D) 1,201 gallons

48. Quint 7 has used 7 gallons of foam in the past 5 minutes. How long will it take Quint 7 to use 100 gallons of foam if it continues pumping at the same rate?

   (A) 75 minutes
   (B) 80.43 minutes
   (C) 84.3 minutes
   (D) 71.42 minutes

49. If there are 22 fire stations and 374 firefighters and all fire stations have the same number of firefighters, how many firefighters are at each station?

(A) 22
(B) 15
(C) 18
(D) 17

50. Engine 12 takes 6 minutes to travel 65 kilometres. How long will it take Engine 12 to travel 50 kilometres?

(A) 5 minutes
(B) 4.5 minutes
(C) 4.6 minutes
(D) 4.7 minutes

51. Eight exposure lines are each flowing 15,000 gallons of water every hour. How much water are the exposure lines combined flowing per hour?

(A) 120,000 gallons
(B) 105,000 gallons
(C) 135,000 gallons
(D) 121,000 gallons

52. If a crew can put out 20 feet of a 350 foot wide forest fire every 10 minutes, how long will it take to put out the whole forest fire?

(A) 180 minutes
(B) 155 minutes
(C) 195 minutes
(D) 175 minutes

53. A firefighting course is 17 units long. It takes 6 days to do the first 10 units. How long will it take to do the last 7 units if each unit takes the same amount of time?

(A) Just over 4 days
(B) Just under 8 days
(C) Just under 9 days
(D) Just over 5 days

54. If Engine 5 can pump 18,750 litres in 15 mintues, how many litres can it pump in 20 minutes?

(A) 24,750 litres
(B) 25,000 litres
(C) 18,750 litres
(D) 25,250 litres

55. If there are about 4 litres in a gallon, how many litres are there in 945 gallons?

(A) 236 ¾
(B) 236 ¼
(C) 232 ¼
(D) 226 ¾

56. When water turns to steam, it expands about 1,000 times. If 10 litres of water are turned to steam while extinguishing a fire, approximately how much steam will remain?

    (A) about 10,000 litres
    (B) about 2,000 litres
    (C) about 11,000 litres
    (D) about 1,000 litres

57. Ladder 1 has been to 36 structure fires in the past 3 months. If they keep going at the same rate, how many structure fires can they expect to go to in the next 8 months?

    (A) about 95 or 96 fires
    (B) about 90 or 91 fires
    (C) about 75 or 76 fires
    (D) about 98 or 99 fires

58. This week, Station 4 had 8 medical calls and 24 other calls. What is the ratio of medical calls to other calls?

    (A) 1/3
    (B) 2/3
    (C) 3/6
    (D) 8/25

59. The fire department has 120 carabiners. If Station 5 has 25% of the carabiners, how many carabiners do they have?

    (A) 25
    (B) 27
    (C) 30
    (D) 32

60. In August, 3 out of 10 rescues involved swiftwater. If this trend stays the same and there are 15 rescues in September, how many rescues can be expected to involve swiftwater?

    (A) 2–3
    (B) 5–6
    (C) 3–4
    (D) 4–5

Section 3—Mechanical Aptitude

DIRECTIONS: Answer Questions 61 through 80 based on the information presented. Choose the best answer for each question and fill in the corresponding bubble on the answer sheet.

61. If gear C is turning clockwise, which gears will turn in the same direction?

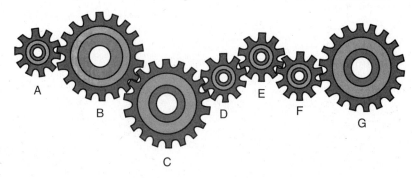

(A) C, A, F

(B) B, C, A

(C) A, C, E, G

(D) B, A, C, G

62. What is the gear ratio of the gears pictured?

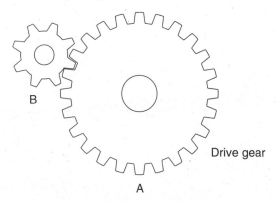

(A) 2:1

(B) 4:3

(C) 3:2

(D) 3:1

SAMPLE TEST 2

63. Which direction will wheel B rotate?

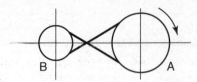

(A) right
(B) clockwise
(C) counterclockwise
(D) none of the above

64. Which ramp is it easiest to push the foam up?

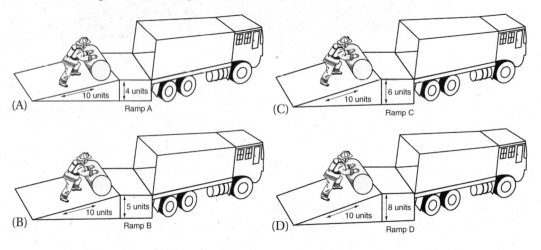

(A) Ramp A — 10 units, 4 units

(C) Ramp C — 10 units, 6 units

(B) Ramp B — 10 units, 5 units

(D) Ramp D — 10 units, 8 units

65. The wheel being driven in the picture below will have _____

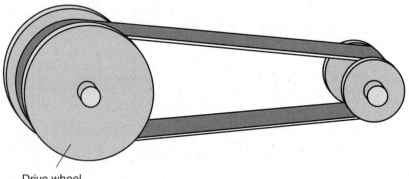

Drive wheel

(A) twice the torque and twice the speed
(B) twice the torque and half the speed
(C) half the torque and twice the speed
(D) half the torque and half the speed

66. Which load feels heavier to a firefighter?

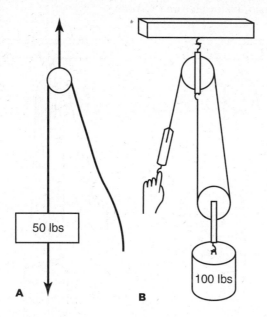

A

50 lbs

B

100 lbs

(A) A
(B) B
(C) cannot be determined
(D) They feel the same

67. In which of the following systems will the load move the least distance if the rope is pulled an equal distance for all three systems?

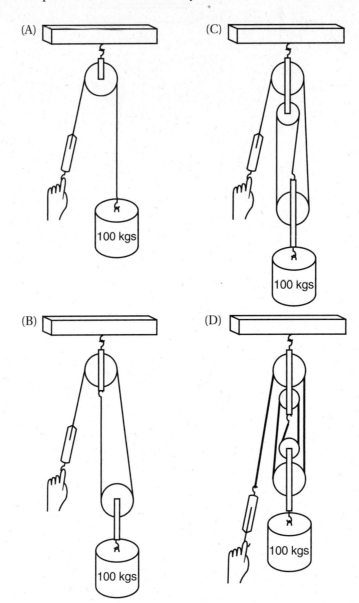

(A)

100 kgs

(C)

100 kgs

(B)

100 kgs

(D)

100 kgs

68. How much effort would a firefighter need to use to remove the bucket from the well?

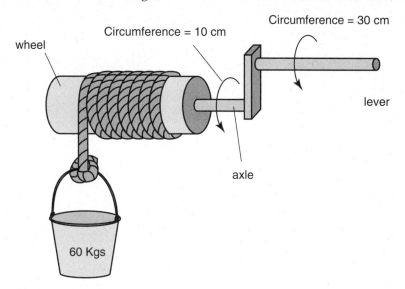

Note: (effort) × (circumference of drive wheel) = (resistance) × (circumference of support wheel)

(A) 30 kgs
(B) 10 kgs
(C) 20 kgs
(D) 15 kgs

69. The longer the handle is on the tire iron, the more _____ will be applied to the nut.

(A) load
(B) torque
(C) levers
(D) weight

70. Which shape, when added to the following shape, forms a triangle?

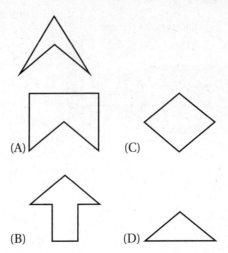

(A)   (C)

(B)   (D)

71. Which shape, when added to the following shape, forms a parallelogram?

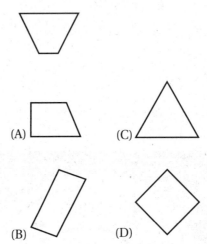

(A)   (C)

(B)   (D)

72. What simple machine is stopping this car from rolling down the hill?

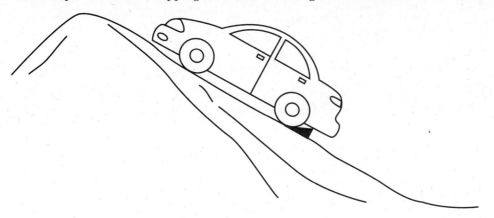

(A) A pulley
(B) A wheel and axle
(C) A wedge
(D) A lever

73. If the drive gear B is turning at 900 rpms, how many rpms will gear A turn at if it is 1/3 the circumference?

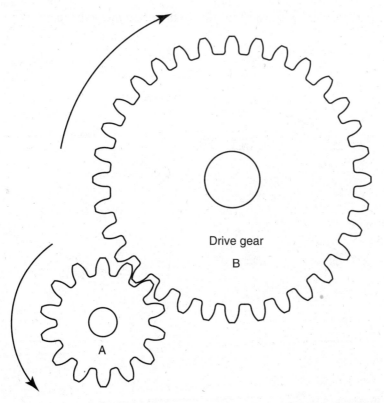

Drive gear

B

A

(A) 900 rpms
(B) 300 rpms
(C) 1,200 rpms
(D) 2,700 rpms

74. If gear A turns at 10 revolutions per minute, how fast will gear C turn?

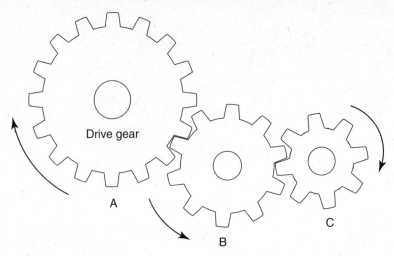

(A) 10 revolutions per minute
(B) 5 revolutions per minute
(C) 4 revolutions per minute
(D) 20 revolutions per minute

75. In which picture will it be easiest for the firefighter to move the load?

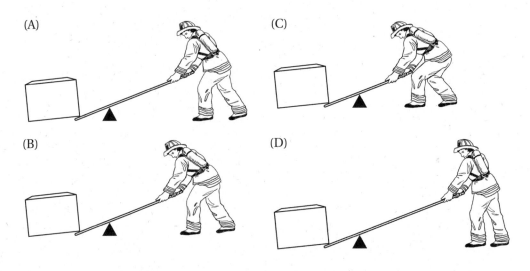

(A)

(B)

(C)

(D)

76. Which screw jack will be easier to turn?

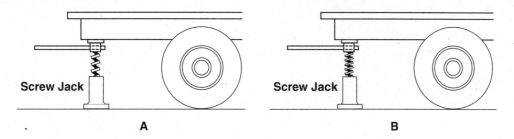

(A) A

(B) B

(C) Both will be the same

(D) Cannot be determined

77. For the dial to point at the number 7, how many degrees does it have to turn clockwise?

(A) 30

(B) 180

(C) 240

(D) 270

78. Where is the force applied on this inclined plane?

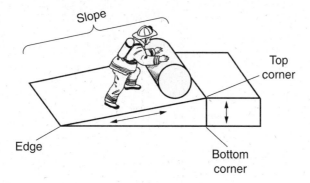

(A) The edge.

(B) The slope.

(C) Top corner

(D) Bottom corner.

SAMPLE TEST 2

79. Which of the following floor plans matches the house?

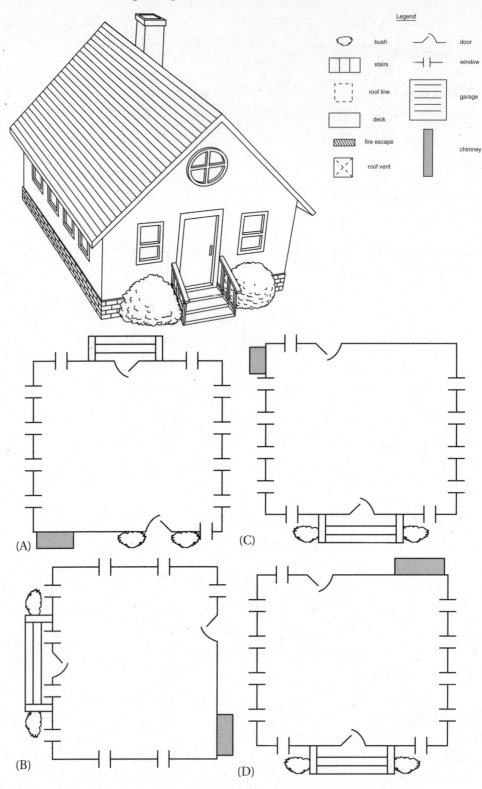

Legend

- bush
- stairs
- roof line
- deck
- fire escape
- roof vent
- door
- window
- garage
- chimney

(A)

(B)

(C)

(D)

SAMPLE TEST 2

80. How long is this house from north to south?

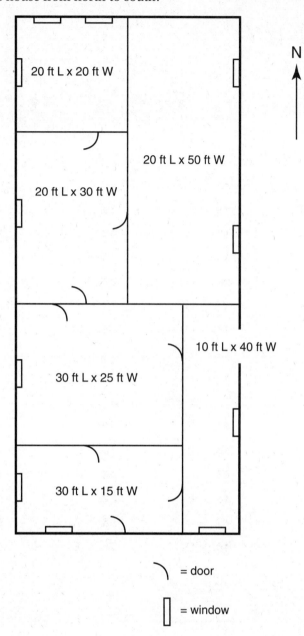

20 ft L x 20 ft W

20 ft L x 50 ft W

20 ft L x 30 ft W

30 ft L x 25 ft W

10 ft L x 40 ft W

30 ft L x 15 ft W

N

⌐ = door

▯ = window

(A) 90 ft.
(B) 105 ft.
(C) 95 ft.
(D) 75 ft.

ANSWER KEY
Test 2

SECTION 1

1.	A	7.	B	13.	D	19.	A	25.	B
2.	C	8.	C	14.	C	20.	D	26.	C
3.	D	9.	C	15.	A	21.	C	27.	A
4.	C	10.	A	16.	D	22.	B	28.	D
5.	C	11.	B	17.	C	23.	D	29.	B
6.	D	12.	C	18.	C	24.	B	30.	D

SECTION 2

31.	C	37.	B	43.	B	49.	D	55.	B
32.	A	38.	A	44.	A	50.	C	56.	A
33.	C	39.	B	45.	C	51.	A	57.	D
34.	C	40.	C	46.	B	52.	D	58.	A
35.	D	41.	B	47.	A	53.	A	59.	C
36.	C	42.	C	48.	D	54.	B	60.	D

SECTION 3

61.	C	65.	C	69.	B	73.	D	77.	D
62.	D	66.	D	70.	D	74.	D	78.	B
63.	C	67.	D	71.	C	75.	D	79.	D
64.	A	68.	C	72.	C	76.	B	80.	A

ANSWER EXPLANATIONS

Section 1:

1. (A) Get their captain to take the phone call. This question asks you to solve a problem. The answer is located in the paragraph: "If the caller is a member of the public who has a question or problem that the rookie firefighter can't immediately help with then the firefighter should pass the call on to the captain."

2. (C) Give the member of the public a copy of form 27-C and the water key. This is an information ordering question. If you read the paragraph, it clearly shows that giving the member of the public a copy of form 27-C and the water key is the last step in the process. See the last step in the paragraph. The word "then" is key.

3. (D) Exhalation. This is the best answer. Death is also a definition for expiration, but it does not fit with the meaning of the information provided.

4. (C) Air brake check sheet and daily truck check form. The maintenance repair form is used only for problems with the truck. "As the Firefighter is checking the truck, he should be filling out his daily truck check form and the air brake check sheet. If the firefighter finds a problem with the truck, he should fill out a maintenance repair form and send it to fire maintenance."

5. (C) Aluminum carabiners do not hold up as well to shock loads as steel carabiners. This question asks the test taker to make inferences from what they have read and reorder some information. The answer is found in this sentence: "Steel carabiners have better locking mechanisms, greater strength, and hold up better to shock loads than aluminum carabiners."

6. (D) All of the above. Answer (A) is mentioned early in the passage. Answers (B) and (C) are mentioned at the end of the passage. The key to correctly answering this question is thoroughly reading the passage.

7. (B) During designated break times, when not involved in an incident, and when inside the fire hall. The information needed to answer this question is found in these three sentences: "Firefighters may use their cell phones during their designated break times only, as long as they are not involved in an incident. Cell phones must be left in the firehall at all times. Under no circumstances will they be allowed away from the firehall (including on the fire truck) during shift hours."

8. (C) There is a gauge that shows the pressure. This answer is found in the sentence: "A gauge on the top of the extinguisher shows that the extinguisher is properly pressurized." None of the other possible answers are mentioned in the passage.

9. (C) In a hydraulic, the water rolls back and can keep objects. This question is asking the test taker to read into the text and find information. If you read the text closely, you will see that the last sentence states "This roll back is dangerous because it can hold an object (e.g., a person) and cause it to be recirculated or "kept" in the hydraulic." This sentence, when combined with the second sentence ("It can also be called hole or a keeper.") is the key to the answer.

10. (A) The spread of a malignant tumor to other tissues in the body away from the original tumor. This answer requires some rearranging of words but is found in the last two sentences of the passage. "A malignant tumor is composed of cells that can break off and spread to other locations in the body. This process is called metastasis."

11. (B) The fire tetrahedron. To find this answer, the test taker must reorder the information in the second, third, and fourth sentences of the passage. "For combustion to occur, four elements are needed. Those elements are heat, fuel, oxygen, and self sustained chemical reaction. These four components together are sometimes called the fire tetrahedron."

12. (C) A reaction that produces energy. This answer is found in the fifth sentence of the passage "Combustion is an exothermic reaction (a reaction that produces energy) . . ."

13. (D) Both A and B. This is mentioned in the sixth sentence of the passage. "The production or release of energy during combustion is usually in the form of heat and light." Kinetic energy is not mentioned in the passage.

14. (C) In a premixed flame, fuel and air have been mixed before combustion, while in a diffusion flame fuel and air are mixed at the site of combustion. Finding this answer requires the reorganization of the sentences in the passage regarding diffusion flames and premixed flames to find their meaning. The answer is found in these sentences: "A premixed flame occurs when fuel and air have been mixed before combustion occurs. A diffusion flame happens when fuel and air mix in the region where combustion takes place."

15. (A) Diffusion flames. This answer is found in the last sentence of the passage. "Most structure fires contain diffusion flames because the fuel (structure and contents) and air mix as the fire grows."

16. (D) 6. 1. Normal 2. Drowning non-swimmer 3. Injured 4. Panic 5. Counterpanic
6. Weak or tired.

17. (C) To help them determine the most appropriate form of rescue. This answer is found in the second sentence of the passage. "It is important for firefighters to be able to recognize the different types of victims to determine the most appropriate form of rescue."

18. (C) Drowning non-swimmers, counterpanic, and weak or tired swimmers. The text related to these types of conscious victims indicates that they are either not able to call for help or that they will usually not be able to call for help. Drowning non-swimmers: "Usually, drowning non-swimmers will not call out for help because any time their mouth is out of the water they are gasping for air." Counterpanic: "They are not vocal." Weak or tired swimmers: "They usually will not be able to call for help." This question requires test takers to reorganize and interpret information.

19. (A) Climbing a ladder. ". . . these victims appear as though they are climbing a ladder . . ." This answer is found under the drowning non-swimmer heading.

20. (D) Both B and C. This answer is found under the weak or tired swimmer heading. "Weak or tired swimmer—This type of victim is often near vertical in the water and very sluggish with wide eyes looking in the direction of safety."

21. (C) Pop them hydraulically. This is mentioned in step 1. "If doors cannot be opened by hand, pop them hydraulically."

22. (B) To check for hidden dangers in the posts. "Step 2—Peel and Peak. Make sure before step three that there are no hidden dangers in the posts that will be cut." None of the other possible answers are mentioned in the passage.

23. (D) Glass removal has been completed. This is mentioned in the opening paragraph. "We can assume that things such as patient protection, glass removal, and seatbelt removal have already been completed." The test taker has to understand the meaning of this sentence.

24. (B) For patient safety. Although the other answers may be correct, this is the only answer mentioned in the text. "If possible, the roof should be removed over the front of the car (in an effort not to pass the windshield over the patient)." This is the type of question that has a BEST answer. Removing the roof over the front of the car is the only option mentioned in the passage. Also, this option is best for patient safety, which common sense dictates is the most important part of this rescue (after rescuer safety).

25. (B) In the parts dump. Step 1 states that "Doors and other parts should be placed in the parts dump after removal." Test takers should realize that a removed door and a removed roof are similar. Therefore, the roof can be considered an "other part."

26. (C) His body has stopped sweating. This question requires the test taker to problem solve, and realize from the definition provided, that a lack of sweat and body fluid in a hot environment will lead to dry skin. "Definition—A failure of the body's heat regulating mechanism that renders the body unable to cool itself. Sweating stops when fluid levels in the body are low. When the body can't sweat, it can't cool itself and body temperature will rise rapidly."

27. (A) There is none. If you look at the history provided for heat stroke and heat exhaustion, both say the same thing: "History—Exposure to a hot, humid environment or extreme heat. Overactivity under hot sun." Therefore, there is no difference between the history of a patient with heat exhaustion and a patient with heat stroke. All of the other answers are true and related to the information provided, but they do not answer the question.

28. (D) Heat prostration. This is explained in the beginning of the text for "Heat Exhaustion (Heat Prostration)."

29. (B) Patients with heat stroke may have convulsions. This question asks for the DIFFERENCE between the symptoms of heat stroke and heat exhaustion. Therefore, the only correct answer is (B). Looking under the Symptoms category for both and noticing that only heat stroke notes that convulsions may occur can verify the answer.

30. (D) Overexposure to heat. This is the best answer to the question. The most relevant information for this question is found in the first sentence of the passage: "Heat exhaustion and heat stroke are serious conditions caused by overexposure to heat."

Section 2:

---

31. (C) 719.5327. This is an addition question. Use column addition to find the correct answer. Don't forget to put the decimal in the correct place when you are adding. See the addition section of Chapter 2 for more information.

Here is how the answer is found:

```
  546.4000
   67.1000
   63.8760
+  42.1567
  719.5327
```

32. (A) 866.901. This is an addition question. Use column addition to find the correct answer. Don't forget to put the decimal in the correct place when you are adding. See the addition section of Chapter 2 for more information.

Here is how the answer is found:

```
856.100
  7.345
+ 3.456
866.901
```

---

33. (C) 177.102. This is a subtraction question. Remember to use subtraction with regrouping. Also remember to subtract only using two numbers at a time. Numbers cannot be stacked like when adding.

Here is how the answer is found:
First

```
  546.98
− 324.20
  222.78
```

Then

```
  222.780
−  45.678
  177.102
```

---

34. (C) 500. This is a division question. It is very important to remember the decimal when answering this question. You can check your answer by using multiplication (500 × .20 = 100). See Chapter 2 for an expanded explanation of division. Another way to answer this question is to divide 100 by 20 (5) and then add two decimal places (500).

35. (D) 1,450,716. This is a multiplication question. Long multiplication should be used to answer this question.

Here is how the answer is found:

$$
\begin{array}{r}
11 \\
441 \\
4562 \\
\underline{\times 318} \\
36496 \\
45620 \\
\underline{1368600} \\
1,450,716
\end{array}
$$

36. (C) 12/15. This question involves adding fractions. Remember to make the denominators the same.

Here is how the answer is found:

3/5 + 3/15 =
9/15 + 3/15 = 12/15

37. (B) 2 6/7. This question involves adding fractions. Remember to make the denominators the same, then add the numerators. Don't forget to simplify the fraction. See Chapter 2 for further explanation of this type of question.

Here is how the answer is found:

7/7 + 6/7 + 2/3 + 1/3
21/21 + 18/21 + 14/21 + 7/21 = 60/21

Simplify—20/7
The answer is 2 6/7

38. (A) –1/12. This question involves subtracting fractions. Remember to make the denominators the same, then subtract the numerator. Don't forget to simplify the answer. See Chapter 2 for further explanation of this type of question.

Here is how the answer is found:

3/12 – 6/24 – 4/48 =
12/48 – 12/48 – 4/48 = –4/48

The answer is –1/12.

39. (B) 8/35. This question involves multiplying fractions. See Chapter 2 for further explanation of how to multiply fractions.

Here is how the answer is found:

2/5 × 4/7 = 8/35

40. (C) 15/32. This question involves multiplying fractions. See Chapter 2 for further explanation of how to multiply fractions.

Here is how the answer is found:

$5/8 \times 3/4 = 15/32$

41. (B) 10. This question asks you to simplify a fraction. 20/2 is the same as 10/1. 10/1 is the same as 10.

42. (C) 4/5. This question involves dividing fractions. Don't forget to simplify the fraction if possible. See Chapter 2 for further explanation of how to divide fractions.

Here is how the answer is found.

$2/5 \div 2/4$
$2/5 \times 4/2 = 8/10$

Simplify—4/5

43. (B) 60. (−176) is a negative being added. This means you have to subtract 176 from 236. Remember that two opposite numbers equal a negative. Chapter 2 contains more detailed information regarding positive and negative integers.

44. (A) 1,185. (−543) is a negative being subtracted. This means that to get the correct answer, 642 has to be added to 543. Remember that two negative numbers equal a positive. Chapter 2 contains more detailed information regarding positive and negative integers.

45. (C) 900 ft. This question asks for a number to be found based on a percentage. The easiest way to answer this question is to convert 30% to a decimal ($\div 100$). $30 \div 100 = .3$. Now multiply 3,000 (ft. of rescue rope) by .3.

$3000 \times .3 = 900$

Another easy way to find the answer to this question is to find 10% of 3000 (300) and multiply that number by 3 to get 30%. $300 \times 3 = 900$.

46. (B) 2:1. This question asks for a ratio. The ratio is 16:8. Like a fraction, this ratio can be simplified further to 2:1.

47. (A) 1,011 gallons. This can be considered a proportion or ratio question. To find the answer, you first need to find the ratio. It is important to know that there are 60 minutes in an hour. Ladder 4 pumped 60,660 gallons in the past hour. The ratio is 60,600 to 60. To correctly answer this question, you will need to simplify the ratio the same way you would simplify a fraction (this is the easiest way; algebra could also be used). See the algebra, ratios, and proportions sections in Chapter 2 for further explanation.

Here is how the answer is found:
The ratio:

$$\frac{60,660 \text{ gallons}}{60 \text{ minutes}}$$

Simplified (top and bottom divided by 60 because there are 60 minutes in one hour)

$$\frac{1,011}{1 \text{ minute}}$$

Another way to find the answer to this question is to divide 60,660 by 60.

48. (D) 71.42 minutes. The ratio in this question is 7 gallons in 5 minutes. 7:5. To find the answer, use algebra and cross multiply. Remember the question is asking how long it will take to use 100 gallons. You can check your answer by checking to see if the equation is equal ($5 \div 7 = 71.42 \div 100$). The algebra, ratios, and proportions sections in Chapter 2 provide further explanation.

Here is how the answer is found:

$$\frac{7 \text{ Gallons}}{5 \text{ minutes}} = \frac{100 \text{ Gallons}}{x}$$
$$7x = 500$$
$$7x \div 7 = 500 \div 7$$
$$x = 71.42$$

49. (D) 17. This is a division question. Divide the number of firefighters (374) by the number of stations (22) to find the correct answer. $374 \div 22 = 17$.

50. (C) 4.6 minutes. The ratio in this question is 65 kilometres in 6 minutes. 65:6. To find the answer, use algebra and cross multiply. You can check your answer by checking to see if the equation is equal. The algebra, ratios, and proportions sections in Chapter 2 provide further explanation.

Here is how the answer is found:

$$\frac{65 \text{ kilometres}}{6 \text{ minutes}} = \frac{50 \text{ kilometres}}{x}$$

$65x = 300$

$65x \div 65 = 300 \div 65$

$x = 4.6$

51. (A) 120,000 gallons. This is a multiplication question. Multiply the gallons per hour by the exposure lines. $15,000 \times 8 = 120,000$.

52. (D) 175 minutes. This is a proportion question. The ratio is 20 feet extinguished every 10 minutes. 20:10. To find the answer, use algebra and cross multiply. You can check your answer by checking to see if the equation is equal. The algebra, ratios, and proportions sections in Chapter 2 provide further explanation.

Here is how the answer is found:

$$\frac{20 \text{ ft.}}{10 \text{ minutes}} = \frac{350 \text{ ft.}}{x}$$

$20x = 3500$

$20x \div 20 = 3500 \div 20$

$x = 175 \text{ minutes}$

53. (A) Just over 4 days. This is a proportion question. The ratio is 6 days to 10 units. 6:10. To find the answer, use algebra and cross multiply. You can check your answer by checking to see if the equation is equal. The algebra, ratios, and proportions sections in Chapter 2 provide further explanation.

Here is how the answer is found:

$$\frac{6 \text{ days.}}{10 \text{ units}} = \frac{x}{7 \text{ units}}$$

$10x = 42$

$10x \div 10 = 42 \div 10$

$x = 4.2 \text{ days}$

The best answer is just over 4 days.

54. (B) 25,000 litres. This is a proportion question. The ratio is 15 minutes to 18,750 litres. 15:18,750. To find the answer, use algebra and cross multiply. You can check your answer by checking to see if the equation is equal. The algebra, ratios, and proportions sections in Chapter 2 provide further explanation.

Here is how the answer is found:

$$\frac{15 \text{ minutes.}}{18750 \text{ litres}} = \frac{20 \text{ minutes}}{x}$$

$$15x = 375,000$$
$$15x \div 15 = 375,000 \div 15$$
$$x = 25,000 \text{ litres}$$

55. (B) 236 ¼. This is a division question. To find the correct answer, divide 945 gallons by 4. $945 \div 4 = 236.25$. Remember when answering the question that .25 is the same as 1/4 (.25 = 25/100). To find the correct answer, you could also multiply by .25 instead of dividing. For more information on division, see Chapter 2.

56. (A) About 10,000 litres. This is a multiplication question. 10 litres times 1000 is 10,000 litres.

57. (D) About 98 or 99 fires. This is a proportion question. The ratio is 36 fires to 3 months. 36:3. To find the answer, use algebra and cross multiply. You can check your answer by checking to see if the equation is equal. Use the algebra, ratios, and proportions sections in Chapter 2 for further explanation.

Here is how the answer is found:

$$\frac{37 \text{ fires}}{3 \text{ months}} = \frac{x}{8 \text{ months}}$$

$$3x = 296$$
$$3x \div 3 = 296 \div 3$$
$$x = 98.66$$

58. (A) 1/3. This is a ratio question. To find the answer, find the ratio (8 medical calls to 2 other calls) and then simplify the ratio the same as you would for a fraction. 8/24 = 1/3.

59. (C) 30. This is a percentage question. To find the answer, multiply the total number by .25 (the percentage as a number). $120 \times .25 = 30$.

60. (D) 4–5. This question can be answered using proportions. The ratio is 3 rescues involving swiftwater to 10 rescues. 3:10. To find the answer, use algebra and cross multiply. You can check your answer by checking to see if the equation is equal. Use the algebra, ratios, and proportions sections in Chapter 2 for further explanation.

Here is how the answer is found:

$$\frac{3 \text{ rescues involving swiftwater}}{10 \text{ rescues}} = \frac{x}{15 \text{ units}}$$

$10x = 45$

$10x \div 10 = 45 \div 10$

$x = 4.5$

The best answer is 4–5.

Section 3:

61. (C) A, C, E, G. When two gears meet, they turn in opposing directions. Internal gears turn in the same direction.

62. (D) 3:1. This answer is correct because the drive gear has to turn 3 times for every 1 time the driven gear turns.

63. (C) Counterclockwise. When the belt is twisted, the wheels spin in opposite directions. See the Belt Drive section of Chapter 2 for more information.

64. (A) Ramp A. This is an inclined plane. The lower the ramp, the easier it will be to push the foam up (assuming all ramps are the same length). See the inclined plane section of Chapter 2 for more information on inclined planes.

65. (C) Half the torque and twice the speed. This answer has to do with gear ratio and belt drives. Refer to the Gears and Belt Drive sections of Chapter 2 for further explanation.

66. (D) They feel the same. The 2:1 system reduces the weight pulled by half, so the firefighter is pulling 50 lbs. in each picture.

67. (D) This load will move the least distance because this system has the greatest mechanical advantage. The load shown in diagram A will move 4 times as far as the load shown in diagram D. See the Pulleys section of Chapter 2 for more information on mechanical advantage.

68. (C) 20 kgs. This is actually a math question, but it is important to also understand how the wheel and axle work in order to answer the question. Sometimes this type of test contains questions in the mechanical aptitude section that are more similar to math questions. This is important to be aware of. To solve the problem, put the numbers in the equation provided and used algebra. Chapter 2 contains the information required to answer this question.

Here is how the answer is found:

(effort) × (circumference of drive wheel) = (resistance) × (circumference of support wheel)
(effort) × 30 = 60 × 10
(effort) × 30 = 600
(effort) × 30 ÷ 30 = 600 ÷ 30
effort = 20

69. (B) Torque. Torque is twisting force. The best answer is torque.

70. (D) This shape completes the triangle.

71. (C) This shape completes the parallelogram.

72. (C) A wedge. A wedge is very similar to an inclined plane except that effort and force are applied on the edge of a wedge (not the slope) and a wedge can move while in use.

73. (D) 2,700 rpm. If the gear is 1/3 the size, it will turn at 3× the speed. This question requires some multiplication. See Chapter 2 for information on math and gears.

74. (D) 20 revolutions per minute. If a gear is half the size of the gear driving it, it will turn at twice the speed. You can count the teeth to find the size of the gears. This question requires some division. See Chapter 2 for information on math and gears.

75. (D) This is a leverage question. The longer the lever is, the easier it will be to lift the weight (as long as it's longer on the correct side of the fulcrum). Information regarding levers is contained in Chapter 2.

76. (B) The pitch on this screw jack is less making it easier to turn. You can tell the pitch is less because the threads are closer together. For more information on screws, see Chapter 2.

77. (D) 270. This dial has to turn 270 degrees to get to the 7.

78. (B) The slope. The force on an inclined plane is applied to the slope. See Chapter 2 for more information.

79. (D) D. This floor plan most closely matches the house. The other options are incorrect. Option A shows the bushes in the wrong place. Option B shows the windows on the front of the house on the side of the house and the windows on the side of the house on the front. Option C shows the chimney in the wrong place.

80. (A) 90 ft. The answer to this question is found by adding up the lengths of each room in a north/south direction.

ANSWERS EXPLAINED

ANSWER SHEET
Test 3

1. Ⓐ Ⓑ Ⓒ Ⓓ	20. Ⓐ Ⓑ Ⓒ Ⓓ	39. Ⓐ Ⓑ Ⓒ Ⓓ	58. Ⓐ Ⓑ Ⓒ Ⓓ
2. Ⓐ Ⓑ Ⓒ Ⓓ	21. Ⓐ Ⓑ Ⓒ Ⓓ	40. Ⓐ Ⓑ Ⓒ Ⓓ	59. Ⓐ Ⓑ Ⓒ Ⓓ
3. Ⓐ Ⓑ Ⓒ Ⓓ	22. Ⓐ Ⓑ Ⓒ Ⓓ	41. Ⓐ Ⓑ Ⓒ Ⓓ	60. Ⓐ Ⓑ Ⓒ Ⓓ
4. Ⓐ Ⓑ Ⓒ Ⓓ	23. Ⓐ Ⓑ Ⓒ Ⓓ	42. Ⓐ Ⓑ Ⓒ Ⓓ	61. Ⓐ Ⓑ Ⓒ Ⓓ
5. Ⓐ Ⓑ Ⓒ Ⓓ	24. Ⓐ Ⓑ Ⓒ Ⓓ	43. Ⓐ Ⓑ Ⓒ Ⓓ	62. Ⓐ Ⓑ Ⓒ Ⓓ
6. Ⓐ Ⓑ Ⓒ Ⓓ	25. Ⓐ Ⓑ Ⓒ Ⓓ	44. Ⓐ Ⓑ Ⓒ Ⓓ	63. Ⓐ Ⓑ Ⓒ Ⓓ
7. Ⓐ Ⓑ Ⓒ Ⓓ	26. Ⓐ Ⓑ Ⓒ Ⓓ	45. Ⓐ Ⓑ Ⓒ Ⓓ	64. Ⓐ Ⓑ Ⓒ Ⓓ
8. Ⓐ Ⓑ Ⓒ Ⓓ	27. Ⓐ Ⓑ Ⓒ Ⓓ	46. Ⓐ Ⓑ Ⓒ Ⓓ	65. Ⓐ Ⓑ Ⓒ Ⓓ
9. Ⓐ Ⓑ Ⓒ Ⓓ	28. Ⓐ Ⓑ Ⓒ Ⓓ	47. Ⓐ Ⓑ Ⓒ Ⓓ	66. Ⓐ Ⓑ Ⓒ Ⓓ
10. Ⓐ Ⓑ Ⓒ Ⓓ	29. Ⓐ Ⓑ Ⓒ Ⓓ	48. Ⓐ Ⓑ Ⓒ Ⓓ	67. Ⓐ Ⓑ Ⓒ Ⓓ
11. Ⓐ Ⓑ Ⓒ Ⓓ	30. Ⓐ Ⓑ Ⓒ Ⓓ	49. Ⓐ Ⓑ Ⓒ Ⓓ	68. Ⓐ Ⓑ Ⓒ Ⓓ
12. Ⓐ Ⓑ Ⓒ Ⓓ	31. Ⓐ Ⓑ Ⓒ Ⓓ	50. Ⓐ Ⓑ Ⓒ Ⓓ	69. Ⓐ Ⓑ Ⓒ Ⓓ
13. Ⓐ Ⓑ Ⓒ Ⓓ	32. Ⓐ Ⓑ Ⓒ Ⓓ	51. Ⓐ Ⓑ Ⓒ Ⓓ	70. Ⓐ Ⓑ Ⓒ Ⓓ
14. Ⓐ Ⓑ Ⓒ Ⓓ	33. Ⓐ Ⓑ Ⓒ Ⓓ	52. Ⓐ Ⓑ Ⓒ Ⓓ	71. Ⓐ Ⓑ Ⓒ Ⓓ
15. Ⓐ Ⓑ Ⓒ Ⓓ	34. Ⓐ Ⓑ Ⓒ Ⓓ	53. Ⓐ Ⓑ Ⓒ Ⓓ	72. Ⓐ Ⓑ Ⓒ Ⓓ
16. Ⓐ Ⓑ Ⓒ Ⓓ	35. Ⓐ Ⓑ Ⓒ Ⓓ	54. Ⓐ Ⓑ Ⓒ Ⓓ	73. Ⓐ Ⓑ Ⓒ Ⓓ
17. Ⓐ Ⓑ Ⓒ Ⓓ	36. Ⓐ Ⓑ Ⓒ Ⓓ	55. Ⓐ Ⓑ Ⓒ Ⓓ	74. Ⓐ Ⓑ Ⓒ Ⓓ
18. Ⓐ Ⓑ Ⓒ Ⓓ	37. Ⓐ Ⓑ Ⓒ Ⓓ	56. Ⓐ Ⓑ Ⓒ Ⓓ	75. Ⓐ Ⓑ Ⓒ Ⓓ
19. Ⓐ Ⓑ Ⓒ Ⓓ	38. Ⓐ Ⓑ Ⓒ Ⓓ	57. Ⓐ Ⓑ Ⓒ Ⓓ	

IPMA STYLE TEST

Section 1: Reading Comprehension

> DIRECTIONS: The following twenty four questions test your ability to read and interpret information from a passage. Fill in the corresponding bubble on the answer sheet.

> DIRECTIONS: Questions 1 through 4 refer to the following passage.

On July 16 at 11:37 A.M., a cooking fire originating on the seventh floor of an 18 story residential building killed 3 people, and injured 14 civilians and 2 firefighters. Firefighters removed approximately 8 people using two tower trucks placed on the A and B sides of the building. They rescued 3 others from the interior of the building. A person using large amounts of cooking oil started the fire when he knocked his wok over and spread flaming oil on the carpet and wall. As the person who started the fire left the suite, he accidently left the door open (it was blocked by a shoe). The fire progressed quickly into the hallway and blocked it, keeping most victims away from the two exits serving the floor. All of the trapped survivors on the fire floor waited on their balconies for rescue. Two of the people who died were overcome by smoke and fire gases in the hallway as they tried to make their way to an exit. The third death has been attributed to a fall. Firefighters believe all deaths that resulted from this fire could have been avoided if the building had fire sprinklers.

The IPMA FF-EL 101 and 102 tests contain 90 questions. However, the sample IPMA test in this book contains only 75 questions due to the difficulty of reproducing Situational Judgment and Vocabulary questions. Please refer to Chapter 1 for details on these types of questions.

1. According to the passage, which of the following is true?

   I.   There was a fire on July 16.
   II. During the fire on July 16, 8 people were rescued using tower trucks.
   III. The fire was in a 16 story building.

   (A) I only
   (B) I and II
   (C) I, II, and III
   (D) None of the above

2. What is this passage describing?

   (A) A fire that happened on July 16.
   (B) Firefighting procedures.
   (C) A medical aid call.
   (D) A fire that took place on July 18.

3. According to the passage, which of the following is true?

   I.   Most of the victims that died in the hallway perished because they couldn't reach the exit
   II. The exit was blocked because of a building collapse.
   III. Eight people died in the fire.

   (A) I only
   (B) I and II
   (C) I, II, and III
   (D) None of the above

4. What started the fire described in the passage?

   (A) motor oil
   (B) gasoline
   (C) castor oil
   (D) cooking oil

DIRECTIONS: Questions 5 and 6 refer to the following passage.

One type of fire detector is the light scatter type fire detector. The light scatter type fire detector works on the principle that when light traverses a transparent medium, its intensity is reduced mostly due to absorption of the light. In a normal clean air state, the light inside a light scatter type fire detector is prevented from reaching the photoelectric cell (which would signal an alarm) by an opaque barrier. When smoke or other suspended particles enter a light scatter type fire detector, they cause the light to "scatter" and reach the photoelectric cell to signal an alarm. Light scatter type fire detectors are designed to signal an alarm if there is a fault in the system to prevent a system fault from causing a missed alarm.

5. What causes a light scatter type fire detector to signal an alarm?

   I.   There is a fault in the system.
   II. Suspended particles enter the detector and cause light to reach the photoelectric cell.
   III. Light travels through the outside of the detector from outside.

   (A) I only
   (B) I and II
   (C) I, II, and III
   (D) None of the above

6. In a light scatter type fire detector, what prevents light from reaching the photoelectric cell in a normal clean air environment?

   (A) Nothing. Light is supposed to reach the cell in a clean air environment.
   (B) There is no photoelectric cell in a light scatter type fire detector.
   (C) A metal band.
   (D) An opaque barrier.

DIRECTIONS: Questions 7 through 9 refer to the following passage.

When a fire truck responds to a call, it will usually respond in one of two ways: routine (sometimes referred to as Code 1) or Code 3. Routine refers to the truck responding to the call as if it were driving somewhere routinely. This type of response is used for less urgent calls such as burning complaints or an assist with a lift that does not involve a medical issue. When a truck responds to a call "routine", it drives normally with its emergency lights and siren deactivated, obeying all the rules of the road. A fire truck will respond Code 3 to calls when the nature of the call is more urgent. For example, a fire truck will respond Code 3 to a structure fire or technical rescue. When responding Code 3, a fire truck will activate its emergency lights and siren and will bypass traffic and traffic lights (keeping within the parameters of the motor vehicle act that relates to Code 3 response). The main reason fire trucks don't always respond to calls Code 3 is for safety. Responding to calls Code 3 is much more dangerous than responding routine.

7. Which of the following are described in the passage as methods of response to a call for a fire truck?

   I.   routine
   II. Code 3
   III. Code 1
   IV. Code 6

   (A) I only
   (B) I and II
   (C) I, II, and III
   (D) I, II, III, and IV

8. Captain Halington receives a phone call at the station from a civilian who reports a serious motor vehicle accident with people trapped at the corner of 1st and Main. The Captain decides to respond to the call immediately. Using the information in the passage, what type of response is Captain Halington most likely to use?

   (A) routine
   (B) code 1
   (C) code 3
   (D) code 6

9. If Code 3 is faster, according to the passage, why don't fire trucks always respond to calls in this manner?

   (A) It's not good for the truck.
   (B) To give firefighters more time to prepare while on route to a call.
   (C) Because of the traffic control act.
   (D) Safety.

DIRECTIONS: Questions 10 through 13 refer to the following passage.

There are six ranks of wildfires in the fire intensity rank system.

Rank 1—Smoldering ground or creeping surface fire.
This is a smoldering ground fire that burns in the ground fuel layer. These fires have no open flame and produce white smoke.

Rank 2—Low vigour surface fire.
This is a fire that burns on the surface or a fire that burns in the surface fuel layer, excluding the crowns of trees. These fires produce a visible open flame.

Rank 3—Moderately vigourous surface fire.

This is a vigorous surface fire with a moderate rate of spread. This fire will have an organized front and may display "candling" along its perimeter or within the fire.

Rank 4—Highly vigourous surface fire.

This type of fire has an organized surface flame front, and has a moderate to fast rate of spread along the ground. These fires produce grey to black smoke.

Rank 5—Extremely vigourous surface fire or active crown fire.

This type of fire has an organized crown fire front, moderate to long-range spotting and independent spot fire growth. These fires produce black or copper smoke.

Rank 6- Extreme fire behavior.

Violent fire behavior occurs with this type of fire. An organized crown fire front, moderate to long-range spotting, and independent spot fire growth are characteristics of this type of fire.

10. A vigorous surface fire that is spreading moderately and displays some candling is what rank of fire?

  (A) Rank 2
  (B) Rank 3
  (C) Rank 4
  (D) Rank 5

11. What rank of fire has no open flame?

  (A) Rank 1
  (B) Rank 2
  (C) Rank 3
  (D) Rank 4

12. According to the passage, which is true of a Rank 5 fire?

  I.   These fires have no open flame and produce white smoke.
  II. These fires produce black or copper smoke.
  III. This is a smoldering ground fire that burns in the ground fuel layer.

  (A) I and II
  (B) II only
  (C) III only
  (D) I and III

13. The passage describes the

  (A) wildland fire system
  (B) wildland fire rank system
  (C) fire intensity rank system
  (D) fire intensity order procedure

DIRECTIONS: Questions 14 and 15 refer to the following passage.

Backdraft is a deflagration caused by the sudden introduction of air into an oxygen deficient atmosphere that contains large amounts of unburned fire gasses. For a backdraft to occur, the fire must be underventilated. Oxygen levels in the compartment will be low and the fire will usually be smoldering. When oxygen is introduced to the compartment, the energy release will be very rapid and will last a short time. Usually, the fire will become fully developed after backdraft occurs due to the change in the ventilation profile.

14. In the passage, the word "compartment" is being used to describe
    (A) The space under the ventilated fire and later where the backdraft takes place.
    (B) A type of flame.
    (C) Oxygen levels.
    (D) A fully developed fire that results from the introduction of oxygen.

15. What type of fire behavior is this passage describing?
    (A) flameover
    (B) fire gas ignition
    (C) smoke explosion
    (D) backdraft

DIRECTIONS: Questions 16 through 18 refer to the following passage.

Firefighter Pownazie and firefighter Bonfacico got back to the fire station after a structure fire at 12:38. They have just finished preparing the truck to go back in service by reloading hose on the truck, cleaning equipment, and making sure the truck is in the same condition it was at the start of their shift. After the captain puts the truck back in service at 12:58, he orders FF. Pownazie and FF. Bonfacico to clean and hang the hose that was used in the fire. The firefighters roll out all the hose in the back parking lot and scrub both sides of the hose down with soap and a turks head. After they have finished rinsing the hose off with water, the next step is to hang the hose in the tower so it can dry out properly and not get moldy. Firefighter Pownazie climbs to the top of the tower to hang the hose. Firefighter Bonfacico ties the hose with a clove hitch and sends it up the tower using a pulley system two to three lengths at a time. Once all the hose has been hung, the firefighters go into the station to prepare themselves for their next call.

16. Overall, what does this passage describe?
    (A) Some of firefighter Pownazie and firefighter Bonfacio's station duties immediately after a structure fire.
    (B) The method firefighter Pownazie and firefighter Bonfacio use for loading hose onto the fire truck.
    (C) How to disinfect SCBA after a structure fire.
    (D) Some of firefighter Pownazie and firefighter Bonfacio's station duties immediately after a vehicle fire.

17. A portion of the passage describes firefighter Pownazie and firefighter Bonfacico hanging hose. Which of the following is true?

    I. Firefighter Pownazie ties the hose with a clove hitch to send it up the tower.

    II. The hose is hung so it will dry.

    III. The hose is sent up the tower 2–3 lengths at a time on a pulley system.

    (A) I and II

    (B) II and III

    (C) III only

    (D) I, II, and III

18. What do the firefighters clean and scrub the hose with?

    (A) a turks head and water

    (B) a specially designed cleaning solution

    (C) soap

    (D) A and C

DIRECTIONS: Questions 19 through 22 refer to the following passage.

When firefighters respond to a fire in a highrise, it is important to pay close attention to the smoke that may accumulate in the stair shaft. Because the stair shafts are a primary and secondary means of escape for tenants of the building and for firefighters, they must be controlled immediately to isolate them from fire and smoke. Sometimes firefighters will use positive pressure ventilation or vertical ventilation to draw smoke from the stair shafts and make them more tenable. Sometimes ventilation can be difficult because as smoke moves up the stair shaft and away from the fire, it cools and will become less buoyant and more difficult to remove. Firefighters must also be careful when entering the fire floor from a stair shaft because the stair shaft may create a negative pressure behind them as they move towards the fire. This can cause smoke and flames to be drawn towards the firefighters.

19. As used in the passage, what does the word tenable mean?

    (A) The word tenable is not used in the passage, only tenants.

    (B) Smoke free.

    (C) Viable, livable, safe.

    (D) Tenables are the people who live in each suite in a highrise.

20. This passage discusses the importance of

    (A) positive pressure attack

    (B) gas cooling in highrise fires

    (C) maintaining a tenable environment in stair shafts during a highrise fire

    (D) firefighters

21. As smoke moves up the stair shaft, it cools and becomes less _____

(A) buoyant

(B) cold

(C) hard to remove

(D) both B and C

22. According to the passage, why must firefighters be careful when they enter the fire floor from the stair shaft?

(A) They don't want to let smoke into the fire floor.

(B) They don't want to let fire into the fire floor.

(C) They want to make sure they have water in their hose.

(D) They may create a negative pressure behind them as they move towards the fire.

DIRECTIONS: Questions 23 and 24 refer to the following passage.

Some areas cannot be safely inhabited by humans because the atmosphere is oxygen deficient. The normal oxygen content in the air is 21%. For the body to function properly, it needs to breathe air that contains at least 18% oxygen (although the person will most likely feel fatigued and have a headache). Anything lower than 18% can cause loss of consciousness or death. Oxygen deficient atmospheres cannot be easily detected without monitoring devices. Firefighters must be careful when operating in areas that may be oxygen deficient.

23. The normal oxygen content in air is

(A) 18%

(B) 14%

(C) 21%

(D) between 17% and 21%

24. How can oxygen deficient atmospheres be identified?

(A) Using monitoring devices.

(B) They cannot be easily identified.

(C) Testing strips.

(D) A and B

Section 2: Interpreting Tables

DIRECTIONS: The questions in this section require you to demonstrate your understanding of the information in the tables provided. Use the table below to answer Questions 25–30

Toxicity of Products of Combustion

Gas Produced	Produced by burning	Effect	Dose/time to be lethal/dangerous
Ammonia	Nitrogen or refrigerants	Irritant	Lethal at .25% to .65% for $\frac{1}{2}$ hour
Carbon dioxide	Almost all fires	Swelling of lungs, breathing issues	Lethal at 10% for several minutes
Carbon monoxide	Almost all fires	Asphyxiation	Lethal at .4% for 1 hour or 1.3% for several minutes
Hydrogen cyanide	Urethane foam, some plastics	Cyanosis	Lethal at .3% for a brief period
Hydrogen sulphide	Hydrocarbons	Respiratory paralysis, nervous system damage.	Lethal at .07%. Dangerous above .002% any time period
Nitrogen dioxide	Nitrates (cellular, inorganic)	Anesthesia and respiratory distress	Lethal at .02% to .07% for several minutes
Sulphur dioxide	Organics that contain sulphur	Irritant	Dangerous at .05% for several minutes

25. According to the table, which of the following are irritants?

    I.   Carbon dioxide
    II. Carbon monoxide
    III. Ammonia
    IV. Sulphur dioxide

    (A) I and II
    (B) II, III, and IV
    (C) III and IV
    (D) III

26. What product of combustion is produced by almost all fires?

    (A) Ammonia
    (B) Carbon monoxide
    (C) Hydrogen cyanide
    (D) Nitrogen dioxide

27. Which product of combustion is described as lethal at 1.3% for several minutes?

(A) Carbon monoxide
(B) Hydrogen cyanide
(C) Carbon dioxide
(D) Sulphur dioxide

28. One effect of hydrogen sulphide is

(A) Respiratory distress
(B) Respiratory paralysis
(C) Cyanosis
(D) All of the above

29. Which of the following is not a gas listed in the table?

(A) Nitrogen dioxide
(B) Sulphur dioxide
(C) Hydrogen dioxide
(D) Carbon dioxide

30. What gas is produced by burning organics that contain sulphur?

(A) Carbon dioxide
(B) Carbon monoxide
(C) Ammonia
(D) Sulphur dioxide

DIRECTIONS: Use the following table to answer Questions 31–34

Truck ID	Number of Firefighters	Amount of 2.5 inch hose	Amount of 5 inch hose
Engine 1	4	1,000 ft.	500 ft.
Engine 2	4	1,000 ft.	500 ft.
Quint 4	5	1,000 ft.	500 ft.
Quint 5	5	1,000 ft.	500 ft.
Rescue 6	4	None	None
Ladder 11	3	500 ft.	500 ft.

31. How many trucks are listed in the table?

(A) 5
(B) 2
(C) 6
(D) 4

32. Which truck carries the least number of firefighters?

(A) Engine 1
(B) Engine 2
(C) Rescue 6
(D) Ladder 11

33. Which truck carries the same amount of 2.5 inch and 5 inch hose?

(A) Engine 1
(B) Quint 5
(C) Rescue 6
(D) Ladder 11

34. What types of fire trucks included in the table carry 1,000 ft. of 2.5 inch hose?

(A) Quints
(B) Ladders
(C) Engines
(D) Both A and C

Section 3: Logical Reasoning

DIRECTIONS: Use the information provided in the passages to draw logical conclusions that answer the questions.

DIRECTIONS: Use the following passage to answer Questions 35 and 36.

Class A fires are fires that burn involving ordinary combustibles. Class B fires involve flammable liquids and gasses. Class C fires involve live electrical equipment. Stored pressure water extinguishers are used only to put out Class A fires. It is important that they are not used on a fire that involves electrical equipment. An AFFF extinguisher can be used for Class A or B fires. A dry chemical extinguisher can be used for Class B or C fires. A halon extinguisher uses a gas (halon) as an extinguishing agent and can be used for Class B or C fires.

35. If a firefighter has to extinguish a Class C fire and has to choose between a dry chemical or AFFF extinguisher, which should he choose?

(A) Neither extinguisher will work.
(B) A halon extinguisher.
(C) A dry chemical extinguisher.
(D) An AFFF extinguisher.

36. If a firefighter, who is told by his Captain to put out a Class B fire without using an extinguisher, uses a gas as an extinguishing agent, which type of extinguisher should he use?

(A) halon
(B) AFFF
(C) stored pressure
(D) B or C (both will work)

DIRECTIONS: Use the following passage to answer Questions 37 and 38.

In his last shift, Firefighter Johnson responded to three medical calls and two structure fires. Firefighter Jones responded to four medical calls and the same amount of structure fires as Firefighter Johnson. Firefighter Smith responded to three more medical calls and one less structure fire than Firefighter Johnson. Firefighter Roberts responded to more medical calls than Firefighter Jones but less than Firefighter Smith and two structure fires.

37. How many medical calls did Firefighter Roberts respond to?

    (A) 3
    (B) 4
    (C) 5
    (D) 6

38. How many structure fires did Firefighter Smith respond to?

    (A) 1
    (B) 2
    (C) 3
    (D) none

DIRECTIONS: Use the following passage to answer Question 39.

Firefighter Blarry forgets his wallet one day and asks Firefighter Benneton to cover his lunch for him. Firefighter Benneton pays $4 for Firefighter Blarry's lunch. Firefighter Blarry tells Benneton he will pay him back the next day. The next day, four firefighters decide to split the bill for lunch at the fire hall. Firefighter Benneton decides to pay for the total bill and then divide it up after lunch. The total bill is $20. Firefighter Benneton tells each firefighter that they owe $5 for lunch. Firefighter Blarry is one of the firefighters who owes money for lunch that day.

39. How much does Firefighter Blarry owe Firefighter Benneton?

    (A) $4
    (B) $10
    (C) $11
    (D) $9

Section 4: Reading Gauges

DIRECTIONS: Base your answers to Questions 40 through 42 on the illustrations provided for each question.

40. What does the gas gauge read?

(A) 3/4 full
(B) 7/8 full
(C) 6/8 full
(D) 5/8 full

41. How many PSI does the gauge read?

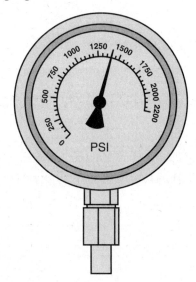

(A) 1,400
(B) 1,500
(C) 1,600
(D) 1,200

42. This voltmeter should read above 10 volts. How many volts above 10 does the voltmeter read?

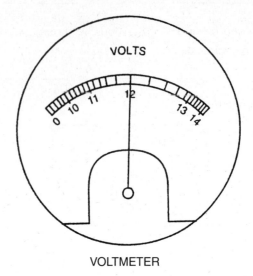

VOLTMETER

(A) 1.5
(B) 2
(C) 2.5
(D) .5

Section 5: Applying Basic Math Rules

DIRECTIONS: Questions 43 through 51 test your basic mathematical skills.

43. Engine 1 carries 3,000 total feet of hose. Engine 2 carries 1,500 total feet of hose. Engine 4 carries 1,200 feet of hose. How much hose do all three trucks carry combined?

(A) 5,500 ft.
(B) 5,700 ft.
(C) 6,000 ft.
(D) 4,500 ft.

44. Firefighter 1 pulls a 150 foot preconnect off the truck as an attack line. Firefighter 2 pulls twice as much hose as firefighter 1 off the truck as an exposure line. How much hose has been removed in total?

(A) 550 ft.
(B) 250 ft.
(C) 300 ft.
(D) 450 ft.

45. Firefighter Jones is at a dumpster fire operating a 125 gpm nozzle off a 250 gallon tank. Assuming he does not close the nozzle and the truck is not connected to a hydrant, approximately how long before Firefighter Jones runs out of water?

(A) just under 3 minutes
(B) about 3 minutes
(C) just over 2 minutes
(D) about 2 minutes

46. A large circular container of gasoline is on fire. The container measures 60 metres across if a straight line is drawn through the middle of the container. What is the circumference of the container?

(A) about 180 metres
(B) about 188 metres
(C) about 120 metres
(D) about 190 metres

47. Engine 7 and Engine 9 are at a structure fire. 950 feet of hose is off Engine 7 and being used at the fire. 1,000 feet of hose is off Engine 9 and being used at the fire. If each length of hose is 50 feet long, how many lengths of hose are off the truck?

(A) 19
(B) 18
(C) 39
(D) 23

48. You have 9 buckets of foam at the station. Five of them are full, 2 are half full, and 2 are three quarters full. How many full buckets of foam do you have?

(A) 8
(B) 8 (with half a bucket remaining)
(C) 7 (with half a bucket remaining)
(D) 7

49. This is a drum of an unknown substance found during a hazardous materials call. It is 80 inches high and 40 inches wide. Assuming it is exactly half full, approximately how much gasoline is in the drum?

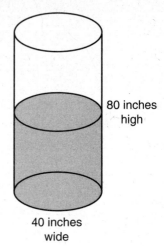

80 inches high

40 inches wide

(A) 50,240 square inches
(B) 52,240 square inches
(C) 100,480 square inches
(D) 120,480 square inches

50. A fire truck takes 16 minutes to travel 60 kilometres, how many minutes will it take the fire truck to travel the remaining 15 kilometres to the fire hall?

(A) 6 minutes
(B) 9 minutes
(C) 8 minutes
(D) 4 minutes

51. A fire department has 134 of their firefighters at a large industrial fire. If the total number of firefighters who work in the fire department is 240, what percentage of firefighters are at the fire?

(A) 54%
(B) 55.8%
(C) 56.9%
(D) 54.3%

Section 6: Mechanical Aptitude

DIRECTIONS: Questions 52 through 57 are based on the illustrations provided for each question.

52. If the drive gear is turning counterclockwise, what direction will gear B turn?

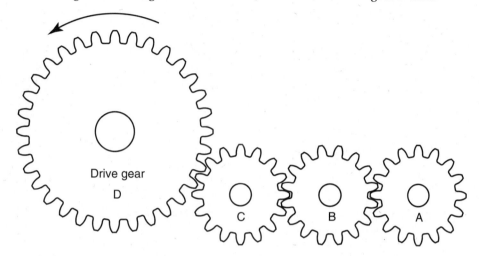

(A) clockwise
(B) counterclockwise
(C) faster
(D) slower

53. In which of the following systems will the load move the most distance if the rope is pulled an equal distance for all three systems?

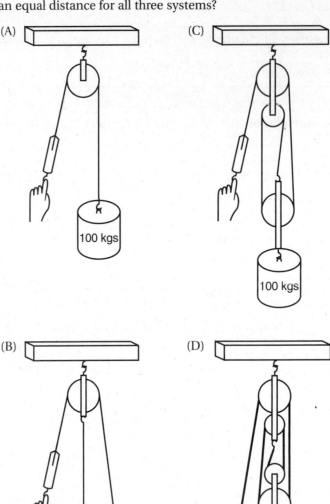

(A)

100 kgs

(C)

100 kgs

(B)

100 kgs

(D)

100 kgs

54. If a belt drive has a drive wheel that is 1/2 the size of the second wheel, how fast will the second wheel turn and how much torque will it have?

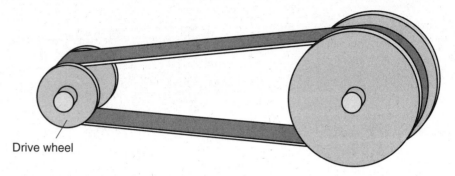

Drive wheel

(A) ¼ the speed, half the torque
(B) ¼ the speed, 4 times the torque
(C) ½ the speed, 2 times the torque
(D) ⅓ the speed, 4 times the torque

55. For the hour hand on this clock to be pointed at the number 8, how many degrees would it have to move?

(A) 360 degrees
(B) 90 degrees
(C) 180 degrees
(D) 30 degrees

56. If gear F is turning clockwise, which gears will turn in the same direction?

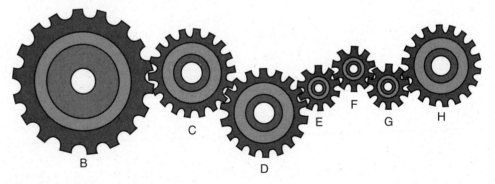

(A) C, D, H
(B) B, D, H
(C) C, E, H
(D) B, D, C, G

57. In which picture will it be easiest for the firefighter to move the load?

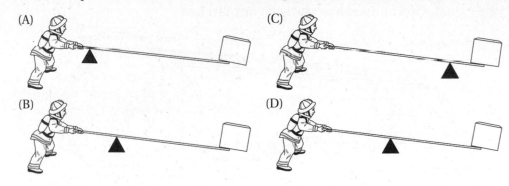

(A)

(C)

(B)

(D)

Section 7: Spatial Sense

> **DIRECTIONS:** Base your answers to Questions 58 through 67 on the illustrations provided and your ability to judge spatial sense.

58. Which of the following four aerial views matches this house?

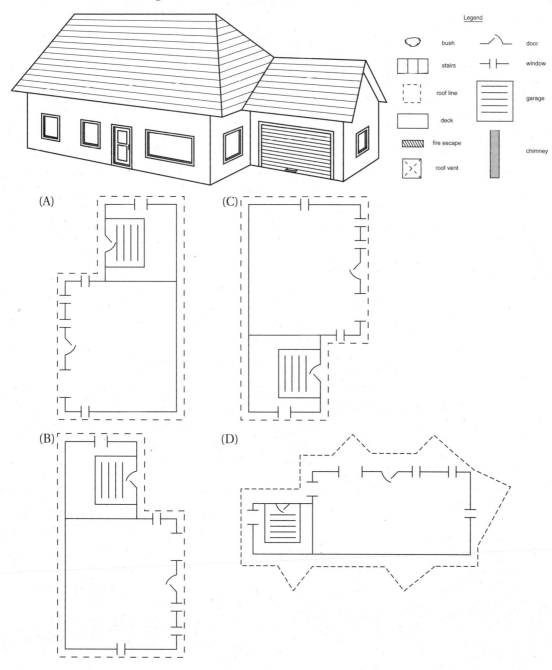

59. Which of the following four aerial views matches this house?

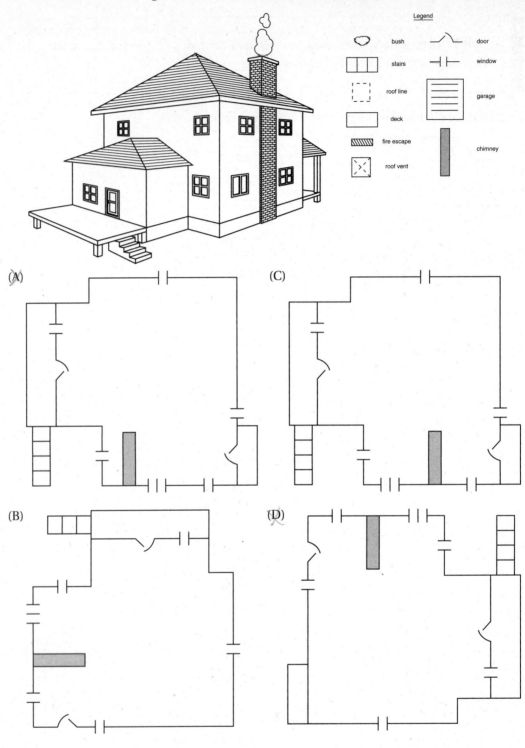

Legend

bush		door	
stairs		window	
roof line		garage	
deck		chimney	
fire escape			
roof vent			

(A)

(C)

(B)

(D)

60. Which of the following four aerial views matches this building?

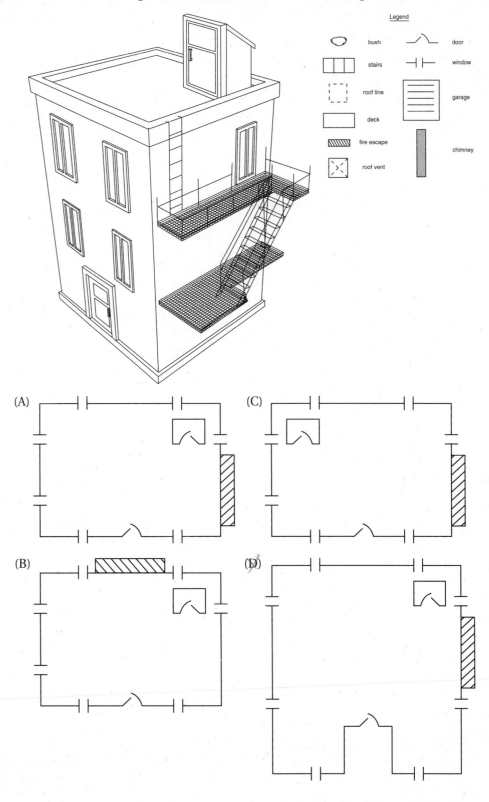

61. Which of the following four aerial views matches this street?

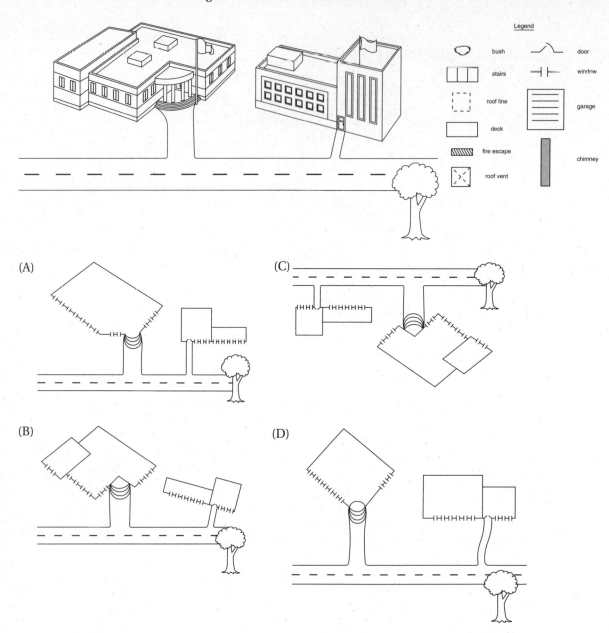

62. Which view shows the perspective of the person in the window of the house?

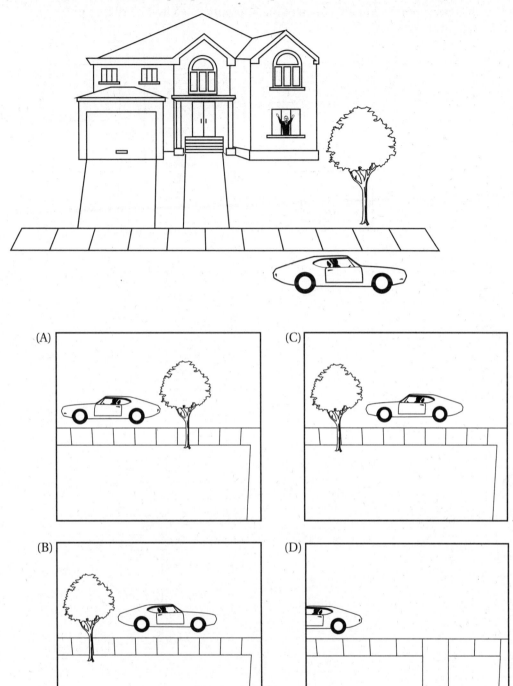

(A)

(C)

(B)

(D)

63. Below are four objects that can be put together based on the numbers on their edges. The objects cannot be flipped. Which of the four options shows the shapes put together correctly?

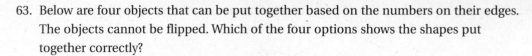
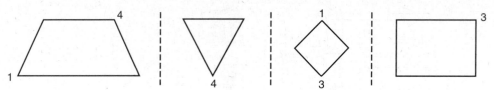

(A)

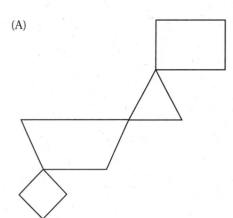

(C)

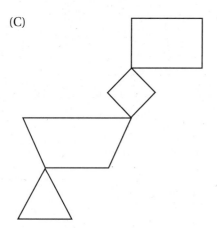

(B)

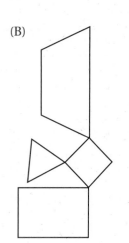

(D)

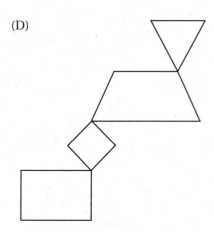

64. Below are four objects that can be put together based on the numbers on their edges. The objects cannot be flipped. Which of the four options shows the shapes put together correctly?

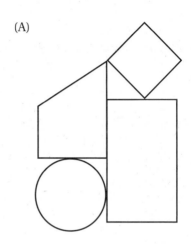 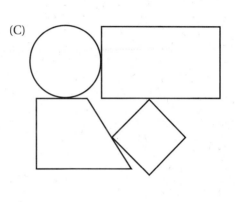

(A)

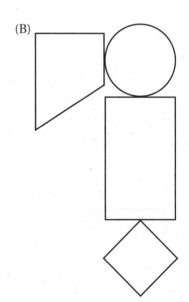

(C)

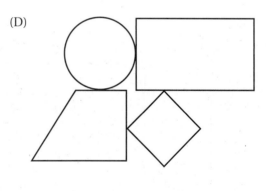

(B)

(D)

65. Below are four objects that can be put together based on the numbers on their edges. The objects cannot be flipped. Which of the four options shows the shapes put together correctly?

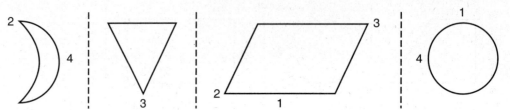

(A)

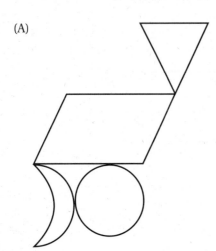

(C)

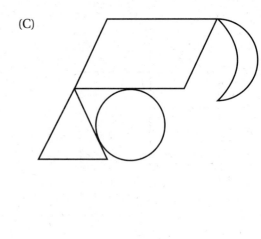

(B)

(D)

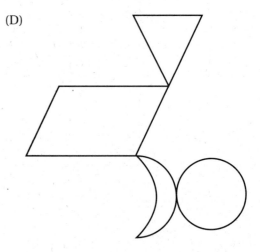

66. Below are four objects that can be put together based on the numbers on their edges. The objects cannot be flipped. Which of the four options shows the shapes put together correctly?

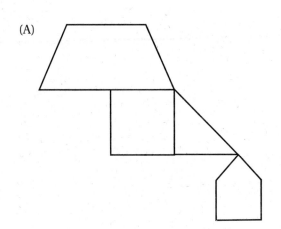
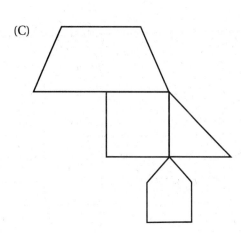

(A)

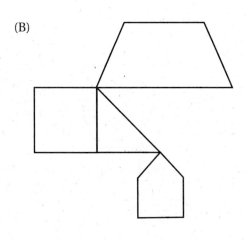

(C)

(B)

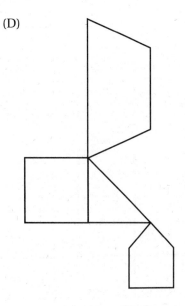

(D)

67. Below are four objects that can be put together based on the numbers on their edges. The objects cannot be flipped. Which of the four options shows the shapes put together correctly?

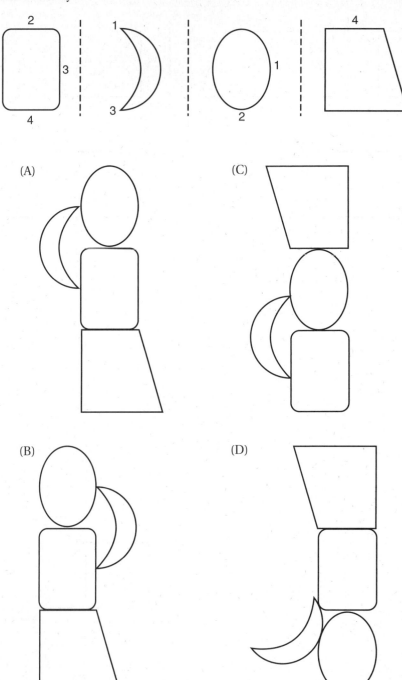

(A)

(B)

(C)

(D)

Section 8: Map Reading

DIRECTIONS: Questions 68 through 75 test your ability to read and interpret maps.

DIRECTIONS: Use the map below to answer Questions 68–72.

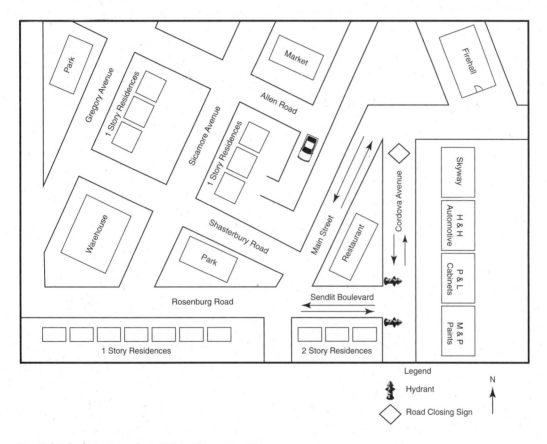

Legend

Hydrant

Road Closing Sign

N

68. Which direction does Main Street run?

   (A) North/South
   (B) East/West
   (C) Northeast/Southwest
   (D) Northwest/Southeast

69. Why can't the fire truck turn right off of Main Street onto Cordova Avenue?

   (A) Construction.
   (B) It's a one way street.
   (C) You can't turn right there.
   (D) The road is closed.

70. What is the shortest route that the fire truck can take to get back to the firehall?

   (A) Left on Allen Road. Left on Gregory Avenue. Left on Shasterbury Road. Left on Main Street.

   (B) Right on Allen Road. Right on Cordova Avenue. Right on Sendlit Boulevard. Right on Main Street.

   (C) Left on Allen Road. Left on Sicamore Avenue. Left on Shasterbury Road. Left on Main Street.

   (D) Left on Allen Road. Left on Sicamore Avenue. Left on Rosenburg Road. Left on Main Street.

71. How many fire hydrants are on the corner of Cordova Avenue and Sendlit Boulevard?

   (A) 1
   (B) 2
   (C) 3
   (D) 4

72. What direction does the fire hall face?

   (A) Northwest
   (B) Southeast
   (C) Southwest
   (D) Northeast

DIRECTIONS: Use the map below to answer Questions 73–75.

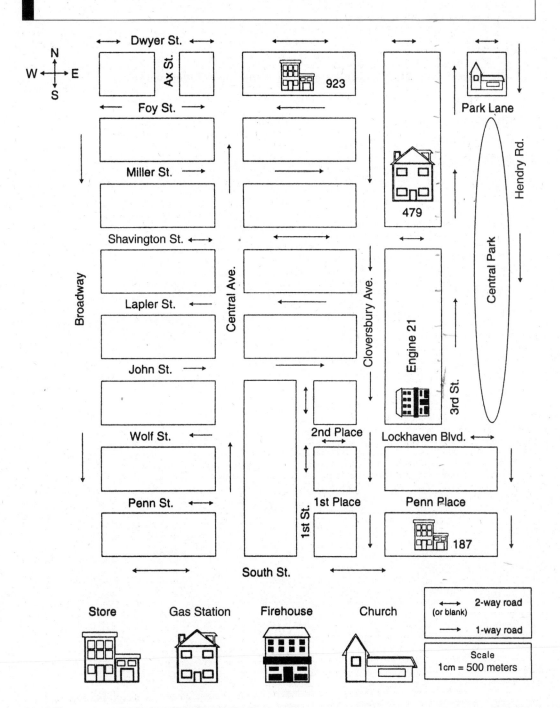

73. What corner is the gas station on?

    (A) Hendry Rd. and Shavington St.

    (B) Hendry Rd. and Cloversbury Ave.

    (C) Cloversbury Ave. and Shavington St.

    (D) Cloversbury Ave. and Lockhaven Blvd.

74. How far is it from the gas station to the fire house?

   (A) 6 km
   (B) 4 km
   (C) 3 km
   (D) 2 km

75. How far is it from the fire house to the fire at the end of Hendry Rd?

   (A) 7.5 km
   (B) 9 km
   (C) 6.5 km
   (D) 8 km

ANSWER KEY
Test 3

SECTION 1

1. B	**6.** D	**11.** A	**16.** A	**21.** A
2. A	**7.** C	**12.** B	**17.** B	**22.** D
3. A	**8.** C	**13.** C	**18.** D	**23.** C
4. D	**9.** D	**14.** A	**19.** C	**24.** A
5. B	**10.** B	**15.** D	**20.** C	

SECTION 2

25. C	**27.** A	**29.** C	**31.** C	**33.** D
26. B	**28.** B	**30.** D	**32.** D	**34.** D

SECTION 3

35. C	**36.** B	**37.** C	**38.** A	**39.** D

SECTION 4

40. C	**41.** A	**42.** B

SECTION 5

43. B	**45.** D	**47.** C	**49.** A	**51.** B
44. D	**46.** B	**48.** C	**50.** D	

SECTION 6

52. B	**54.** C	**55.** B	**56.** B	**57.** C
53. A				

SECTION 7

58. B	**60.** A	**62.** C	**64.** C	**66.** A
59. C	**61.** B	**63.** D	**65.** A	**67.** B

SECTION 8

68. C	**70.** C	**72.** A	**74.** C	**75.** D
69. D	**71.** B	**73.** C		

1. **(B)** I and II. Option III is incorrect because the fire was in an 18-story building. All of the information needed to answer the question is found in the first two sentences: "On July 16 at 11:37 A.M., a cooking fire originating on the seventh floor of an 18-story residential building killed 3 people, and injured 14 civilians and two firefighters. Firefighters removed approximately 8 people using two tower trucks . . ."

2. **(A)** A fire that happened on July 16. Answer (A) is the best option. Answer (B) is incorrect because no actual procedures are described. Answer (C) is incorrect because this passage describes a fire. Answer (D) is incorrect because the date is incorrect (according to the passage, the fire described happened on July 16, not July 18).

3. **(A)** I only. Only the first statement is true. This question can be answered using two pieces of information in the passage. It is known that three people died in the fire from the first sentence ("On July 16 at 11:37 A.M., a cooking fire originating on the seventh floor of an 18-story residential building killed 3 people . . ."). That information is combined with the information in the 8th sentence: "Two of the people who died were overcome by smoke and fire gases in the hallway as they tried to make their way to an exit." The conclusion is that most (2/3) of the victims that died in the hallway perished because they couldn't reach the exit. Options II and III are incorrect.

4. **(D)** Cooking oil. This answer is found in the 4th sentence: "A person using large amounts of cooking oil started the fire when he knocked his wok over . . ."

5. **(B)** I and II. Options I and II are true because they are mentioned in the passage: "Light scatter type fire detectors are designed to signal an alarm if there is a fault in the system . . ." and "When smoke or other suspended particles enter a light scatter type fire detector they cause the light to 'scatter' and reach the photoelectric cell to signal an alarm." Option III is incorrect because it is not mentioned in the passage.

6. **(D)** An opaque barrier. This answer can be found by rearranging the information in the third sentence of the passage: "In a normal clean air state the light inside a light scatter type fire detector is prevented from reaching the photoelectric cell (which would signal an alarm) by an opaque barrier."

7. (C) I, II, and III. To answer this question correctly requires a careful reading of the passage. Routine response is also called Code 1. This along with the rest of the information required to answer the question is learned from the first sentence: "When a fire truck responds to a call it will usually respond in one of two ways: routine (sometimes referred to as Code 1) or Code 3." For this type of question, it is important to read the entire passage and be sure another mode of response is not mentioned.

8. (C) Code 3. Some problem solving is required to answer this question. It is clear that fire trucks will respond Code 3 to more urgent calls: "A fire truck will respond Code 3 to calls when the nature of the call is more urgent. For example, a fire truck will respond Code 3 to a structure fire or technical rescue. When responding Code 3, a fire truck will activate its emergency lights and siren and will bypass traffic and traffic lights . . ." A motor vehicle accident with trapped victims is an urgent call. This is common sense. Based on both pieces of information, we know that a Code 3 response is the best option.

9. (D) Safety. None of the other options are mentioned in the passage. The last two sentences in the passage contain the information needed to answer the question correctly: "The main reason fire trucks don't always respond to calls Code 3 is for safety. Responding to calls Code 3 is much more dangerous than responding routine."

10. (B) Rank 3. A Rank 3 fire most closely matches the description in the question. "Rank 3—Moderately vigourous surface fire. This is a vigorous surface fire with a moderate rate of spread. This fire will have an organized front and may display 'candling' along its perimeter or within the fire."

11. (A) Rank 1. This information is found under the Rank 1 heading. "Rank 1—Smoldering ground or creeping surface fire. This is a smoldering ground fire that burns in the ground fuel layer. These fires have no open flame and produce white smoke."

12. (B) II only. This answer can be found by closely reading the passage and determining that only option II is contained under the Rank 5 heading. "Rank 5—Extremely vigourous surface fire or active crown fire. This type of fire has an organized crown fire front, moderate to long-range spotting and independent spot fire growth. These fires produce black or copper smoke."

13. (C) The fire intensity rank system. This information is found in the heading for the passage. "There are six ranks of wildfires in the fire intensity rank system."

14. (A) The space under the ventilated fire and later where the backdraft takes place. The test taker should be able to come to this conclusion by reading the entire passage, particularly the third and fourth sentences, "Oxygen levels in the compartment will be low and the fire will usually be smoldering. When oxygen is introduced to the compartment the energy release will be very rapid and will last a short time."

15. (D) Backdraft. This is explained throughout the entire passage.

16. (A) Some of firefighter Pownazie and firefighter Bonfacico's station duties immediately after a structure fire. The most important word in the question is "overall." The correct answer is what the firefighters were doing in general or on the whole.

17. (B) II and III. We know these are correct because both answers are mentioned in the passage. ". . . the next step is to hang the hose in the tower so it can dry out properly . . ." and "firefighter Bonfacico ties the hose with a clove hitch and sends it up the tower using a pulley system two to three lengths at a time." We know that answer I is incorrect because firefighter Bonfacico ties the hose (see previous quote), not firefighter Pownazie (he is up the tower: "Firefighter Pownazie climbs to the top of the tower to hang the hose.")

18. (D) A and C. "The firefighters roll out all the hose in the back parking lot and scrub both sides of the hose down with soap and a turks head. After they have finished rinsing the hose off with water . . ."

19. (C) Viable, livable, safe. This is the best option. The other options are incorrect. Option B is known to be definitely incorrect because smoke removal has already been mentioned in the sentence that uses the word tenable. "Sometimes firefighters will use positive pressure ventilation or vertical ventilation to draw smoke from the stair shafts and make them more tenable."

20. (C) Maintaining a tenable environment in stair shafts during a high-rise fire. This is what the passage describes overall. None of the other options are mentioned in that context.

21. (A) Buoyant. This information is found in the fourth sentence: ".. . . as smoke moves up the stair shaft and away from the fire it cools and will become less buoyant . . ." The other answers also do not fit grammatically.

22. (D) They may create a negative pressure behind them as they move towards the fire. This answer can be found in the last two sentences of the passage. "Firefighters must also be careful when entering the fire floor from a stair shaft because the stair shaft may create a negative pressure behind them as they move towards the fire. This can cause smoke and flames to be drawn towards the firefighters."

23. (C) 21%. The answer can be found by reading the second sentence of the paragraph. "The normal oxygen content in the air is 21%."

24. (A) Using monitoring devices. This answer is found in the fourth sentence of the passage, "Oxygen deficient atmospheres cannot be easily detected without monitoring devices." The information contained in option B is in the passage, but it does not answer the question. Therefore option B is incorrect.

Section 2

25. (C) III and IV. Both ammonia and sulphur dioxide are listed as irritants under the effects column of the table.

26. (B) Carbon monoxide. In the table, carbon monoxide is listed as one of two products of combustion produced by almost all fires.

27. (A) Carbon monoxide. Under the dose/time to be lethal/dangerous column of the table, carbon monoxide is the only product of combustion listed as lethal at 1.3% for several minutes.

28. (B) Respiratory paralysis. This is the only choice of the possible answers that is listed in the table as an effect of hydrogen sulphide.

29. (C) Hydrogen dioxide. This question is asking for a gas NOT listed in the table. Hydrogen dioxide is not listed in the table.

30. (D) Sulphur dioxide. According to the "Produced by burning" section of the table, this is the only gas that is produced by burning "organics that contain sulphur."

31. (C) 6. The table lists 6 trucks. To answer the question, count the trucks listed in the Truck ID column.

32. (D) Ladder 11. Ladder 11 carries 3 firefighters. The other trucks carry 4 or 5 firefighters.

33. (D) Ladder 11. Ladder 11 has 500 ft. of 2.5 inch hose and 500 ft. of 5 inch hose.

34. (D) Both A and C. The table indicates in the 2.5 inch column that both engines and Quints carry 1,000 ft. of 2.5 inch hose.

Section 3

35. (C) A dry chemical extinguisher. Only a dry chemical extinguisher and an AFFF extinguisher are available (a halon extinguisher is not available to the firefighter). According to the passage, AFFF extinguishers are not for Class C fires. Therefore, a dry chemical extinguisher is the best choice.

36. (B) AFFF. This is the best answer. This is the only option that would be appropriate. Halon uses a gas extinguishing agent. Stored pressure can be used only to put out Class A fires.

37. (C) 5. To find out how many medical calls Firefighter Roberts responded to, you have to find out how many medical calls Firefighter Jones and Firefighter Smith responded to ("Firefighter Roberts responded to more medical calls than Firefighter Jones but less than Firefighter Smith."). Firefighter Jones responded to 4 medical calls ("Firefighter Jones responded to four medical calls"). Firefighter Smith responded to 6 medical calls (this is known because Firefighter Smith responded to "three more medical calls than Firefighter Johnson" (who responded to three medical calls). Now we know that Firefighter Roberts went to 5 medical calls because the only number more than 4 but less than 6 is 5.

38. (A) 1. This is known because Firefighter Smith responded to one less structure fire than FF Johnson ("Firefighter Smith responded to three more medical calls than Firefighter Johnson and one less structure fire."). Firefighter Johnson responded to 2 structure fires (". . . Firefighter Johnson responded to three medical calls and two structure fires."). Therefore, Firefighter Smith responded to 1 structure fire (2 − 1 = 1).

39. (D) $9. Firefighter Blarry owes Firefighter Benneton $4 from the day before and $5 from the current day. The total is $9.

Section 4

40. (C) 6/8. The gauge is 6/8 of the way towards full.

41. (A) 1,400. The gauge reads closest to 1,400 PSI.

42. (B) 2. This voltmeter reads 12 volts. 12 is 2 more than 10 (12 − 10 = 2).

Section 5

43. (B) 5,700 ft. This is an addition question. 3,000 + 1,500 + 1,200 = 5,700

44. (D) 450 ft. This is an addition and multiplication question.

Firefighter 1 pulled 150 ft.

Firefighter 2 pulled 300 ft. This is the multiplication portion. This firefighter removed twice as much hose as firefighter 1.

$150 \times 2 = 300$

Therefore 450 ft of hose was removed in total. 150 + 300 = 450.

45. (D) About 2 minutes. If you are flowing water at 125 gpm (gallons per minute), after 2 minutes you will have used 250 gallons. Your tank contains 250 gallons. The best answer is about 2 minutes.

46. (B) About 188 metres. To find the answer to this question, you need to understand how the circumference of a circle is found. Pi times diameter = circumference. $3.14 \times 60 = 188.4$. Therefore, the distance around the container (circumference) is about 188 metres.

47. (C) 39. This is an addition and division question. First add 950 to 1,000 (950 + 1,000 = 1,950). To find the correct answer, divide 1,950 (total hose) by 50 (length of hose). $1,950 \div 50 = 39$. To learn more about addition, division, and order of operations, see Chapter 2.

48. (C) 7 (with half a bucket remaining). This is an adding fractions question. Five buckets are full (1/1 + 1/1 + 1/1 + 1/1 = 1/1). Two buckets are half full (1/2 + 1/2). Two buckets are three quarters full (3/4 + 3/4). To answer the question make the denominator the same and add up the fractions.

1/1 + 1/1 + 1/1 + 1/1 + 1/1 + 1/2 + 1/2 + 3/4 + 3/4 =
4/4 + 4/4 + 4/4 + 4/4 + 4/4 + 2/4 + 2/4 + 3/4 + 3/4 = 30/4

Simplify the fraction: 7½.

49. (A) 50,240 square inches. To solve this problem, you need to find the volume of the drum (cylinder) and then divide by 2 (because the drum is half full). First, determine the area of the circle, then multiply it by the height of the cylinder. The volume of a cylinder is found by the formula (3.14 (pi)) × (radius sq.) × height.

The easiest way to do this is to first convert the diameter (width of drum) to a radius by dividing by 2:

40 divided by 2 = 20

Next find the area of the top of the drum (circle).

3.14 (20 × 20 = 400)
3.14 × 400 = 1,256

Now multiply the area of the circle (top of the drum) by the height of the drum.

1,256 × 80 = 100,480

Now divide by 2 (the drum is half full) and you will have your answer:

100,480 divided by 2 = 50,240

50. (D) 4 minutes. This question can be solved by recognizing that 16:60 is the same ratio as 4:15. See the ratio and proportions section of Chapter 2 for more information regarding this type of question.

51. (B) 55.8%. To find the answer to this question, first recognize that a fraction is involved (134/240). To find the percentage, divide the top number by the bottom number and then multiply by 100. 134 ÷ 240 = .558. .558 × 100 = 55.8. Finally add the % sign. To check your answer, multiply .558 × 240.

Section 6

52. (B) Counterclockwise. When two gears meet, they turn in opposite directions.

53. (A) This load will move the most distance because this system has the least mechanical advantage. The load shown in diagram A will move 4 times as far as the load shown in diagram D. See the Pulleys section of Chapter 2 for more information on mechanical advantage.

54. (C) ½ the speed, 2 times the torque. This answer has to do with gear ratio and belt drives. Refer to the Gears and Belt Drive sections of Chapter 2 for further explanation.

55. (B) 90 degrees.

56. (B) B, D, H. When two gears meet, they turn in opposite directions. Internal gears turn in the same direction.

57. (C) C. This is a leverage question. The closer the fulcrum is to the weight, the easier it will be to lift the weight. Information regarding levers is contained in Chapter 2.

Section 7

58. (B) The other views are not of the same house. Option A shows the garage in the wrong place. Option C is a mirror image. Option D shows the wrong roof line.

59. (C) The other views are incorrect. Option A shows the chimney in the wrong spot. Option B shows an incorrect stair length and the back deck is missing. Option D shows the back deck in the wrong spot.

60. (A) The other views are incorrect. Option B shows the fire escape in the wrong place. Option C shows the roof exit in the wrong place. Option D is the wrong shape and does not match the building.

61. (B) This matches correctly. The other options are incorrect. Options A and D show the wrong building shapes. Option C shows the buildings on the wrong side of the street.

62. (C) This is the correct answer. Option A shows a tree in the wrong place. Option B shows the car in the street facing the wrong direction. Option D shows the wrong perspective (from the wrong window).

63. (D) This option shows the shapes in the correct orientation.

64. (C) This option shows the shapes in the correct orientation.

65. (A) This option shows the shapes in the correct orientation.

66. (A) This option shows the shapes in the correct orientation.

67. (B) This option shows the shapes in the correct orientation.

Section 8

68. (C) Northeast / Southwest. This is known because the direction of north is provided in the bottom right corner of the map.

69. (D) The road is closed. This is known because of the road closing sign.

70. (C) Left on Allen Road. Left on Sicamore Avenue. Left on Shasterbury Road. Left on Main Street. This is the shortest distance.

71. (B) 2.

72. (A) Northwest.

73. (C) Cloversbury Ave and Shavington St.

74. (C) 3 km. This is based on the scale on the map. 1 cm = 500 metres. You can use a scrap piece of paper or your pencil like a ruler (draw the measurements from the scale onto the "ruler") to measure the 6 cm between the gas station and the fire house, if it helps. It's important to know that there are 1,000 metres in a kilometre. 6 cm = 3,000 metres = 3 km.

75. (D) 8 km. This is based on the scale on the map. 1 cm = 500 metres. You can use a scrap piece of paper or even your pencil like a ruler (draw the measurements from the scale onto the "ruler") to measure the 6 cm between the gas station and the fire house, if it helps; just turn the "ruler" 90 degrees at the corner. It's important to know that there are 1,000 metres in a kilometre. 16 cm = 8,000 metres = 8 km.

ANSWER SHEET
Test 4

SECTION 1

1. Ⓐ Ⓑ Ⓒ Ⓓ   6. Ⓐ Ⓑ Ⓒ Ⓓ   11. Ⓐ Ⓑ Ⓒ Ⓓ   16. Ⓐ Ⓑ Ⓒ Ⓓ
2. Ⓐ Ⓑ Ⓒ Ⓓ   7. Ⓐ Ⓑ Ⓒ Ⓓ   12. Ⓐ Ⓑ Ⓒ Ⓓ   17. Ⓐ Ⓑ Ⓒ Ⓓ
3. Ⓐ Ⓑ Ⓒ Ⓓ   8. Ⓐ Ⓑ Ⓒ Ⓓ   13. Ⓐ Ⓑ Ⓒ Ⓓ   18. Ⓐ Ⓑ Ⓒ Ⓓ
4. Ⓐ Ⓑ Ⓒ Ⓓ   9. Ⓐ Ⓑ Ⓒ Ⓓ   14. Ⓐ Ⓑ Ⓒ Ⓓ   19. Ⓐ Ⓑ Ⓒ Ⓓ
5. Ⓐ Ⓑ Ⓒ Ⓓ   10. Ⓐ Ⓑ Ⓒ Ⓓ   15. Ⓐ Ⓑ Ⓒ Ⓓ   20. Ⓐ Ⓑ Ⓒ Ⓓ

SECTION 2

21. Ⓐ Ⓑ Ⓒ Ⓓ   30. Ⓐ Ⓑ Ⓒ Ⓓ   39. Ⓐ Ⓑ Ⓒ Ⓓ   48. Ⓐ Ⓑ Ⓒ Ⓓ
22. Ⓐ Ⓑ Ⓒ Ⓓ   31. Ⓐ Ⓑ Ⓒ Ⓓ   40. Ⓐ Ⓑ Ⓒ Ⓓ   49. Ⓐ Ⓑ Ⓒ Ⓓ
23. Ⓐ Ⓑ Ⓒ Ⓓ   32. Ⓐ Ⓑ Ⓒ Ⓓ   41. Ⓐ Ⓑ Ⓒ Ⓓ   50. Ⓐ Ⓑ Ⓒ Ⓓ
24. Ⓐ Ⓑ Ⓒ Ⓓ   33. Ⓐ Ⓑ Ⓒ Ⓓ   42. Ⓐ Ⓑ Ⓒ Ⓓ   51. Ⓐ Ⓑ Ⓒ Ⓓ
25. Ⓐ Ⓑ Ⓒ Ⓓ   34. Ⓐ Ⓑ Ⓒ Ⓓ   43. Ⓐ Ⓑ Ⓒ Ⓓ   52. Ⓐ Ⓑ Ⓒ Ⓓ
26. Ⓐ Ⓑ Ⓒ Ⓓ   35. Ⓐ Ⓑ Ⓒ Ⓓ   44. Ⓐ Ⓑ Ⓒ Ⓓ   53. Ⓐ Ⓑ Ⓒ Ⓓ
27. Ⓐ Ⓑ Ⓒ Ⓓ   36. Ⓐ Ⓑ Ⓒ Ⓓ   45. Ⓐ Ⓑ Ⓒ Ⓓ   54. Ⓐ Ⓑ Ⓒ Ⓓ
28. Ⓐ Ⓑ Ⓒ Ⓓ   37. Ⓐ Ⓑ Ⓒ Ⓓ   46. Ⓐ Ⓑ Ⓒ Ⓓ   55. Ⓐ Ⓑ Ⓒ Ⓓ
29. Ⓐ Ⓑ Ⓒ Ⓓ   38. Ⓐ Ⓑ Ⓒ Ⓓ   47. Ⓐ Ⓑ Ⓒ Ⓓ

SECTION 3

56. Ⓐ Ⓑ Ⓒ Ⓓ   58. Ⓐ Ⓑ Ⓒ Ⓓ   59. Ⓐ Ⓑ Ⓒ Ⓓ   60. Ⓐ Ⓑ Ⓒ Ⓓ
57. Ⓐ Ⓑ Ⓒ Ⓓ

General Firefighter Test 1
Section 1: Reading Comprehension

DIRECTIONS: The following twenty questions test your ability to read and interpret information from a passage. Fill in the corresponding bubble on the answer sheet.

DIRECTIONS: Questions 1–7 are based on the following passage.

Firefighter Ferguson is a member of Engine 4 and is attending a structure fire at 3:45 A.M. in a two story wood frame house at 1452 Glendale Dr. Other units attending the fire are Engine 6, Engine 9, Quint 5, Tower 1, and a Command Vehicle. Each engine and Quint has four firefighters (including officers) on it. The ladder has a lieutenant and two firefighters. The command vehicle is on scene with just the officer in Command. Firefighter Ferguson is ordered to enter the fire and complete a primary search with firefighter Johnson. Firefighter Ferguson enters the house with firefighter Johnson through the front door on the B side of the building and starts a right hand search. As firefighter Ferguson moves through what appears to be the living room, he looks under the thermal layer and can see the seat of the fire just past the bottom of a staircase. The fire appears to be in the kitchen in the C/D corner of the house. The crew from engine 9 is attacking the fire. Firefighter Ferguson continues his search into a room with several toys on the floor and a single bed against the wall. As he is searching the room, he hears engine 9 inform command over the radio that the fire is extinguished. They will be performing hydraulic ventilation out of the C side of the building and checking for fire extension. When firefighter Ferguson reaches the bed, he finds an unconscious child wearing red pajamas under the bed. As firefighter Ferguson pulls the child out from under the bed, his partner radios command to inform them that they have found a victim and are in the process of removing him from the building. Firefighter Johnson leads the way while firefighter Ferguson follows with the victim. Firefighter Ferguson and firefighter Johnson remove the victim from the house using the same door they came in from. As firefighter Ferguson carries the victim into the front yard, firefighters from Quint 5 take the victim from him and begin a medical assessment.

1. What type of ventilation does engine 9 use in the kitchen after the fire is extinguished?

   (A) vertical ventilation
   (B) hydraulic ventilation
   (C) horizontal ventilation
   (D) positive pressure ventilation

2. What floor did firefighter Ferguson find the victim on?

   (A) first floor
   (B) second floor
   (C) third floor
   (D) unknown

3. Most likely, what type of room did firefighter Ferguson find the victim in?

   (A) kitchen
   (B) bathroom
   (C) living room
   (D) bedroom

4. How many firefighters (including chiefs and officers) are likely to be at this structure fire?

   (A) 20
   (B) 19
   (C) 21
   (D) 14

5. When did engine 9 inform command that the fire was extinguished?

   (A) Before firefighter Ferguson found the victim
   (B) After firefighter Ferguson found the victim
   (C) After the fire
   (D) They didn't

6. What corner of the house does engine 9 attack the fire in?

   (A) A/B
   (B) B/C
   (C) C/D
   (D) D/A

7. How many firefighters are on Quint 5?

   (A) 1
   (B) 5
   (C) 3
   (D) 4

DIRECTIONS: Questions 8–13 are based on the following passage:

The Incident Command System

The Incident Command System is a system designed for successful management of resources at emergency scenes. Effective and efficient organization is essential for success at an emergency scene. The ICS consists of standard operating procedures for managing personnel, equipment, and communications.

The California Department of Forestry and Fire Protection and several other agencies throughout California and the United States designed the Incident Command System in the early 1970s. The system was put together in response to several large fires that destroyed wild land and structures in southern California. The Incident Command System was designed to allow for a clear command system that allowed multiple agencies to work towards a common goal. With a clear command system, various agencies could arrive at an emergency scene and integrate themselves without confusion.

The Incident Command System starts being used from the time the emergency incident starts and finishes at the time when the need for on scene operations and management no longer exists. The organization of the Incident Command System can be adjusted based on the progression of the incident. Because of this, the ICS can be used for any type or size of emergency incident.

8. The Incident Command System is a system designed for successful management of resources at _____ scenes.

    (A) auto extrication
    (B) medical
    (C) social
    (D) emergency

9. The ICS consists of standard operating procedures for managing personnel, _____, and communications.

    (A) public
    (B) firefighters
    (C) equipment
    (D) water flow

10. When was the Incident Command System designed?

    (A) The early 1970s
    (B) The early 1990s
    (C) The late 1980s
    (D) 2005

11. Why was the Incident Command System designed?

    (A) To make it clear who is in charge.
    (B) As part of a project at UCLA
    (C) To allow for a clear command system that allows multiple agencies to work towards a common goal.
    (D) By the California Department of Forestry and Fire Protection and several other agencies throughout California and the United States.

12. When does the ICS system stop being used at an emergency scene?

    (A) When the need for on scene operations and management no longer exists.
    (B) When all victims are recovered.
    (C) When the second due company arrives.
    (D) When the fire is struck.

13. What size emergency incident can the Incident Command System be used for?

    (A) Large scale emergency incidents only.
    (B) Only small emergency incidents.
    (C) Any size of emergency incident.
    (D) The Incident Command System is used only for small medical incidents.

When entering a duty trade, a personnel movement form (PMF) must be filled out and emailed to your officer. Firefighters should also write their duty trade in the day book and print off a copy of the PMF and put it in the duty trade binder in the hall they are stationed at. Your officer will forward the PMF to the captain at #1 hall who will enter the information into Telestaff. When entering a PMF, firefighters must find coverage with a matching skill code and give at least 6 days notice. If a firefighter has an emergency and would like to enter a duty trade with less than 6 days notice, he or she can contact the duty chief and ask permission.

14. When entering a duty trade, what form must be filled out?

(A) a personal movement form
(B) a duty trade form
(C) a shift swap form
(D) the day book

15. Who enters the PMF in Telestaff?

(A) the duty chief
(B) the firefighter
(C) the captain at hall #1
(D) the senior firefighter on shift

16. How many days notice should a firefighter give when entering a PMF?

(A) 9
(B) 6
(C) 3
(D) It doesn't matter.

17. Who can authorize a duty trade with less than 6 days notice?

(A) the station officer
(B) the #1 hall captain
(C) the duty chief
(D) the senior firefighter on shift

Natural anchors are often used during technical rescues. Trees are frequently used as anchors. For a tree to be a viable natural anchor, several conditions must be met. First, it is important that the tree is alive. A dead tree is very unpredictable and should not be used. Thoroughly inspect the tree before use. Make sure it is green and in good condition all the way to the top. Secondly, if a tree is used as an anchor, it must be big enough and provide a deep root system. Some large trees may have very shallow root systems. If you are not sure about a species, do not use it. Do not use a tree that is suspect in any way.

18. What is an example of a natural anchor?

 (A) a tree
 (B) a steel beam
 (C) an eye bolt
 (D) a concrete pillar

19. What is an example of a tree that should not be used as an anchor?

 (A) If it is dead.
 (B) If it is very large.
 (C) If it has a deep root system.
 (D) If the tree looks suspect.

20. According to the passage, which one of the following statements is true?

 (A) Small trees are good anchors.
 (B) Natural anchors are never used during technical rescues.
 (C) Large trees can have shallow root systems.
 (D) Even if a tree is suspect, it can still be used as an anchor.

Section 2: Mathematics

DIRECTIONS: Answer Questions 21 through 55 by choosing the best answer for each question and filling in the corresponding bubble on the answer sheet.

21. Rescue 4 carries 300 total feet of rope. Engine 2 carries 250 total feet of rope. Engine 4 carries a total of 250 ft. of rope. How much rope do all three trucks carry combined?

 (A) 700 ft.
 (B) 800 ft.
 (C) 750 ft.
 (D) 850 ft.

22. Seven fire trucks carry 300 ft. of hose each. Combined they carry 2,100 ft. of hose. If one truck is removed, how much hose remains?

 (A) 2,100 ft.
 (B) 1,800 ft.
 (C) 1,900 ft.
 (D) 2,000 ft.

23. Station 5 had 191 fires last year. Station 1 had three times as many fires as Station 5. How many fires did Station 1 have?

 (A) 463
 (B) 563
 (C) 573
 (D) 574

24. There are 14 fire stations in your municipality. Each station is staffed with 4 firefighters per shift with the exception of Station 1, which has 7 firefighters. How many firefighters work per shift?

    (A) 56
    (B) 53
    (C) 59
    (D) 21

25. During a trail rescue, 6 firefighters are carrying a rescue basket with one patient weighing 210 pounds. Approximately how much weight is each firefighter carrying?

    (A) 29 pounds
    (B) 35 pounds
    (C) 30 pounds
    (D) 34 pounds

26. Engine 6 uses 5/8 of a full tank at a car fire. How full is the tank now?

    (A) 1/2 full
    (B) 3/8 full
    (C) 2/8 full
    (D) 5/16 full

27. Engine 7 is using a water tower to pump from. For every one foot of elevation, water pressure exerts .434 pounds per square inch. The storage tank is 97 feet above the truck. How much pressure will the water exert when it enters the truck?

    (A) About 42 pounds per square inch
    (B) About 54 pounds per square inch
    (C) About 47 pounds per square inch
    (D) About 32 pounds per square inch

28. A fire truck has 37/100 of its water left. What percentage of water is left?

    (A) 27%
    (B) 37%
    (C) 74%
    (D) 32%

29. 19 of the 326 firefighters that work in the municipality are injured. About what percentage of firefighters are injured?

    (A) 85%
    (B) 8%
    (C) 6%
    (D) 2%

10. (A) The early 1970s. This answer is found in the second paragraph: "The California Department of Forestry and Fire Protection and several other agencies throughout California and the United States designed the Incident Command System in the early 1970s."

11. (C) To allow for a clear command system that allowed multiple agencies to work towards a common goal. This answer is found in the second paragraph: "The Incident Command System was designed to allow for a clear command system that allowed multiple agencies to work towards a common goal." Notice that the correct answer provides more specific information. Answer (D) does not fit grammatically with the question.

12. (A) When the need for on scene operations and management no longer exists. The answer to this question is found in the third paragraph: "The Incident Command System starts being used from the time the emergency incident starts and finishes at the time when the need for on scene operations and management no longer exists."

13. (C) Any size of emergency incident. The answer to this question is found in the third paragraph: ". . . the ICS can be used for any type or size of emergency incident."

14. (A) A personnel movement form. This information is found in the first sentence of the passage: "When entering a duty trade a personnel movement form (PMF) must be filled out and emailed to your officer."

15. (C) The captain at hall #1. This information is contained in the passage: "Your officer will forward the PMF to the captain at #1 hall who will enter the information into Telestaff."

16. (B) 6. The information required to answer this question is contained in the passage: "When entering a PMF firefighters must find coverage with a matching skill code and give at least 6 days notice."

17. (C) The duty chief. The information required to answer this question is contained in the passage: "If a firefighter has an emergency and would like to enter a duty trade with less than 6 days notice, they can contact the duty chief and ask permission."

18. (A) A tree. The passage makes it clear that a tree is considered a natural anchor. Also, the other three options are not natural.

19. (A) If it is dead. This is confirmed by the fifth sentence of the passage: "A dead tree is very unpredictable and should not be used."

20. (C) Large trees can have shallow root systems. This answer is found in the ninth sentence of the passage: "Some large trees may have very shallow root systems."

Section 2

21. (B) 800 ft. This is an addition question. Use column addition to find the correct answer. Don't forget to put the decimal in the correct place when you are adding. See the addition section of Chapter 2 for more information.

$300 + 250 + 250 = 800$

22. (B) 1800 ft. This is a subtraction question. To find the answer, subtract the truck that is removed from the total. Remember to use subtraction with regrouping.

$2{,}100 - 300 = 1{,}800$.

23. (C) 573. This is a multiplication question. To find the answer, multiply the number of fires Station 5 had by 3.

This is how the answer was calculated:

$$\begin{array}{r} 2 \\ 191 \\ \times\ 3 \\ \hline 573 \end{array}$$

24. (C) 59. This question involves addition, subtraction, and multiplication. The easiest way to answer this question is to first multiply the 14 stations by 4 firefighters each. $14 \times 4 = 56$. Next, find out how many extra firefighters are at station 1. $7 - 4 = 3$. Finally, add those extra firefighters to the total. $56 + 3 = 59$. You could also find the answer to this question by writing down the numbers at each station and adding them all up.

25. (B) 35 pounds. This is a division question. To find the answer, divide 210 pounds by 6 firefighters. $210 \div 6 = 35$.

26. (B) 3/8 full. This question asks you to subtract fractions. To find the answer, subtract 5/8 of a tank from a full tank (1/1).

Here is how the answer is calculated:

$1/1 - 5/8 =$
$8/8 - 5/8 = 3/8$

27. (A) About 42 pounds per square inch. This question is a multiplication question. To find the answer, multiply the height by the pressure exerted (97 × .434). If you want, add the decimal after. .434 × 97 = 42.1. 42 is the best answer.

28. (B) 37%. This question asks for a percentage. To find the answer, first realize that you have a fraction (37/100). The next step is to simply divide the top number by the bottom number, then multiply by 100.

Here is how the answer is calculated:

37 ÷ 100 = .37
.37 × 100 = 37 (just add the %)

29. (C) 6%. This question asks for a percentage. To find the answer, first realize that you have a fraction (19/326). The next step is to simply divide the top number by the bottom number, then multiply by 100.

Here is how the answer is calculated:

19 ÷ 326 = .058
.058 × 100 = 5.8 (just add the %).

Just round up 5.8% to 6% and you know that *about* 6% of the firefighters are injured.

30. (D) Just over 3 minutes. If you are flowing water at 95 gpm (gallons per minute), after three minutes you will have used 285 gallons and 15 gallons remaining (3 × 95 = 285). The best answer is just over 3 minutes.

31. (B) 1,800. To solve this problem, you need to find the area of the floor shown and then multiply by 2 (the question asks for the total area of the house, indicating two floors).

Area = length × width.
Length = 45
Width = 20
45 × 20 = 900
900 × 2 = 1,800

ANSWERS EXPLAINED

32. (B) 27.5%. This question asks for a fraction to be converted to a percentage. Eight firefighters are rope rescue technicians out of 29 total. 8/29. To convert the fraction to a percentage, divide 8 by 29 and then multiply by 100.

Here is how the answer is calculated:

$8 \div 29 = .2758$
$.2758 \times 100 = 27.58$

27.5% is the best answer.

---

33. (B) 19. This question asks for a number to be found based on a percentage. The easiest way to answer this question is to convert 2% to a decimal ($\div$ 100). $2 \div 100 = .02$. Now multiply 950 (total firefighters) by .02. $950 \times .02 = 19$. If you want to check your answer, divide 19 by 950.

---

34. (B) 6.8 minutes. The ratio in this question is 70 kilometres in 8 minutes. $70:8$. To find the answer, use algebra and cross multiply. You can check your answer by checking to see if the equation is equal. The algebra, ratios, and proportions sections in Chapter 2 provide further explanation.

Here is how the answer is calculated:

$$\frac{70 \text{ kilometres}}{8 \text{ minutes}} = \frac{60 \text{ kilometres}}{x}$$
$70x = 480$
$70x \div 70 = 480 \div 70$
$x = 6.85$

35. (D) 30 gallons. To solve this problem, you need to find the volume of the drum (cylinder) and then divide by 2 (because the drum is half full). First, determine the area of the circle, then multiply it by the height of the cylinder. The volume of a cylinder is found by the formula (3.14 (pi)) × (radius sq.) × height.

The easiest way to do this is to first convert the diameter (width of drum) to a radius by dividing by 2:

20 divided by 2 = 10

Next, find the area of the top of the drum (circle)

3.14 (10 × 10 = 100)
3.14 × 100 = 314

Now, multiply the area of the circle (top of the drum) by the height of the drum.

314 × 50 = 15,700 (an easy way to figure this out in your head is to multiply 314 by 100 and then divide by 2)

Now you must convert your measurement into a measure of volume (gallons)

1 gallon = 277.42 cubic inches

Divide 15,700 by 277.42 to find out how many gallons are in the drum.

15,700 divided by 277.42 = 56.59. (You most likely won't have a calculator during a firefighter exam. To make the answer easier to find, round down to 275 and just add or multiply until you get to a number close to 15,700, e.g., 275 × 57 = 15,675).

Now, divide by 2 (the drum is half full) and you will have your answer:

56.59 divided by 2 = 28.30
Or 57 divided by 2 = 28.5

The closest answer is 30.

---

36. (D) 600 metres. The ratio in this question is 900 metres travelled to 3 minutes. To find the answer, use algebra and cross multiply. The algebra, ratios, and proportions sections in Chapter 2 provide further explanation.

Here is how the answer is calculated:

$$\frac{3 \text{ minutes}}{900 \text{ metres}} = \frac{2 \text{ minutes}}{x}$$
$$3x = 1,800$$
$$3x \div 3 = 1,800 \div 3$$
$$x = 600$$

37. (D) 40%. To find the answer, first add up the total calls from the first day shift:

4 + 1 + 3 + 2 = 10

Percentages are fractions:

10/10 calls is 100%
4/10 calls is 40%

An easy way to understand this is to add a 0 to each number

100/100 calls is 100%
40/100 calls is 40%

---

38. (B) 50%. To find the answer, first add up the total calls over the two dayshifts:

4 + 1 + 3 + 2 + 5 + 1 + 2 = 18

Next, find the total number of medical aid calls:

4 + 5 = 9

Now find the answer by recognizing that:
9 is half of 18 (or 50%)

---

39. (C) About 87 litres. The ratio in this question is 270 minutes to 180 litres. To find the answer, use algebra and cross multiply. The algebra, ratios, and proportions sections in Chapter 2 provide further explanation.

Here is how the answer is calculated:

$$\frac{270 \, \text{minutes}}{180 \, \text{litres}} = \frac{130 \, \text{minutes}}{x}$$

$270x = 23{,}400$

$23{,}400 \div 270 = 270 \div 270x$

$86.6 = x$

The best answer is about 87 minutes.

---

40. (C) 286¼. This is a division question. To find the correct answer, divide 1,145 gallons by 4. $1{,}145 \div 4 = 286.25$. Remember when answering the question that .25 is the same as 1/4 (.25 = 25/100). To find the answer, you could also multiply by .25 instead of dividing. For more information on division, see Chapter 2.

41. (C) 4 miles. This can be considered a proportion or ratio question. To find the answer, you first need to find the ratio. For this question, the truck will travel 12 miles every 3 minutes. The ratio is 12 to 3. To correctly answer this question, you will need to simplify the ratio the same way you would simplify a fraction (this is the easiest way, although the answer can also be calculated using algebra). See the algebra, ratios, and proportions sections in Chapter 2 for further explanation.

Here is how the answer is calculated:
The ratio:

$$\frac{12 \text{ miles}}{3 \text{ minutes}}$$

Simplified (top and bottom divided by 3)

$$\frac{4 \text{ miles}}{1 \text{ minute}}$$

42. (D) 3 : 1. There are 3 firefighters for every captain. See the ratios section of Chapter 2 for more information.

43. (B) 24 hours. This is a proportion question. The ratio is 8 hours to 2 sections. 8 : 2. To find the answer, use algebra and cross multiply. You can check your answer by checking to see if the equation is equal. The algebra, ratios, and proportions sections in Chapter 2 provide further explanation.

Here is how the answer is calculated:

$$\frac{8 \text{ hours}}{2 \text{ sections}} = \frac{x}{6 \text{ sections}}$$
$$2x = 48$$
$$2x \div 2 = 48 \div 2$$
$$x = 24 \text{ hours}$$

44. (A) 11/41. This is a ratio question. Because the ratio can't be reduced any further, it is 11/41.

45. (D) Acetone. Acetone is the only fuel listed in which 11 falls in its flammable range (2.6–12.8). Carbon monoxide is too rich and propane is too lean.

46. (B) Kerosine. At 0.7, kerosine has the lowest flammable limit.

47. (C) 4.5%. 1.2% is too lean for gasoline to ignite. At 11.6% and 7.8%, the mixture is too rich to ignite.

48. (C) 16. This is a percentage question. To find the answer, multiply the total number by .20 (the percentage as a number). $80 \times .20 = 16$.

49. (C) 109,900. This is a multiplication question. Multiply the gallons per hour by the exposure lines. $15,700 \times 7 = 109,900$.

50. (B) 10,950 gallons. This is a proportion question. To find the answer, you first need to find the ratio. It is important to know that there are 60 minutes in an hour. Engine 15 pumped 14,600 gallons in the past hour. The ratio is 14,600 to 60. See the algebra, ratios, and proportions sections in Chapter 2 for further explanation.

Here is how the answer is calculated:

$$\frac{14,600 \text{ gallons}}{60 \text{ minutes}} = \frac{x}{45}$$
$$14,600 \times 45 = 657,000 = 60 \times x = 60x$$
$$657,000 \div 60 = 60x \div 60$$
$$10,950 = x$$

The answer could also be found by multiplying 10,950 by .75. This is because 45 minutes is ¾ of one hour.

51. (D) 4 fires. This can be considered a proportion or ratio question. To find the answer, you first need to find the ratio. Engine 8 has had 24 fires in 48 shifts. The ratio is 24 to 48 (which can be reduced to 1/2). To correctly answer this question, you will need to simplify the ratio the same way you would simplify a fraction (this is the easiest way; algebra can also be used to solve this question). See the algebra, ratios, and proportions sections in Chapter 2 for further explanation.

Here is how the answer is calculated:
The ratio:

$$\frac{24 \text{ fires}}{48 \text{ shifts}}$$

Simplified:

$$\frac{4 \text{ fires}}{8 \text{ shifts}}$$

This answer can also be calculated by recognizing that Engine 8 is averaging 1 structure fire every 2 shifts.

52. (A) 19. This is a division question. To find the correct answer, divide 950 (total hose) by 50 (length of hose). To learn more about division, see Chapter 2.

53. (A) 720 feet. This is a perimeter question. To find the perimeter, add up the lengths of all the sides. 300 + 300 + 60 + 60 = 720. For more information regarding perimeter, see Chapter 2.

54. (D) 18,000 feet. This is an area question. Area = Length × Width. 300 × 60 = 18,000. For more information regarding area, see Chapter 2.

55. (B) 1,080,000 feet. This is a volume question. Volume = Length × Width × Height. 300 × 60 × 60 = 1,080,000. For more information regarding volume, see Chapter 2.

Section 3

56. (D) This option is correct. Option A is incorrect because the deck is in the wrong place. Option B is incorrect because the roofline is incorrect. Option C is incorrect because the entrance is in the wrong place.

57. (C) This option is correct. Option A is incorrect because it is a mirror image and in the wrong orientation. Option B is incorrect because the entrance is in the wrong spot. Option D shows the roof vents in the wrong place.

58. (A) This option is correct. Option B shows the second and third building in the wrong place and the sixth building isn't set back properly. Option C shows the front exit of the third building in the wrong place. Option D is missing the fire escape on the fourth building.

59. (B) This option is correct. Option A shows the path curving incorrectly. Option C shows the mailbox in the wrong place. Option D is a mirror image and is incorrect for that reason (everything is backwards).

60. (D) This option is correct. Option A is incorrect because the bush in the front yard is in the wrong place. Option B shows the driveway on the wrong side of the yard. Option C is from the wrong perspective (too high and from the wrong side of the house).

ANSWER SHEET
Test 5

SECTION 1

1. Ⓐ Ⓑ Ⓒ Ⓓ
2. Ⓐ Ⓑ Ⓒ Ⓓ
3. Ⓐ Ⓑ Ⓒ Ⓓ
4. Ⓐ Ⓑ Ⓒ Ⓓ

5. Ⓐ Ⓑ Ⓒ Ⓓ
6. Ⓐ Ⓑ Ⓒ Ⓓ
7. Ⓐ Ⓑ Ⓒ Ⓓ
8. Ⓐ Ⓑ Ⓒ Ⓓ

9. Ⓐ Ⓑ Ⓒ Ⓓ
10. Ⓐ Ⓑ Ⓒ Ⓓ
11. Ⓐ Ⓑ Ⓒ Ⓓ
12. Ⓐ Ⓑ Ⓒ Ⓓ

13. Ⓐ Ⓑ Ⓒ Ⓓ
14. Ⓐ Ⓑ Ⓒ Ⓓ
15. Ⓐ Ⓑ Ⓒ Ⓓ

SECTION 2

16. Ⓐ Ⓑ Ⓒ Ⓓ
17. Ⓐ Ⓑ Ⓒ Ⓓ
18. Ⓐ Ⓑ Ⓒ Ⓓ
19. Ⓐ Ⓑ Ⓒ Ⓓ
20. Ⓐ Ⓑ Ⓒ Ⓓ
21. Ⓐ Ⓑ Ⓒ Ⓓ
22. Ⓐ Ⓑ Ⓒ Ⓓ

23. Ⓐ Ⓑ Ⓒ Ⓓ
24. Ⓐ Ⓑ Ⓒ Ⓓ
25. Ⓐ Ⓑ Ⓒ Ⓓ
26. Ⓐ Ⓑ Ⓒ Ⓓ
27. Ⓐ Ⓑ Ⓒ Ⓓ
28. Ⓐ Ⓑ Ⓒ Ⓓ
29. Ⓐ Ⓑ Ⓒ Ⓓ

30. Ⓐ Ⓑ Ⓒ Ⓓ
31. Ⓐ Ⓑ Ⓒ Ⓓ
32. Ⓐ Ⓑ Ⓒ Ⓓ
33. Ⓐ Ⓑ Ⓒ Ⓓ
34. Ⓐ Ⓑ Ⓒ Ⓓ
35. Ⓐ Ⓑ Ⓒ Ⓓ
36. Ⓐ Ⓑ Ⓒ Ⓓ

37. Ⓐ Ⓑ Ⓒ Ⓓ
38. Ⓐ Ⓑ Ⓒ Ⓓ
39. Ⓐ Ⓑ Ⓒ Ⓓ
40. Ⓐ Ⓑ Ⓒ Ⓓ

SECTION 3

41. Ⓐ Ⓑ Ⓒ Ⓓ
42. Ⓐ Ⓑ Ⓒ Ⓓ
43. Ⓐ Ⓑ Ⓒ Ⓓ
44. Ⓐ Ⓑ Ⓒ Ⓓ
45. Ⓐ Ⓑ Ⓒ Ⓓ

46. Ⓐ Ⓑ Ⓒ Ⓓ
47. Ⓐ Ⓑ Ⓒ Ⓓ
48. Ⓐ Ⓑ Ⓒ Ⓓ
49. Ⓐ Ⓑ Ⓒ Ⓓ
50. Ⓐ Ⓑ Ⓒ Ⓓ

51. Ⓐ Ⓑ Ⓒ Ⓓ
52. Ⓐ Ⓑ Ⓒ Ⓓ
53. Ⓐ Ⓑ Ⓒ Ⓓ
54. Ⓐ Ⓑ Ⓒ Ⓓ
55. Ⓐ Ⓑ Ⓒ Ⓓ

56. Ⓐ Ⓑ Ⓒ Ⓓ
57. Ⓐ Ⓑ Ⓒ Ⓓ
58. Ⓐ Ⓑ Ⓒ Ⓓ
59. Ⓐ Ⓑ Ⓒ Ⓓ
60. Ⓐ Ⓑ Ⓒ Ⓓ

General Firefighter Test 2

Section 1—Learning, Remembering, and Applying Written Information

> DIRECTIONS: Set a timer and study the following passage for 5 minutes. When the time is up, turn the page and begin the test. DO NOT look back at the passage.

Firefighters often use ladders at fires, during rescues, and for many other functions of fire-fighting. It is essential for competent firefighters to have a good understanding of the parts of a ladder, how it works, and the correct procedures for raising and positioning a ladder.

Fire department ladders are generally stronger and built to withstand more abuse than ladders used in other industries. This is to provide an extra level of safety for firefighters and the public. The construction, design, and testing of fire department ladders is covered by NFPA 1931—Standard on Design of and Design Verification Tests for Fire Department Ground Ladders.

There are several types of ladders used by fire departments. The most frequently used ground ladder is the 24′ extension ladder. The main parts of a 24′ extension ladder are:

Beams—These could also be called the rails of the ladder. These are the two long portions of the ladder that are connected by the rungs.

Rungs—These are the parts of the ladder used to climb on. They connect the beams.

Bed section—This is the wider section of the ladder.

Fly Section—This is the section of the ladder that is extended using the halyard.

Halyard—This is the rope used for extending and retracting the ladder.

Butt—This can also be called the heel of the ladder. This is the bottom tip of the ladder.

Butt Spurs—Pieces of metal attached to the butt of the ladder to help stop the ladder from slipping.

Dogs—These can also be called Pawls. These are the locks that hold the fly section in place when it is extended.

Heat Sensor—These are small stickers placed in several places on the inside of the beam of the ladder. When they are exposed to extreme heat they will change color and indicate that the ladder needs testing to see if it has been compromised.

Tip—This is the top of the ladder. The opposite of the butt.

A 24′ extension ladder has two sections and is adjustable in length. Standard procedures are used for raising a 24′ ladder. This increases safety and ensures all firefighters have a uniform standard while working together. The basic steps for a one person 24′ ladder raise are:

1.	Shoulder or underarm carry to the building. Spot the ladder.
2.	**Place the butt of the ladder into the building with the fly up.**
3.	Check for overhead hazards.
4.	Grasp the ladder 2nd rung from the top facing away from the building.
5.	Lift with your legs and pivot into the ladder hitting every rung as the ladder is raised.

6.	Grasp the 2nd and 5th rungs of the ladder and pull the butt 12 to 18 inches away from the building (plus overhang).
7.	Untie the halyard.
8.	Extend the ladder keeping the tip off the building and your shoulder on the beam.
9.	Rotate the ladder 180° so the fly is facing out. Keep one foot on the beam and eye contact with the tip as the ladder rotates.
10.	Tie off the halyard on two easily accessible rungs using a clove hitch and an overhand safety. Excess halyard should be placed between the ladder and the building (can be tied off if possible).
11.	Grasp the 2nd and 5th rungs and pull the ladder away from the building to the proper climbing angle (1/4 the length of the extended ladder plus overhangs).
12.	Before climbing the ladder check five things: 1) Proper climbing angle (stand on bottom rung, hands on rung in front of you, arms should be parallel with the ground) 2) Halyard is tied off 3) Ladder has 4 points of contact 4) Dogs are locked 5) There is a butt man
13.	Ladder is ready to climb.

When raising ground ladders, firefighters have several options for how to position the ladder depending on the situation. Listed below is the proper ladder positioning for roof operations, for window rescue operations, for window ventilation operations, and for window hose stream operations.

Roof Operations—If a firefighter is going onto a roof, he or she should be sure to have 3–5 rungs of the ladder above the roofline. This makes the ladder easier to see in an emergency. Before a firefighter steps onto a roof, he or she should sound the roof using a hand tool (e.g., an axe).

Window Rescue Operations—When setting a ladder up for window rescue operations, firefighters should place the tip of the ladder just below the window sill. The tip of the ladder can be wedged under the sill to increase stability.

Window Ventilation Operations—When setting up a ladder for window ventilation, the ladder should be set up with the tip of the ladder even to the top of the window. The ladder should be set up on the windward side of the window (to avoid smoke when the window is broken). When breaking a window for ventilation, a firefighter should first do a leg lock on the opposite side of the ladder he or she is working on. Next, the firefighter should notify other firefighters that he or she is "breaking glass" and strike the window with an axe in the upper corner of the window closest to him (to prevent his hand/arm from entering the window and glass from striking them).

Window Hose Stream Operations—When operating a hose stream through a window from a ladder, the tip should be placed just above and directly over the window opening (unless heavy smoke and/or flames are showing). Firefighters should position themselves safely on the ladder using a leg lock or ladder belt. A bucking strap can be attached to a rung and used to make hose handling easier.

1. Why are fire department ladders generally stronger and built to withstand more abuse than ladders used in other industries?

    (A) Because they are made of a different material than other ladders.
    (B) To provide an extra level of safety for firefighters and the public.
    (C) The extra weight holds them more firmly to the ground because of gravity.
    (D) All of the above.

2. What governing body covers the construction, design, and testing of fire department ladders?

    (A) IFSAC
    (B) NIST
    (C) IAFF
    (D) NFPA

3. According to the passage you just studied, what is the most frequently used ground ladder?

    (A) 24′ extension ladder
    (B) roof ladder
    (C) attic ladder
    (D) pompier ladder

4. Where are the heat sensors located?

    (A) on the inside of the dogs
    (B) on each rung
    (C) built into the halyard
    (D) on the inside of the beam

5. According to the instructions, when the butt of the ladder is placed into the building in preparation for a 24′ ladder raise, which direction should the fly be facing?

    (A) up
    (B) down
    (C) it doesn't matter
    (D) none of the above

6. Extend the ladder keeping your eye on the tip and your _____ on the beam.

   (A) hand
   (B) head
   (C) shoulder
   (D) none of the above

7. Before climbing the ladder, what five things should you check?

   (A) That you have four points of contact, the dogs are locked, the halyard is tied off, you have a butt man, and you have a proper climbing angle.
   (B) That you have three points of contact, the dogs are locked, the halyard is tied, you have a butt man, and you have a proper climbing angle.
   (C) That you have four points of contact, the dogs are locked, the halyard is tied off, you have a butt man, and that you have a hose with you.
   (D) That you have two points of contact, the dogs are locked, the halyard is tied off, and you have a proper climbing angle.

8. According to the study material, how many rungs should be placed above the roof line when working on a roof?

   (A) 5–6
   (B) 3–5
   (C) 4–5
   (D) 5–10

9. Before a firefighter climbs onto a roof from a ladder, what should he do?

   (A) Throw his tools on.
   (B) Tell the butt man he isn't needed any more.
   (C) Sound the roof using a hand tool.
   (D) Put on his SCBA.

10. What is one reason that you would wedge the tip of a ladder under a window sill during rescue operations?

    (A) To stop it from flexing.
    (B) You should never do this.
    (C) To test its strength.
    (D) To increase stability.

11. According to the study material, why should a ladder be set up on the windward side of a window when a firefighter is ventilating?

    (A) To stay away from the glass.
    (B) So the firefighter can hear better.
    (C) To avoid smoke.
    (D) All of the above.

12. What should a firefighter say before she breaks glass during window ventilation?

    (A) "Heads up."
    (B) "Look up."
    (C) "Striking Glass."
    (D) "Breaking Glass."

13. When breaking glass for ventilation, what part of the window should the firefighter strike?

    (A) The top corner closest to him.
    (B) The bottom corner closest to him.
    (C) The top corner furthest from him.
    (D) The bottom corner furthest from him.

14. When operating a hose stream through a window, when would you not place the ladder tip just above and directly over the window opening?

    (A) Heavy smoke is coming from the window.
    (B) It is raining extremely hard.
    (C) Flames are coming from the window.
    (D) Both A and C are correct.

15. According to the information provided, when positioning themselves on a ladder for hose stream operations, should firefighters use a leg lock or a ladder belt?

    (A) both should be used
    (B) either option can be used
    (C) leg lock
    (D) ladder belt

Section 2: Mathematics

> DIRECTIONS: Answer Questions 16 through 40 by choosing the best answer for each question and filling in the corresponding bubble on the answer sheet.

16. Five fire trucks carry 500 feet of hose each. Combined, how much hose do they carry?

    (A) 2,500 ft.
    (B) 3,000 ft.
    (C) 4,000 ft.
    (D) 2,000 ft.

17. A barrel of gasoline containing 40 gallons falls over and spills. When the barrel is righted, only 7 gallons remain. How many gallons of gasoline were spilled?

    (A) 27 gallons
    (B) 7 gallons
    (C) 33 gallons
    (D) 23 gallons

18. The truck you work on carries 800 feet of hose. After a fire, 150 feet of hose remains on the truck. How much hose was used at the fire?

   (A) 550 feet
   (B) 600 feet
   (C) 650 feet
   (D) 700 feet

19. There are 15 firefighters and 5 fire trucks. If an even amount of firefighters are on each fire truck, how many firefighters will be on each truck?

   (A) 3
   (B) 5
   (C) 4
   (D) 7

20. There are 22 fire stations in your municipality. Each station is staffed with 4 firefighters per shift with the exception of Station 14 which has 12 firefighters. How many firefighters work per shift in your municipality?

   (A) 96
   (B) 92
   (C) 88
   (D) 98

21. There are 3 fire trucks in your station. Each truck carries 23 lengths of 1.75 inch hose. Combined, how much 1.75 inch hose do all three trucks carry?

   (A) 60 lengths
   (B) 62 lengths
   (C) 69 lengths
   (D) 68 lengths

22. You have 6 buckets of foam at the station. Three of them are full, 1 is half full, and 2 are three quarters full. How many full buckets of foam do you have?

   (A) 4
   (B) 3
   (C) 6
   (D) 5

23. Engine 4 is using a water tower to pump from. For every one foot of elevation, water pressure exerts .434 pounds per square inch. The storage tank is 70 feet above the truck. How much pressure will the water exert when it enters the truck?

   (A) 31.42
   (B) 30.38
   (C) 32.68
   (D) 30.39

24. Ten firefighters are at a technical rescue. Three firefighters go off to set up the main line and safety. One firefighter sets off to be the rescuer. What percentage of firefighters remains?

(A) 10%

(B) 15%

(C) 60%

(D) 75%

25. There are 35 firefighters at a fire. Twenty percent of them are doing an interior attack. How many firefighters are doing an interior attack?

(A) 7

(B) 8

(C) 28

(D) 27

26. The assistant fire chief wants to know how much weight the rescue team would be required to pull to raise a 450 pound victim up a cliff. He tells you to use a 5:1 mechanical advantage system. Approximately how much weight will be pulled?

(A) 45 pounds

(B) 90 pounds

(C) 80 pounds

(D) 100 pounds

27. If 50 feet of hose were cut into 4 equal sections, how long would each piece of hose be?

(A) 13 feet

(B) 12.5 feet

(C) 10 feet

(D) 5 feet

28. If there are 16 fire stations and 352 firefighters and all fire stations have the same number of firefighters, how many firefighters are at each station?

(A) 20

(B) 19

(C) 18

(D) 22

29. A large circular container of diesel is on fire. The container measures 80 metres around. What is the distance from edge to edge of the container if a straight line is drawn through the middle of the container?

(A) About 25½ metres

(B) About 24 metres

(C) About 29 metres

(D) About 30 metres

30. There is about .946 of a litre in one quart. How many litres are there in 90 quarts?

(A) 84.8
(B) 86.75
(C) 85.14
(D) 84.23

31. If a firefighter attends 4,678 of a possible 5,200 calls, what percentage of calls did he attend?

(A) About 94%
(B) About 90%
(C) About 85%
(D) About 70%

32. Ladder 12 has used 17 gallons of foam in the past 10 minutes. Approximately long will it take Ladder 12 to use 200 gallons of foam if it continues pumping at the same rate?

(A) 97 minutes
(B) 133 minutes
(C) 117 minutes
(D) 142 minutes

33. A fire truck takes 23 minutes to travel 24 kilometres, how many minutes will it take the fire truck to travel the remaining 11 kilometres to the firehall?

(A) 8–9 minutes
(B) 12–14 minutes
(C) 9–10 minutes
(D) 10–11 minutes

34. A package of an unknown powder is found at a hazmat call. The package is 20 cm long, 10 cm wide, and 10 cm high. If the package is about 60% full, how much powder is in the package?

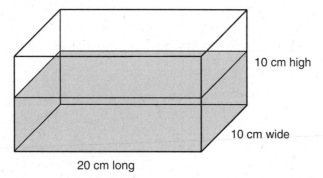

10 cm high

10 cm wide

20 cm long

(A) 1,000 cubic centimetres
(B) 1,200 cubic centimetres
(C) 1,100 cubic centimetres
(D) 1,400 cubic centimetres

35. A technical rescue course is 18 units long. It took 4 days to do the first 8 units. How long will it take to do the last 10 units if each unit takes the same amount of time?

(A) 3 days
(B) 8 days
(C) 9 days
(D) 5 days

36. Eight of the firefighters at Station 7 have been firefighters for less than 2 years. There are 112 total firefighters working at Station 7. What percent of firefighters at Station 7 have been firefighters for less than 2 years?

(A) 7.1%
(B) 6.9%
(C) 8%
(D) 3.9%

37. When water turns to steam, it expands about 1,000 times. If 35 litres of water are turned to steam while extinguishing a fire, approximately how much steam will be produced?

(A) About 30,000 litres
(B) About 45,000 litres
(C) About 35,000 litres
(D) About 11,000 litres

38. The fire department has 3,000 ft. of rescue rope. How much is 10% of that rope?

(A) 300 ft.
(A) 600 ft.
(A) 900 ft.
(A) 1,000 ft.

39. In January, 2 out of 11 fires involved rescues. If this trend stays the same and there are 14 fires in February, how many fires can be expected to involve rescue?

(A) 2–3
(B) 5–6
(C) 3–4
(D) 4–5

40. The following house is on fire and the attic is full of fire gasses. How much fire gas is in the attic?

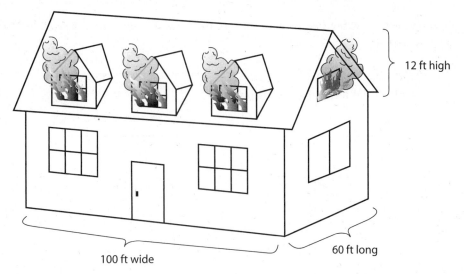

12 ft high

100 ft wide

60 ft long

(A) 21,400 cubic feet
(B) 36,000 cubic feet
(C) 20,610 cubic feet
(D) 21,600 cubic feet

Section 3: Mechanical Aptitude

DIRECTIONS: Questions 41 through 60 are based on the illustrations provided for each question.

41. Which load feels lighter to the firefighter?

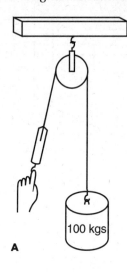
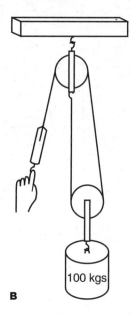

(A) A
(B) B
(C) They feel the same
(D) Cannot be determined

42. Which ramp is easiest to push the car up?

(A)

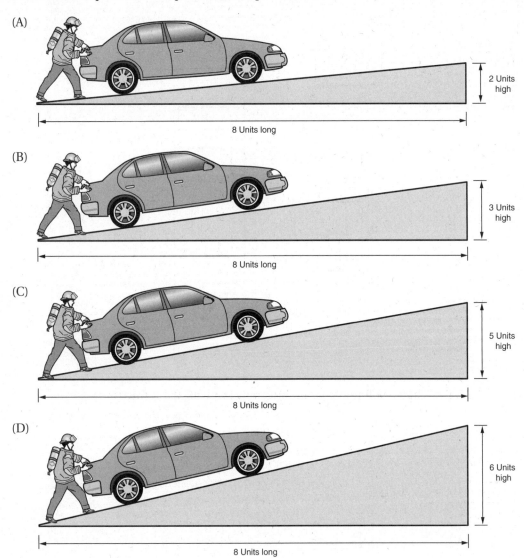

2 Units high

8 Units long

(B)

3 Units high

8 Units long

(C)

5 Units high

8 Units long

(D)

6 Units high

8 Units long

43. Which shape, when added to the following shape, forms a square?

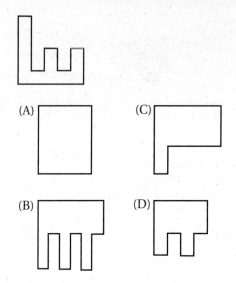

(A)

(C)

(B)

(D)

44. If gear A turns at 8 revolutions per minute, how fast will gear B turn?

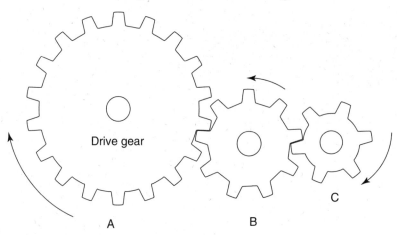

(A) 17 revolutions per minute
(B) 15 revolutions per minute
(C) 14 revolutions per minute
(D) 16 revolutions per minute

45. The gear being driven in the picture below will have _____

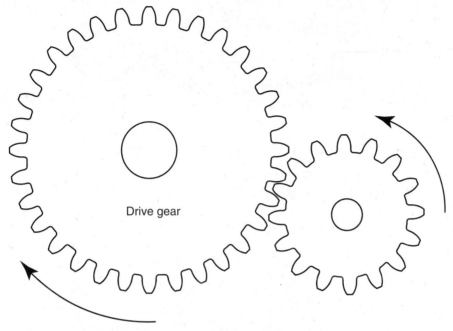

Drive gear

(A) twice the torque and twice the speed as the drive gear.
(B) twice the torque and half the speed as the drive gear.
(C) half the torque and twice the speed as the drive gear.
(D) half the torque and half the speed as the drive gear.

46. What is the gear ratio of the following gears?

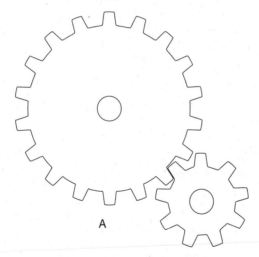

A

Drive gear

(A) 2:1
(B) 3:1
(C) 2:3
(D) 1:8

47. Wheel A will turn _____ and Wheel C will turn _____.

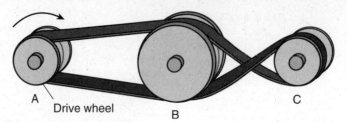

(A) clockwise, clockwise
(B) counterclockwise, clockwise
(C) clockwise, counterclockwise
(D) counterclockwise, counterclockwise

48. What does this gauge read?

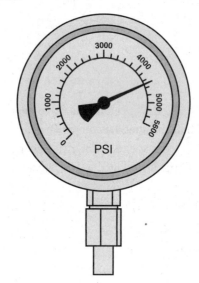

(A) 4,100
(B) 4,250
(C) 4,450
(D) 4,200

49. Which direction will wheel B rotate?

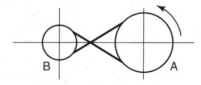

(A) clockwise
(B) counterclockwise
(C) left
(D) None of the above

50. Which wheel turns faster?

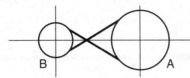

(A) Wheel A

(B) Wheel B

(C) They turn at the same speed.

(D) Cannot be determined

51. In which picture will it be easiest for the firefighter to move the load?

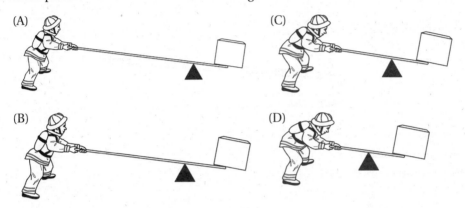

(A)

(C)

(B)

(D)

52. Which of the following is not a simple machine?

(A) pry bar

(B) screw driver

(C) car battery

(D) door wedge

53. Which screw jack will be harder to turn?

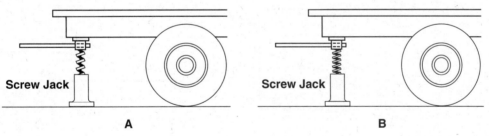

Screw Jack   Screw Jack

A   B

(A) A

(B) B

(C) Cannot be determined

(D) Both will be the same

54. Moving the weight on the left in towards the weight on the right will _____.

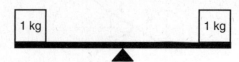

(A) cause the weight on the right to raise
(B) cause the weight on the left to lower
(C) cause the weight on the right to lower
(D) do nothing

55. The crowbar below is a _____.

(A) lever
(B) inclined plane
(C) screw
(D) pulley

56. Of the wedges below, which one can produce the most force?

(A)

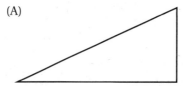

(C)

(B)

(D)

57. The axe below is usually used as a _____.

(A) wheel and axle
(B) screw
(C) wedge
(D) pulley

58. The following pulley system provides a mechanical advantage of _____.

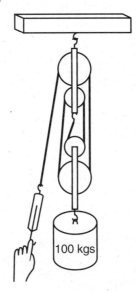

100 kgs

(A) 3:1
(B) 4:1
(C) 5:2
(D) 2:1

59. Which direction will gear B turn if gear A turns clockwise?

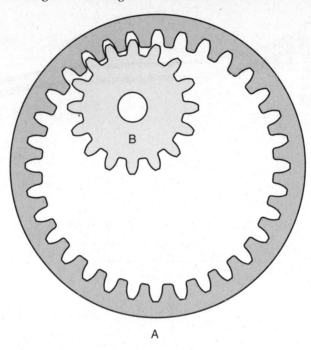

(A) The opposite direction to gear A.

(B) The same direction as gear A.

(C) Counterclockwise.

(D) It will not turn.

60. If wheel A is turning clockwise, what direction will wheel H turn?

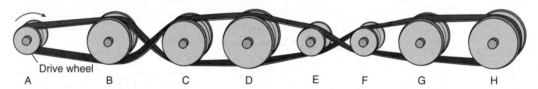

(A) counterclockwise

(B) it will not turn

(C) clockwise

(D) none of the above

ANSWER KEY
Test 5

SECTION 1

1. B	4. D	7. A	10. D	13. A
2. D	5. A	8. B	11. C	14. D
3. A	6. C	9. C	12. D	15. B

SECTION 2

16. A	21. C	26. B	31. B	36. A
17. C	22. D	27. B	32. C	37. C
18. C	23. B	28. D	33. D	38. A
19. A	24. C	29. A	34. B	39. A
20. A	25. A	30. C	35. D	40. B

SECTION 3

41. B	45. C	49. A	53. A	57. C
42. A	46. A	50. B	54. C	58. B
43. D	47. C	51. A	55. A	59. B
44. D	48. C	52. C	56. D	60. C

ANSWER EXPLANATIONS
Section 1

1. (B) To provide an extra level of safety for firefighters and the public. This answer is provided in the second sentence of the second paragraph.

2. (D) NFPA. This answer is provided in the third sentence of the second paragraph.

3. (A) 24′ extension ladder. This answer is provided in the second sentence of the third paragraph.

4. (D) On the inside of the beam. This answer is mentioned in the first sentence of the heat sensor heading.

5. (A) Up. The answer to this question is contained in step number 2 of the steps for raising a 24′ ladder in the fourth paragraph.

6. (C) Shoulder. The answer to this question is contained in step number 8 of the steps for raising a 24′ ladder in the fourth paragraph.

7. (A) That you have four points of contact, the dogs are locked, the halyard is tied off, you have a butt man, and you have a proper climbing angle. The answer to this question is contained in step number 12 of the steps for raising a 24′ ladder in the fourth paragraph. This question can also be answered by process of elimination. D can be ruled out because it only offers four things to check instead of five. Next, if you compare answers A, B and C, you will see that all three are very similar. The difference is that answers B and C contain one different answer from A while the rest are the same. By process of elimination, you can find the correct answer is A.

8. (B) 3–5. This answer is located in the first sentence under the Roof Operations heading.

9. (C) Sound the roof using a hand tool. This answer is located in the third sentence under the Roof Operations heading. Notice that the correct answer contains slightly more information than the other answers (sometimes this can be a hint towards the correct answer).

10. (D) To increase stability. This answer is located in the second sentence under the Window Rescue Operations heading.

11. (C) To avoid smoke. This answer is found in the second sentence of the Window Ventilation Operations. All of the above is not a correct answer because neither option A nor option B is mentioned in the study material. Also, neither of these answers is correct. Glass may move due to wind, but firefighters position themselves to avoid it while wearing PPE. Neither the windward nor the leeward side would impact a firefighter's hearing.

12. (D) "Breaking Glass." This answer is located in the fourth sentence under the Window Ventilation Operations heading.

13. (A) The top corner closest to him. This answer is located in the fourth sentence under the Window Ventilation Operations heading.

14. (D) Both A and C are correct. This answer is found in the first sentence of the Window Hose Stream Operations.

15. (B) Either option can be used. This answer is found in the second sentence of the Window Hose Stream Operations.

Section 2

16. (A) 2,500 ft. The answer to this question can be calculated using addition or multiplication.

Addition:

```
   500
   500
   500
   500
 + 500
  2500
```

Multiplication:

```
 500
×  5
2500
```

17. (C) 33 gallons. This is a subtraction question. Subtract what remains in the barrel (7 gallons) from what was in the barrel originally (40 gallons). 40 – 7 = 33. You could also work through the answers, adding the remaining gasoline to the potential answers to see which answer adds up to 40 gallons.

18. (C) 650 feet. This is a subtraction question. Subtract the remaining hose from the original hose. 800 – 150 = 650. You could also work through the answers, adding the remaining hose to the potential answers to see which answer adds up to 800 feet.

19. (A) 3. This is a division question. 15 ÷ 3 = 5. You can check your answer by multiplying 3 × 5 = 15.

20. (A) 96. This question involves addition, subtraction, and multiplication. The easiest way to answer this question is to first multiply the 22 stations by 4 firefighters each. 22 × 4 = 88. Next, find out how many extra firefighters are at station 14. 12 – 4 = 8. Finally, add those extra firefighters to the total. 88 + 8 = 96. You could also find the answer to this question by writing down the numbers at each station and adding them all up.

21. (C) 69 lengths. This is a multiplication question. 23 × 3 = 69. The answer can also be found by adding 23 three times. 23 + 23 + 23 = 69.

22. (D) 5. This is an adding fractions question. Three buckets are full (1/1 + 1/1 + 1/1). One bucket is half full (1/2). 2 buckets are three quarters full (3/4 + 3/4). To answer the question, make the denominator the same and add up the fractions.

1/1 + 1/1 + 1/1 + 1/2 + 3/4 + 3/4 =
4/4 + 4/4 + 4/4 + 2/4 + 3/4 + 3/4 = 20/4

Simplify the fraction 5/1 = 5

23. (B) 30.38. This question is a multiplication question. To find the answer, multiply the height by the pressure exerted (70 × .434). If you want, add the decimal after. .434 × 70 = 30.38.

24. (C) 60%. This question asks for a fraction to be converted to a percentage. First, add the firefighters who are occupied (mainline, safety, and rescuer). 3 + 1 = 4. Next, subtract the occupied firefighters from the total. 10 – 4 = 6. Now you have a fraction 6/10 (you may realize you have 60% at this point). To convert the fraction to a percentage, divide 6 by 10 and then multiply by 100.

25. (A) 7. This question asks for a number to be found based on a percentage. The easiest way to answer this question is to convert 20% to a decimal (÷ 100). 20 ÷ 100 = .2. Now, multiply 35 (total firefighters) by .2.

$35 \times .2 = 7$.

26. (B) 90 pounds. To find the answer to this question, you will need to find out what 20% of 450 is (5/1 = .20). $450 \times .20 = 90$.

27. (B) 12.5 feet. To find the correct answer to this question, use division. $50 ÷ 4 = 12.5$. See Chapter 2 for more information on division.

28. (D) 22. This is a division question. Divide the number of firefighters (352) by the number of stations (16) to find the correct answer. $352 ÷ 16 = 22$.

29. (A) About 25½ metres. To find the answer to this question, you need to understand how the circumference of a circle is found. Pi times diameter = circumference. To calculate diameter using circumference, divide the circumference by pi. $80 ÷ 3.14 = 25.47$. The best answer is 25½.

30. (C) 85.14. This is a multiplication question. To find the answer, multiply 90 quarts by .946. Chapter 2 contains more information on multiplication.

31. (B) About 90%. This question asks for a percentage. To find the answer, first realize you have a fraction (4,678/5,200). The next step is to simply divide the top number by the bottom number, then multiply by 100.

32. (C) 117. The ratio in this question is 17 gallons in 10 minutes. 17:10. To find the answer, use algebra and cross multiply. Remember the question is asking how long it will take to use 200 gallons. You can check your answer by checking to see if the equation is equal. The algebra, ratios, and proportions sections in Chapter 2 provide further explanation.

Here is how the answer is calculated:

$$\frac{17\,\text{gallons}}{10\,\text{minutes}} = \frac{200\,\text{gallons}}{x}$$
$17x = 2000$
$17x ÷ 17 = 2000 ÷ 17$
$x = 117.64$, or approximately 117 minutes.

33. (D) 10–11 minutes. This question involves a proportion. Because one ratio (23 minutes to travel 24 kilometres) is known, the equation can be solved. See the algebra, ratios, and proportions sections in Chapter 2 for further explanation.

Here is how the answer is found:

$$\frac{23 \, \text{minutes}}{24 \, \text{kilometres}} = \frac{x \, \text{minutes}}{11 \, \text{kilometres}}$$

$$253 = 24x$$

$$253 \div 24 = 24 \div 24x$$

$$10.54 = x$$

34. (B) 1,200 cubic centimetres. To find the answer to this question, first find the volume of the package. Volume equals Length × Width × Height:

Volume = $20 \times 10 \times 10 = 2{,}000$.

Next, find out what 60% of 2,000 is:

$2{,}000 \times .6$ (60% = 60/100) = 1,200.

35. (D) 5 days. This is a proportion question. The ratio is 4 days to 8 units. 4 : 8. To find the answer, use algebra and cross multiply. You can check your answer by checking to see if the equation is equal. The algebra, ratios, and proportions sections in Chapter 2 provide further explanation.

Here is how the answer is found:

$$\frac{4 \, \text{days}}{8 \, \text{units}} = \frac{x}{10 \, \text{units}}$$

$$8x = 40$$

$$8x \div 8 = 40 \div 8$$

$$x = 5 \, \text{days}$$

36. (A) 7.1%. This is a percentage question. To find the answer, first realize you have a fraction (8/112). The next step is to simply divide the top number by the bottom number, then multiply by 100. $8 \div 112 = 0.071$. $0.071 \times 100 = 7.1$.

37. (C) About 35,000 litres. This is a multiplication question. 35 litres times 1,000 is 35,000 litres.

38. (A) 300 ft. This question asks for a number to be found based on a percentage. The easiest way to answer this question is to convert 10% to a decimal (÷ 100). 10 ÷ 100 = .1. Now, multiply 3,000 (ft. of rescue rope) by .1.

$3,000 \times .1 = 300.$

Another easy way to find the answer to this question is to remove a 0 from 3,000 (because 10% has 1 less 0 than 100%).

39. (A) 2–3. This question can be answered using proportions. The ratio is 2 fires involving rescue to 11 fires. 2 : 11. To find the answer, use algebra and cross multiply. You can check your answer by checking to see if the equation is equal. See the algebra, ratios, and proportions sections in Chapter 2 for further explanation.

Here is how the answer is found:

$$\frac{2\,\text{fires involving rescue}}{11\,\text{fires}} = \frac{x}{14\,\text{fires}}$$
$$11x = 28$$
$$11x \div 11 = 28 \div 11$$
$$x = 2.5$$

The best answer is 2–3.

40. (B) 36,000 cubic feet. This question involves finding the volume of a triangular shape. To answer this question, first find the area of the triangular portion:

Area = ½ base × vertical height.
Area = ½ (60 × 12) = ½ (720) = 360

Next, multiply the area by the length of the triangular shape:

$360 \times 100 = 36,000$

Section 3

41. (B) The 2 : 1 system reduces the weight pulled by half so the firefighter is pulling less in picture B.

42. (A) Ramp A. This is an inclined plane. The higher the ramp, the more difficult it will be to push the car up (assuming all ramps are the same length). See the inclined plane section of Chapter 2 for more information on inclined planes.

43. (D) This shape completes the square.

44. (D) 16 revolutions per minute. If a gear is half the size of the gear driving it, it will turn at twice the speed. You can count the teeth to find the size of the gears. This question requires some division. See Chapter 2 for information on math and gears.

45. (C) Half the torque and twice the speed as the drive gear. This answer has to do with gear ratio. Refer to the Gears section of Chapter 2 for further explanation.

46. (A) 2 : 1. The drive gear turns 1 time for every 2 times the driven gear turns.

47. (C) Clockwise, counterclockwise. All of the pulleys turn the same direction until the twist in the pulley. Refer to the Belt Drive section of Chapter 2 for further explanation.

48. (C) 4,450. The gauge points closest to 4,450 psi.

49. (A) Clockwise. When the belt is twisted, the wheels spin in opposite directions. See the Belt Drive section of Chapter 2 for more information.

50. (B) Wheel B. The smaller wheel will turn faster. See the Belt Drive section of Chapter 2 for more information.

51. (A) This is a leverage question. The longer the lever is, the easier it will be to lift the weight (as long as it's longer on the correct side of the fulcrum). Information regarding levers is contained in Chapter 2.

52. (C) Car battery. A (lever), B (screwdriver), and D (wedge) are all simple machines.

53. (A) The pitch on this screw jack is steeper than on the other screw jack, so this makes it harder to turn. You can tell the pitch is steeper because threads are wider apart. For more information on screws, see Chapter 2.

54. (C) Cause the weight on the right to lower. This is a lever. The correct answer is based on leverage. See Chapter 2 for more information regarding leverage.

55. (A) Lever. This is an example of a lever. See Chapter 2 for more information regarding leverage.

56. (D) This wedge has the sharpest edge. The sharper the edge of a wedge, the more force it can produce. For more information on wedges, see Chapter 2.

57. (C) Wedge. An axe is a wedge. For more information on wedges, see Chapter 2.

58. (B) 4:1. This system provides a 4:1 mechanical advantage. Remember the phrase ODD load EVEN anchor. See Chapter 2 for more information on pulleys and mechanical advantage systems.

59. (B) The same direction as gear A. Inner gears turn the same direction as the gear they are inside. See Chapter 2 for further explanation of gears.

60. (C) Clockwise. This question involves a belt drive. There are two twisted belts. Each twisted belt changes the direction the wheel spins. Therefore, wheel H turns the same direction as wheel A. For more information on Belt Drives see Chapter 2.

MOVE TO THE HEAD OF YOUR CLASS
THE EASY WAY!

Barron's presents **THE E-Z SERIES** (formerly THE EASY WAY SERIES)—specially prepared by top educators, it maximizes effective learning while minimizing the time and effort it takes to raise your grades, brush up on the basics, and build your confidence. Comprehensive and full of clear review examples, **THE E-Z SERIES** is your best bet for better grades, quickly!

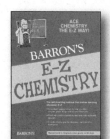

Available at your local book store
or visit **www.barronseduc.com**

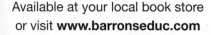

Barron's Educational Series, Inc.
250 Wireless Blvd.
Hauppauge, NY 11788
Order toll-free: 1-800-645-3476
Order by fax: 1-631-434-3217

In Canada:
Georgetown Book Warehouse
34 Armstrong Ave.
Georgetown, Ontario L7G 4R9
Canadian orders: 1-800-247-7160
Order by fax: 1-800-887-1594

(#45) R8/13

Prices subject to change without notice.